W E

S

OLE

Bridgirdle

W
8A
W
48

BURHAM OVERY

WELLS-NEXT-THE-SEA

RKET

the turn of the tide

the turn of the tide

North Norfolk's Saltmarsh Coast

Edited by Ian Scott

Dedication

This book is dedicated to the Norfolk families who have preserved the wild and cultural heritage of the Saltmarsh Coast; to the incomers who understand they have much to learn from them and realise that sustainable communities of outsiders and insiders must be grounded in mutual respect; and to those who have never been to North Norfolk but who know and care for other vulnerable places.

Copyright text © 2005 Ian Scott and the Contributors
Copyright photos © 2005 Campbell MacCallum
Copyright endpaper map © 2005 Godfrey Sayers
Copyright drawings © 2005 Janet Beckett and Keith McDougall

Designed by Graham Hiles, Station Farmhouse, Barney

First published 2005 by JJG Publishing
Sparrow Hall
Hindringham
Fakenham
Norfolk NR21 0DP

ISBN 1 899163 794

Printed in China through Coloreraft Ltd., Hong Kong.

Contents

Foreword – by Lady Buxton

For all of us fortunate to live by the marshland coast, this book is an array of highly informed views on our special paradise. It's remarkable that twenty writers with the same literary objective can be so diverse. All the authors in this book are fervent lovers of North Norfolk, yet they all write about such different subjects and aspects of the place they might be scattered in far-flung parts of the planet. This says a great deal for the beauty and fascination of our beloved haven.

What is interesting is that some writers want to keep things as they are and resist change, whereas others want to help people grasp new opportunities and march with the times. Norfolk, and particularly its north coast, has suffered less change than most of England, because it was almost an island in past centuries, when the Fens stretched to Cambridge. Even after the era of great drainage, you could still not pass through North Norfolk, you could only go there and come back again. Thus the inhabitants and the natural environment remained comparatively isolated, and less vulnerable to outside pressures and to what has come to be known as progress.

It is not difficult to find oneself in harmony with all the authors, because wherever one stands in the debate we all love this coastal paradise, whatever we feel should be done about it. It is not only the human race that imposes change and may be destructive; nature itself never stands still. Many centuries ago much of it here was mainly forest or swamps.

Now this beautiful, tranquil and mellow coastline, with its hinterland of soft landscape and gentle hills, is threatened by social changes. Since these changes are mainly in aid of social satisfaction and pleasure, is it conceivable that someone can suddenly blow a whistle and stop so-called progress? I think not. Other solutions, with compromise, need to be found.

So long as the human race is based on motoring, people will pour through here on sunny weekends because practically everyone now has a car. This does not only apply to Europe; I have experienced gridlock at lunchtime in Nairobi and in many parts of Africa and the Americas. Soon it will be China. Can any Government put a stop to that? Obviously not, so we now have to accept the rising tide of motorists and visitors in our North Norfolk haven as the norm.

The best we can hope for now is to educate the masses to understand and appreciate the countryside and the natural environment. And that's not easy when most politicians are town bred and, senior ministers particularly, know next to nothing about the countryside and always spend their holidays abroad. Three-quarters of the population are brought up and live in urban areas and do not understand that open country has to be more carefully and sensitively managed than towns if the rest of nature is to flourish. Managing land and wilderness for nature is far more complex and delicate than sweeping and tidying urban areas, but the urban population does not think so and seems to consider that countryside and wilderness is just there to be used as they wish.

Coming as I do from the Rocky Mountains in America, it could hardly be more of a contrast to put one's roots down in North Norfolk. You might think that one would feel completely out of it on a low coastline after growing up at 6000 feet a thousand miles from the sea. And probably one might suppose that someone moving from the Norfolk coast to Colorado might feel similarly displaced and excluded moving from here to the beautiful mountains.

But for me that misses the point. For country people and those brought up close to the rest of nature, it is not the difference in scenery, or altitude or the part of the world that counts so much, but the state of the environment itself. How close is one or the other to unspoilt nature? How close are the threats to wild mountains and how easy is it to go bird watching, or looking for bears or porcupines or whatever? And similarly over here on a smaller scale, how well are the natural resources conserved and how imminent are the threats from 'progress'?

It seems to me that in both cases nature has earned and is given a very high profile and priority, and wherever you are you can enjoy nature and wildlife close by and feel a part of the natural world. I think that that is what matters most for country people wherever they hail from.

So I feel privileged, as a North Norfolk resident of only twenty years, to be able to welcome this rich, varied and fascinating collection of essays by such an illustrious group of Norfolk authors, brilliantly assembled by Ian Scott whose own writings we know so well.

At the time I was reading these selections, I saw this poster in an office:

Coming together is a beginning
Keeping together is progress
Working together is success.

This engaging book is a beginning. Our working together is the hope for this saltmarsh coast we each cherish in our own way.

Kathleen Buxton,
Stiffkey

Ian Scott

Ian Scott was introduced to the Saltmarsh Coast when he visited the Wells home of his future wife Glynis in 1962. After their marriage in 1964 they lived mainly abroad for much of the next thirty years but in 1974 bought a cottage in Binham where, each summer, their children grew Norfolk roots. They moved to Wells when the Granary was converted in the 1990s. Ian retired as a Director of the World Bank in 1996 and now divides his time between academia, consulting, writing, messing about with (mostly wooden) boats and long distance motor rallies (South America in 2001, London-Sydney in 2005). Ian has written three books, chapters in several others and numerous articles on topics ranging from economic development, urbanisation, management and organisation, classic boats and the North Norfolk coast, to American politics. He lives on Wells Quay and in Virginia, USA.

A Vulnerable Place

Ian Scott

My first encounter with a vulnerable place came when, as a child of eleven, I met the Isle of Purbeck in Dorset. It was actually a peninsula, not an island, but in 1951 it was a place apart. I loved it at once and in my teenage years often cycled there from my home in London. Twenty years later I wanted to share it with my Norfolk wife. Corfe Castle, Langton Matravers and Rime Intrinsica were still on the map but their magic had evaporated. This once special place had been homogenised with the rest of Southern England.

Twenty years later our family discovered another island, this time a real one, five miles off the coast of Massachusetts. Martha's Vineyard was and is a magical place and the contrast with the southern part of strip-malled, neon-lighted, billboarded Cape Cod, that not long before had been much like the Vineyard, was overwhelming.

Why, we asked, was it so different? Because, we learned, the people who lived there, few of whom were anybody's idea of social conservatives, had fought to preserve the uncommon blend of landscape, townscape, seascape, beachscape and pondscape that reflected tradition, celebrated diversity and embraced a rich, distinctive and laid back lifestyle that made the Vineyard what it was.

The island had changed as it had been discovered and populated by summer visitors. But the year-rounders and the part-timers had developed a generally harmonious, tolerant and mutually appreciative culture. And both groups knew where to draw the line on change.

There is a tendency to encapsulate the history of the conservation of Martha's Vineyard in the celebrated 1960s fight to keep McDonalds restaurants off the island. Vineyarders had nothing against hamburgers but saw McDonalds as a Trojan horse: McDonalds today, Burger King tomorrow, House of Pancakes the day after, strip malls the year after that. It looked like snobbery but the real issue was not Big Macs. It was the threat of homogenisation that would begin with the first order for a cheeseburger and fries and end when the Vineyard looked like Cape Cod.

The saltmarsh coast

The Isle of Purbeck and Martha's Vineyard are respectively three hundred and three thousand miles from North Norfolk. Yet the economic, cultural, social, environmental and aesthetic issues, the commercial pressures and the stakes were much the same in the 1950s (Purbeck) and 60s (Vineyard) as they are in North Norfolk today. And the different outcomes – failure in Purbeck, success on the Vineyard – bound the range of plausible futures for the Saltmarsh Coast.

The North Norfolk coast is as distinctive as any similar-length stretch of shoreline and adjacent countryside in the world. The endpapers of this book show that from Holme-next-the-Sea where soft red cliffs give way to muddy deposits that support Europe's largest semi-contiguous saltmarsh, its inland boundary curves south by east towards the King's Lynn – Cromer road (the A148) then east by north back to the coast where, beyond Salthouse, the saltmarshes are replaced by crumbling chalk cliffs. There are no signs to tell the visitor he has arrived or she is about to leave. Yet most people, if not on their first visit, then on their second or third, develop an intuitive sense of where it begins and ends.

The area straddles parts of two District Councils (North Norfolk and West Norfolk) and two parliamentary constituencies (North Norfolk and North-West Norfolk). It also straddles parts of an Area of Outstanding Natural Beauty, a Special Area of Conservation and a Site of Special Scientific Interest. The area does not coincide precisely with any of them. But then administrative and political boundaries rarely coincide with geographical and historical realities and in North Norfolk they cut randomly across the geological, geomorphological, architectural, economic, cultural and social characteristics that bind the area together and distinguish it from everywhere else. Parish level census data provide the basis for the demographic and economic profile of the Saltmarsh Coast in this chapter that show both its internal similarities and external contrasts.

The dominant physical features of this place apart are a network of creeks that fill quickly and empty slowly every twelve hours; sand and mud flats that reach to the far horizon; and dissected hummocks that are seasonally quilted with samphire, sea lavender and other salt-loving vegetation. Above the intense life of the creek bottoms, the marsh is home to waders, ducks, geese, terns and gulls and highflying larks.

Small parts of saltmarsh have been reclaimed as fresh water marsh. But most of it has survived as one of Britain's last remaining wildernesses. Because it is wild it is untamed; because it is untamed it can be dangerous; and because it can be dangerous it offers an exotic and exciting contrast with the orderly countryside behind it.

The coastal settlements of North Norfolk exist because the saltmarsh is intersected by winding tidal channels that at one time provided sheltered deepwater harbours, some more than a mile from the open sea (which is why Wells, Holme and Cley are 'next-the-sea' rather than 'on-sea'). Most of these settlements have been there for at least a thousand years, as have the villages that, two to five miles apart, dot the just-inland landscape. Until railways and roads improved in the 19th century the inland as well as the coastal settlements accessed the rest of England, the Low Countries and the Baltic through the marsh-protected ports and harbours of Thornham, Brancaster, Burnham, Holkham, Wells, Stiffkey, Morston, Blakeney, Wiveton, Cley and Salthouse. Partly as a result of natural processes and partly because of human interventions, none are now commercial ports and Cley, Wiveton and Holkham have not had access to the sea for more than 200 years.

The history of this area has been shaped by its geography. It is all-of-a-piece today because it shares a largely common past. For those of us who live here now it is an almost mystical blend of wild and tamed: a saltmarsh that looks much as it looked at the start of the last millenium; a well-tended arable landscape; and well-loved villages built with brick, flint, carrstone and chalk-rock that came from the ground beneath them.

Some people with remarkably short memories argue that the only significant changes to have occurred here since 1960 lie in the shifting sands of one of the world's most dynamic foreshores where spits, bars, dunes and even hills come and go from one year to the next. But while it is true that the saltmarsh today is much as it was, it is nonsense to pretend the cultivated and cultural landscapes to the

The Granary, Wells

3

south have not changed.

In the forty odd years I have known it the area has changed in many ways. A place that forty years ago was all but unknown has become a bolthole for the almost rich and would-be famous. A place where, forty years ago, properties changed hands for fractions of London prices now has one of the hottest housing markets in the country. A place that, forty years ago, had thriving agriculture and fishing is increasingly dependent on service trades. A place that, forty years ago, had a sprinkling of retirees and lots of growing families now has a population that is ageing faster than that of most places on the planet.

Because census definitions have changed, it is impossible to track the pace and extent of change with great accuracy. But there is sufficient partial evidence to validate the premise that North Norfolk is not the same place it was in the 1960s and that the pace of change is accelerating. Looking at them and taking stock of my own thoughts and feelings as the millennium ended, it seemed to me the pace and implications of demographic, economic, social and environmental change had accelerated enough to threaten the essence of the place. A few of its most fashionable villages had been radically altered; it seemed only a matter of time before others went the same way.

The book

In December 2000, I concluded it was time for a book about the cultural erosion of the Saltmarsh Coast with the (I thought) plausible aim of getting people to wake up and take notice before it was too late. With the lessons of Purbeck and the Vineyard at the back of my mind, I talked to friends and neighbours and learned from them that the area was more vulnerable in more ways than I had thought.

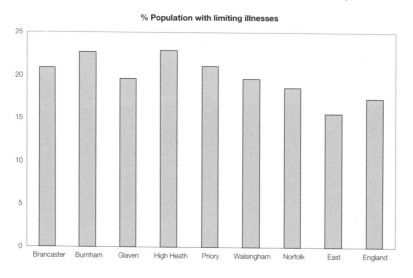

% Population with limiting illnesses

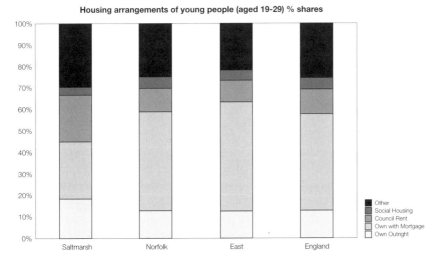

Housing arrangements of young people (aged 19-29) % shares

They told me about the implications of global warming and the pros and cons of 'managed retreat'; about the threats to the rural landscape from price competition and European agricultural policy; about the continued depletion of fish stocks and policies that promised further depletion; about threats to traditional country sports; about threats to migrant bird habitats brought about by changing farming practises; about threats to health, education and social services from rising costs….

They told me about many issues and argued that many of them had many sides. And it became obvious that if there were to be a new book about North Norfolk I could not write it. Partly because I had already written *A Month of Summers*[1] and more importantly because I could not hope to authentically reflect the contrasting perspectives it would have to capture. I knew of only two ways to do that. One was for an author to record a cross-section of thoughts and feelings in conversations with a representative group of people. The other was for an editor to recruit a group of authors who could speak authoritatively about the issues.

Having worked on many projects with multiple authors I knew the risks of that approach but decided I would rather take those risks than set myself up for comparison with Ronald Blythe[2]. So I set about finding authors who shared my concern for the future of the place, who knew what they were talking about, who were willing to be candid and who were willing to tolerate the inevitable ambiguities and probable frustrations of an enterprise for which I knew no precedents.

In due course I found them. Twenty of them. All had the crucial attributes I was looking for. And they were certainly diverse. In fact, apart from those attributes and a marked propensity to travel (the authors spent weeks or months in America,

---

[1] *A Month of Summer*, Terence Dalton, Lavenham, 1964
[2] *Akenfield: Story of an English Village*, Ronald Blythe, Pantheon Books, London, 1969

Argentina, Australia, Austria, Bolivia, Brasil, Canada, Chile, China, New Zealand, Peru, Russia, Uganda, Uruguay and South Africa while the book was being written) they had little in common.

In fact I gradually realised that our perceptions of the Saltmarsh Coast varied to the extent it was, for each of us, an ultimately different place. We had experienced it in different ways, at different times, over different periods. We had seen it through the prism of different interests. We had interpreted it in light of different values, priorities and concerns. And we had started our never-ending journeys from different towns and villages[3]. This place hangs together because it has a largely common history and geography. But the view from Wiveton is not quite the same as the view from Wells or Walsingham; what you see is affected by where you sit.

Some of the authors have lived their entire lives on the Saltmarsh Coast; some were born here, went away, and came back; some came as adults; some began as summer children. Some are intimate with one village; some know the whole area as though it were one. Some work mainly with their hands; some with their heads; some with both; and some stopped working years ago. Some have specific interests; some are interested in just about everything.

I knew in advance the book could not deal with all the forces that might shape the future of the Saltmarsh Coast. But then the aim was not to produce a primer but to show how and why the area was physically, socially and culturally fragile and to arouse a largely passive and in some ways complacent community to the threats and opportunities that, in the absence of action, could transform it in less time than most people might imagine.

Questions, questions

In my professional life I have found that when confronted by change – in places, in organisations, public and private, large and small, in customs and conventions and in policies, procedures and practices – a remarkable number of people, including many who should know better, have a perverse and lemming-like tendency to glue onto answers without first defining questions.

If there is broad agreement about the question and everyone agrees on the answer there is little point in arguing the toss. But if the question is poorly defined or if there are different views about its relevance or priority the invariable result of going straight to the answer is muddle, waste and frustration. The question must come first.

I had a slate of questions about the future of North Norfolk that seemed to me both urgent and important. But the authors had questions too. So rather than try

---

[3] Binham, Blakeney, Brancaster, the Burnhams (Market, Norton and Overy Staithe), Holkham, Langham, Sculthorpe, Wells and Wiveton

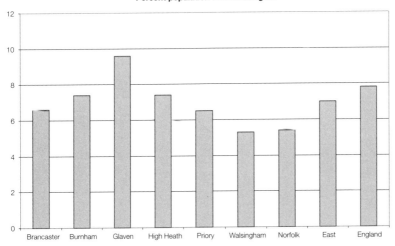

Percent population with first degree

to select the questions myself (although I made the odd suggestion), I asked them to choose their own, relying on their commitment to the issues and on their diversity to flush out the right ones – which is to say the questions most readers would likely see as critical.

A special case, a case in point

Every place is a special case because every location is unique. But drawing an analogy with some of Orwell's pigs some places are more unique than others. Homogenisation and globalisation have blunted distinctions and have made some issues almost ubiquitous; with local variations they crop up time and again. An assessment of issues arising in one place echo in others.

The fact that a special case can also be a case in point was brought home to me by *'A Place in the Country'* (1985)[4], a book about the processes of economic, social and cultural change in the by then relict County of Rutland. The changes in Rutland were remarkably similar – although the details were different – to those that had already transformed Gloucestershire and would soon creep across Cornwall. So while the book was about Rutland it was also about, among other places, Norfolk, because the economic, social and cultural changes there resembled the changes that by 1990 were well under way here. Rutland was both a special case and an example of a generic one.

With the exceptions of things like power generation schemes that wipe places off the planet, business closures that stop economic pulses and new roads that spoil unspoiled landscapes, changes in rural landscapes, cultures, economies and societies are rarely if ever the product of grand designs, government fiats or

---

[4] *A Place In The Country*, Nigel Ducker and Huw Davies, Michael Joseph, London, 1990

orchestrated transformations. They are smaller, subtler and more incremental. They result from hundreds and thousands of decisions by households and small firms to buy and sell houses, shops, hotels, restaurants and other small businesses, to farm or not to farm, to fish or not to fish, to retire early or buy a country retreat. And they invariably go unreported, even unnoticed, until someone contrasts the way things are with the way things were – by which time the sum of their effects is often irreversible.

The public sector naturally has a role in rural change. It invests in public services, facilities and infrastructure. It creates plans and strategies that provide frameworks for the decisions of firms and households. But the gradual changes that have occurred in rural England over the last several hundred years owe little to grand (or even small) designs or the generally uncoordinated actions of national, regional and local governments.

Some of the most important public sector decisions that have shaped the face of North Norfolk were taken long before anyone was talking about tides of change. Notably those about transport infrastructure taken in the 1960s when North Norfolk was still its old and comfortable self, second homes few and telecommuters unheard of.

A notable example was the Norfolk County Council's decision, made after lengthy debate in the 1950s, to improve the King's Lynn – Cromer road (A148) rather than the coast road (A149). Another was the national government's decision to build the M11 which, with complementary improvements to the A11 and other roads, reduced journey times from London to less than three hours and, in the 1980s, brought North Norfolk within the London weekend belt.

In North Norfolk, as elsewhere, the public sector proposes, the private sector disposes. It is one thing for government (national, county, district or town) to

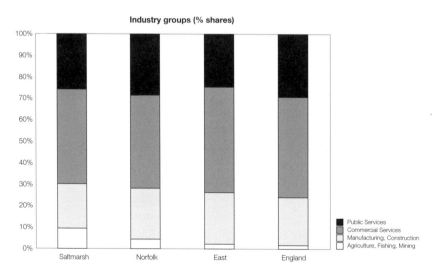

create amenities, facilities and incentives, another for the private sector to use them. The main impact of strategies developed by County and District Governments and an astonishing array of quasi-public bodies – the National Trust, the Nature Conservancy, English Nature, English Heritage, the Norfolk Coast Partnership – has been to control excesses, prevent atrocities and provide sometimes conflicting frameworks for private sector decisions.

In detail, these arrangements are idiosyncratic to North Norfolk. But give or take a nuance or two, planning controls are planning controls and the roles of the public and private sectors are much the same as in most of the modern world. And just as things that happened last year in Cornwall, the year before in Dorset and the year before that in Gloucestershire are relevant to Norfolk today, this book about what could happen here tomorrow may echo in places I have never even heard of.

The big issue

The most obvious changes in the Saltmarsh Coast in recent decades are direct and indirect results of the fact that local families with long and strong roots in the community have been partially replaced by people who have moved here from elsewhere. These demographic changes and the economic, social and cultural changes that have come with them have strained the fabric of what not long ago was an arguably feudal yet tight-knit society. The strains are measured in tensions, jealousies and resentments. Some can be explained by local standoffishness towards strangers. Some by the crassness of incomers. Some by the fact that people who were born here, retired here and live here on a part-time basis do not understand each other very well.

Local people and incomers exchange greetings, meet in community organisations, visit each other's houses and chew over questions that come to the surface, sometimes in heated public debates. Many such issues – housing, schooling, transport, health, jobs, – are dealt with from different and sometimes contrasting perspectives in this book. But the big issue that is rarely if ever discussed is who, if anyone, 'owns' this place.

Only those who have lived in real communities know what most people in

today's urbanised world are missing. The distinguishing feature of communities is that people who live in them know and care about the other people who live and work in them. As recently as the 1960s life in a typical North Norfolk village was in some ways very different than it had been fifty years earlier when village houses lacked running water, indoor sanitation and mains electricity. But it was in other ways very similar. Most of the people living in it would have been born, if not there, then not far away. Most would have worked, if not there, then not far away. Most of their immediate families would have lived, if not there, then not far away. And most of their ancestors would have lived and died, if not there, then not far away.

Fast forward forty-five years and some North Norfolk villages are shadows of their recent selves. Few have expanded. Apart from 'infilling' most of the buildings were there in 1960. But look closer at the double-glazing, conservatories, rebuilt walls, central heating and insulated roofs. Look inside at designer kitchens, master bedrooom suites, jacuzzi bathrooms and original art. Look outside and see the heated pool. Look in the garage and see this year's Range Rover and last year's Porsche. Talk to the new owners. Ask where they spend the rest of the week or year. Find out where they work. Learn about their children's schools. And understand why local transport, local schools, local jobs and local health care are not on their agendas; they are in this place but are not of this place.

In 1960 there was no doubt who owned North Norfolk. It belonged to people whose forebears had lived there for centuries. They were the literal and unself-conscious embodiment of a traditional culture. Visitors came and went, mostly in summer and mostly for the day. People moved in and out in relatively small numbers. It was not yet a magnet for retirees. On winter nights most houses in most villages had glowing windows and coal smoke poured from their chimneys.

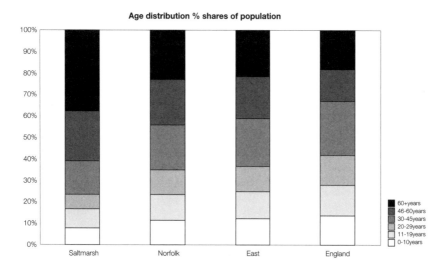

Age distribution % shares of population

Now, more houses and cottages in its fashionable villages are dark than lit from Monday to
Friday. More than half the houses in some villages are owned by people who live there only at
weekends and in longer summer holidays when the
villages are transformed by foreign voices, attitudes and
consumer preferences.

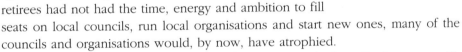

Some local people wish outsiders had never
discovered the place. But if retirees and weekenders had not bought the village houses no
longer needed by farm workers, some would have
stood empty. If they had not come, more village
shops would have closed, more builders and decorators would be less busy, more local pubs, restaurants and hotels would not have been upgraded
and new jobs would not have offset those lost in
agriculture, fishing and manufacturing. And if
retirees had not had the time, energy and ambition to fill
seats on local councils, run local organisations and start new ones, many of the
councils and organisations would, by now, have atrophied.

Although born-here local people still chair most Parish Councils, incomers will,
if recent trends continue, eventually take over. And that is the heart of the matter.
Because if the character of a place reflects its natural and built environments and
the distinctive culture of the people who live there, and if the people who live
there are eventually out-numbered, out-spent, out-voted and out-organised by
incomers there comes a time at which it is no longer the same place. It becomes
a husk, a shell, and ultimately a sham.

The risk this could happen in North Norfolk is now real despite the fact few
people welcome the prospect. Local people fear it because it means the loss of
their heritage. Many incomers do not like it either because they came for the
culture as well as the natural and built environment. If the essence of this place is
lost it will not be lost because most people want that to happen but because
circumstances conspire to bring about change that is ultimately beyond anyone's
control.

Faced with comparable realities local communities in other places have
responded in different ways. Some have burned property owned by incomers.
Some have hurled insults, waved placards and written offensive letters. Some have
grumbled to each other and written to local newspapers. Some have said nothing,
admitting defeat.

Yet if local people do not, can not or will not stand up for preservation and
conservation, who will? Certainly not incomers with an imperfect grasp of the past

11

and a tenuous understanding of local sensibilities wrapped in misplaced nostalgia for things that never were and places that never existed.

Authenticity flows from continuity that can come only from those who remember the way things were, the people who were here before and the great and sometimes awful events in the life of a place such as the great flood that devastated the North Norfolk coast (and other North Sea coasts) in 1953. They remember them because they are part of their personal experiences.

Continuity is a burden and local people can shed it. But they cannot share it with even the most industrious incomers. Because no matter how hard the incomers work to understand their adopted environments (cherishing the mistaken notion they can become local if only they try hard enough) they can never replicate the implicit knowledge that is in the bones of truly local people – including those who grew up here, went away and came back.

But it is one thing to say local people have a unique burden, another to contemplate the facts that not all of them accept it and that those who do sometimes act their parts in counterproductive ways, just as those who envy them, despite good intentions, frequently get it wrong.

Local people behave counterproductively when they reject everything proposed by outsiders as wrong, misguided or motivated by greed rather than altruism; when they confuse compromise with weakness; when they attack incomers' ideas only because they come from incomers; when they refuse to seek public offices in which they could make a difference preferring instead to shout from the side-lines; when they ignore the opportunities that often come with threats; when they strike futile Canute-like postures towards the tides of change; when they oppose the reality that in their lifetimes things have changed and will continue to change whether they like it or not; when they fail to realise that local communities can

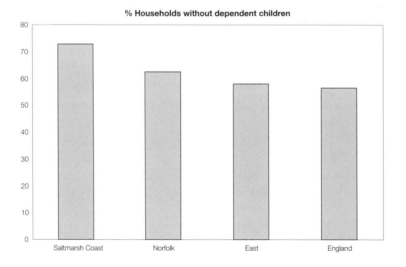

% Households without dependent children

affect and direct change if only they will get their collective acts together; when they focus on their differences with each other rather than their differences with outsiders; and when they are unwilling to fight for the conditions – above all affordable housing – that must be satisfied if they are to live here.

Outsiders get it wrong when they patronise local people; when they assume that because some local people have less formal education they are less intelligent; when they fail to listen to local voices; when they impose their interpretations of local history on the people whose history it is; when they fail to understand that when local people seem reticent to speak they are simply reflecting the self-effacing modesty that is part of their culture; when they ignore local precedents; when they mistake silence for acceptance; when they insist they know better because they have more experience of the world; when they denigrate local customs, conventions and practices they find offensive; when they want to change the very things that make this place so distinctive; when they gush about a place that never was; when they are unwilling to work with and through local people to help the local economy adapt to changing circumstances; when they fail to bite their tongues when criticised for being too pushy; and when they do not listen to the people to whom the essence of this place belongs.

North Norfolk would remain what it is if the incomers went away. But it would not remain what it is if the incomers took over. Local people are the key to the future of North Norfolk and places like it. Their families preserved the environment, built the villages, and transferred speech, attitudes and values to their children. They therefore have special rights because this place ultimately belongs to them.

So when incomers who have been here for the famous five minutes start gushing about things that have been familiar to local people for generations as though their insights had led them to new discoveries, it is small wonder local people wish they would shut up. When incomers start apologising to weekend guests because they have to drive through local authority housing estates that 'lower the tone of the place', it is not surprising that local people wish they would go away. When incomers send party invitations that say they are 'planning to invite a few locals for a bit of colour', it is only to be expected local people will feel insulted. When incomers complain about kitchen smells from the pub in Binham that has been serving food and drink for four hundred years, you can understand why local people want to chuck them out. When incomers in a middle class housing development at Brancaster make it known they 'do not want locals', the locals are inevitably outraged. And when newly arrived incomers say things like[5]: 'There are just tons of clever, talented creative people and all working jolly hard to stay here'... 'the joy of living in North Norfolk is that it IS so cosmopolitan'... 'what is great is the combination of (its outstanding natural beauty) and its coolness – yes it is funky and hip and happening and chi-chi'... and 'you have to be seen queuing for something in Burnham Market'....you can understand why local people wish they would keep their thoughts to themselves.

At one time I thought an organising principle for this book might be a fault line between local people or 'born heres' and incomers or 'come heres'. I later realised that 'born heres' do not necessarily think common thoughts or share common feelings and that it is no less absurd to tar all 'come heres' with the same brush.

There are no easy answers to the questions posed in this book. And answers will remain elusive in the absence of a constructive dialogue between those who fear the implications of change and those who are shaping it. Meanwhile the forces of change will grind on. Entrepreneurs will see opportunities others have ignored. Improvers will try to improve things that do not need improving. There will be more degrees of separation between those who want to stay and those who want to come. House prices will continue to rise. Tensions will continue to increase. So it is time for those who want to preserve the essence of this place to start talking to each other – and to the incomers.

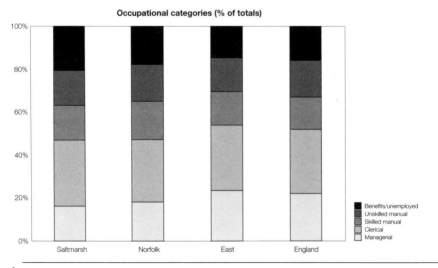

Occupational categories (% of totals)

_____

[5] From *North Norfolk Living*, Summer 2004

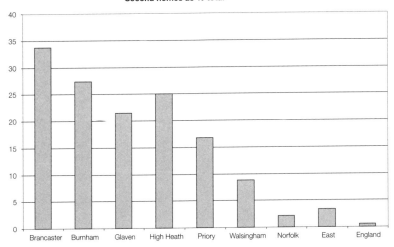

Second homes as % total

In the early 1970s a property developer bought a large Georgian house called 'Normans' in Wells-next-the-Sea and built half a dozen new houses in what had been its grounds. He called the development 'Invaders Court' and named the houses for the successive waves of invaders – Romans, Saxons, Danes, Vikings, Jutes – who, having stormed ashore, settled here and contributed to the local gene pool.

None of the invaders were welcomed as they pillaged, burned and raped. But in due course they mingled, adding distinctive outlooks, customs and practices to those they found. The latest invaders came on the M11 and the A47 rather than by sea. They did not pillage or burn; they just pushed property prices through the roof of the big blue sky.

If 'Invaders Court' were built today and there were room for another house it might be called 'Yuppies'. By comparison with their predecessors, today's invaders are a tame lot. Yet some members of the local community view them with a milder form of the same suspicion and hostility with which the Icenae met the Romans and the Saxons met the Vikings. Bearing in mind those invaders eventually resolved their differences with the people they invaded it may not be too much to expect the current invaders to do likewise. They should, because if they don't they will wake up one day to find most of the really local people have been driven out of their homeland by inaccessible property prices. They will then have it all to themselves. And they will find it is no longer the place they came to. They will own the theme park but will have lost the theme.

Andrew Bloomfield

Andrew Bloomfield was born at Holkham in 1967, went to school in Wells, trained and worked as a printer in Fakenham and elsewhere before becoming a summer Warden on Holkham Nature Reserve. As 'Rattlesnake Bloomfield' he also became a part time professional wrestler but decided writing about and photographing birds was safer than being hurled about by 17-stone freaks. His hobby became his career and he has travelled widely in search of birds, most recently in Uganda. His publications on area bird life include *The Birds of Holkham* (Pica Press, 1999). He lives at Sculthorpe.

Here Today, Gone Tomorrow?

Andrew Bloomfield

Looking back on my upbringing in the 1970s, I often think it could not have been any finer. Born as a shepherd's son in a tied cottage in Holkham Park would not perhaps seem the ideal beginning for many of the present generation, but to me it was wonderful.

The world around me, despite seeming vast at the time, was in fact unbelievably small. About three thousand acres within nine miles of wall to be precise. Understandably, everything seemed quite familiar and insular. Then the only threats were avoiding the gamekeepers in the woods – the nearest a youngster got to real life.

At that time the estate still boasted a large workforce in all its departments. Its cottages were all inhabited by its staff; farm workers, building maintenance, gamekeepers and woodsmen. Many were either distantly related or came from large families who had been there just as long as my own (my mother's family roots at Holkham date back to the 1700s). All seemed as one in both attitude and upbringing and a sense of community spirit prevailed that could never be underestimated. For a child in such a relatively isolated environment, with few friends of the same age, the only natural thing seemed to be to join in with day-to-day chores and (at the time unknowingly) begin a journey of appreciation of the natural history of the land where I lived. My youth was spent enjoying the freedom of being able to wander wherever I wanted across fields and through woods, although much of my life revolved around the daily routines of my father and his sheep. Depending on the season it would be lambing, shearing, feeding, moving the flock, penning them in or training sheep dogs; enough to ensure boredom was never an issue. Despite never being a wealthy man and working himself into an early grave, my father lived for the most part a satisfying and contented life, out in the fresh air without any of the constraints of modern life.

I loved every minute, becoming aware of the landscape, the wildlife, the weather and above all the characters. And what characters there were. They all had their tales to tell and all were uttered in a wonderful broad accent, with expressions and words that would undoubtedly be quite alien to many of today's new residents and youngsters. Farm labourers such as Bernie Beaumont, 'Big' John Mallett, and Bob Sizeland, gamekeepers Arbo Gent, Basil Goffin, Eric Newstead and Billy Rowe, while who could forget Aunt Deb, organist in the Methodist chapel (a converted granary!)? I became tuned in to their wry observations of life and dry sense of humour; qualities that only seem to be so pronounced amongst genuine country folk. All of course were different, but to me they all fitted neatly into the environment and were as much a part of it as the fallow deer, the beech trees and the Obelisk in the centre of the park. As life progressed and my horizons broadened, I soon realised they were not entirely unique. Every village, hamlet and farm had its own equally wise old characters. These were the true inhabitants of North Norfolk. They helped shape it and they would have been quite out of place anywhere else.

School in nearby Wells was equally enjoyable. Most pupils came from similar backgrounds, their parents either working on the land, fishing, the building trade or in local factories. Most of us felt our future was to follow in their footsteps. One thing I soon learnt at school was how a Norfolk accent was often thought of as quaint and seemingly unacceptable. Naturally a few of us revelled in it. It felt good to speak in a dialect that some of the teachers just could not comprehend; it gave us a strong sense of proud uniqueness. Despite much ridicule from some of the staff and pupils who had moved here from elsewhere, I was determined not to alter my pronunciation and vocabulary. Why should I? It was part of my heritage, and yet it seemed then as it does now that a broad Norfolk accent was something only to be laughed at. I could not and still have not worked out why a London or Northern accent is deemed acceptable in Norfolk, more so it seems than our own! What was always in one way wonderful and insulting in another was the way the accent was impersonated by others. Very few could (and still cannot) imitate it convincingly. Unfortunately with fewer youngsters these days mixing with the old characters, it is a dying accent. What we hear today is far more watered down and it is obvious that many of our former expressions and phraseology will be lost for good.

For me, Wells school provided another bonus. Not only was there an agricultural science teacher with nearly as much enthusiasm for his subject as for rapping knuckles with the split end of his ruler, but it also had a bird club. The two combined helped to install a deep love of natural history in me that has yet to wane. It opened up a whole new world, from the wide open wilderness of the saltings at Wells and Stiffkey, to the bird-filled marshes of Titchwell and Cley and the stark splendour of the dunes at Scolt Head and Burnham Overy. Seeing terns in abundance, marsh harriers in their high-flying, sky-dancing display flight and bushes full of migrant song birds left me overwhelmed by the fact that so much could be seen only a few miles away from home. It made me certain from a very young age that here was my place. I had no ambitions to be rich or famous, just to enjoy all the aspects of the land where I was fortunate enough to have been born. My love of the North Norfolk countryside and its flora and fauna, its abundance of country characters and above all my family roots, left me with no desire ever to leave.

My initial journey into life might have been slightly different from those of some of my contemporaries but upon leaving school I was left with the same hard decisions about what to do with my future. The North Norfolk of my childhood was a good grounding in many aspects of life, but in the wider world it was soon apparent just how fast the region was changing and how difficult things were becoming for local people, particularly youngsters.

Nowadays many local youngsters, particularly those with ambitions, opt to move away, lured by higher wages, further education or simply to undertake opportunities that do not exist here. Those who do decide to stay face the uncertainty of finding local work. Farming and fishing, the traditional cornerstones of the region's employment, have been the subject of much technological, political and economical change and consequently no longer offer the opportunities they once did. Over-fishing, lessening quotas, stricter regulations and foreign competition have changed the face of the latter. Farming similarly has been affected by increasing mechanisation and competition from subsidized foreign crops.

As time moves on it seems the nail is being driven ever further into the coffin of agricultural employment. A perfect example in how quickly and how much things have changed is Shammer Farm, near North Creake. In the mid-1980s it still employed well over 20 local men. Manual hoeing and sprout picking were still carried out, bales were stacked by hand and pigs and cattle were kept. Temple's Farm in Wells had its own carrot-processing factory that created extra employment. In the short space of 15 years Shammer Farm's workforce was down to only half a dozen workers and it had no pigs or cattle. Thanks to continental prices it was no longer viable for Temple's to grow carrots and the factory closed. It is a sad fact that the area's villages now offer hardly any of the forms of employment that initially made them what they were.

This lack of choice has forced relocation, which in turn has led to other changes; the closure of village shops, pubs and schools and ultimately the demise of communities. Quality of life for those few still able to earn a living from the land has also been greatly affected by the smaller workforce. Longer hours, something the fledgling trade unions fought hard to combat in former years, have once more become the norm.

Further problems for locals seeking work in agriculture have been created by the upsurge in foreign immigrant workers, who are attractive to many employers because of their willingness to accept paltry wages. Many farmers also find it more cost effective to utilise agricultural contractors as opposed to buying expensive machinery and employing extra men. Often the only option for youngsters if they are unable to find a trade apprenticeship is to accept low paid work from the handful of nearby factories or shops, bars, hotels and anything the ever-growing tourist industry might produce. It can be argued that tourism does produce a multitude of local jobs, but the fact that many are seasonal and invariably low-paid make them unsuitable for anyone wishing to either start a family or buy a house. Things have worsened further since the millennium. More foreign competition, not only in the low-skilled factory labour market but also in the up- market bars and hotels. Add to this a great desire by some employers to enlist well-educated students (in their summer breaks) from anywhere except locally and the problem looks set to last. Such factors mean that many youngsters are forced to travel further afield to find work and ultimately end up leaving the area.

The only glimmer of hope may be that with the boom in second and more affluent homes there will always be demand for building maintenance, electricians, plumbers, decorators, gardeners and other support services. With few apprenticeships available locally and few housing options for young adults, the question is whether any of those who can provide these services will be able to live locally or will they come from elsewhere?

Looking back at the time that has passed since I left school in 1984, it soon becomes obvious that North Norfolk is no longer the place it once was. Quite frighteningly, some places and aspects of life have changed beyond all recognition. Many reasons can be cited such as political decisions, economics, climate change, social factors and technological progress. Change is of course one of life's certainties and is not unique in any way to North Norfolk. The fact that it has happened so quickly in an area that once had such a pronounced identity makes it all the more unpopular amongst the local population. Equally despised is the fact that change was in many ways driven by the area's growing popularity among affluent newcomers and second home owners. This, along with the demise of local employment, has been the biggest catalyst of change.

Whilst seaside towns such as Cromer, Hunstanton and Sheringham have been holiday resorts since Victorian times, most of the North Norfolk coast was for a long while rather more undesirable to the masses. Its abundance of picturesque navigable harbours, its miles of unspoilt beaches and its wild and weather-beaten marshes were once a relatively well kept secret, appreciated only by the more 'exclusive' sailing fraternity or 'eccentric' naturalists, wildfowlers and birdwatchers.

Above all it was still just as much a place of work as of play.

Gradually, however, the allure of North Norfolk's subtleties and rural setting became more mainstream. The growing popularity of Blakeney and Wells soon extended to the smaller villages, initially on the coast, soon to be followed by the adjacent villages inland. With house prices cheap in comparison to those in many other places around the country, what started as a trickle turned into a spiralling avalanche. By the end of the 1980s and into the 1990s the flood of incomers who purchased holiday homes, second homes and retirement homes seemed more akin to an invasion. While tourism undoubtedly has its benefits, for many locals the negative issues that soon began to emerge, gradually outweighed the positive ones.

The issue that is having the greatest impact and quite honestly looks like it might never be solved is the lack of affordable houses for locals who were brought up in North Norfolk and want to remain here. Rapidly ascending house prices since the 1980s is of course nothing unique; it is a nationwide problem for anyone trying to get onto the property ladder. What has heightened the dilemma here is the fact that most working class locals earn very poor wages. Whereas in the past

many farm labourers would live in tied cottages, the lack of such employment has taken this option away.

Some landowners have also been forced into selling these 'surplus' cottages to supplement their lessening incomes. With many unused barns, farm buildings and Methodist chapels falling into a steady state of decline, the last decade has seen an ever-increasing number of them converted into living accommodation. It is a crying shame to see such wonderful old buildings that once had so much character and were integral parts of North Norfolk's history and landscape, no longer used for the purposes for which they were built. Everyone agrees that it is far better to see them used than to be left to disintegrate (although how much of their character remains is debatable) and such is the price of their restoration and their ultimate desirability to the wealthy incomer, they will never be places for low paid locals to live in.

Mortgages are often beyond the reach of youngsters and it now seems very sadly that rented accommodation is becoming equally expensive or is simply not available to the extent it once was. Many of the area's council houses, once the answer to every lowly paid family's housing problems, have been sold to tenants and then ultimately private buyers (some eventually becoming holiday homes) to such a degree that trying to rent one is now virtually impossible. Those that are still council owned seem to be handed out wholesale to unmarried mothers or 'problem' families from elsewhere. Such a policy naturally creates further resentment amongst locals genuinely in search of a home, while it has been known on frequent occasions to encourage teenage girls to perhaps began life on the wrong footing and become pregnant thus ensuring the probability of being housed. With nothing much except a small (by comparison) number of housing association dwellings as an alternative, the future looks decidedly bleak.

What has added to and in many cases fuelled the problem is the aforementioned popularity of the area to incomers. Those fortunate enough to have sold their houses elsewhere at inflated prices or are just plain rich, have been able to snap up any house that springs up on the local housing market seemingly without any worry or concern, thus effectively banishing many poorly paid locals as mere bystanders, devoid of any chance at competing.

One of many examples of outsiders' attitudes to the local housing problem concerns a good friend of mine born and bred in a house on Front Street in Burnham Market. Both his father and his father's father had been born there too. As time has progressed the street has increasingly been taken over by incomers, with very few locals now in residence. The dogged determination of some outsiders to take over the whole street became increasingly clear to my friend's father. For almost his whole life he worked locally as a stockman and like many of his generation never had any desire to move. Several times each year however, he would have people beg him to sell his property for cash, money no object. He would always refuse, sometimes (unsurprisingly) not too politely, particularly if they were persistent in their attempts. On one occasion he was told, 'the street would see the back of him' followed quite laughably by letters of complaint about the early morning crowing of his cockerels, which even went to great detail in listing dates, times and frequency of their crowing! Naturally he ignored such futile attempts, saying the only way they would see him gone was when he died. Unfortunately he died suddenly in 2002, thus depriving the community of another irreplaceable local character.

The story did not end there, however, as both his widow, his son and his daughter received letters only a month or two after his death, from a family in London unknown to them, desperate to move to Burnham Market, begging them to sell. It just shows how thick skinned and thoughtless incomers often are. They assume money is the answer to everything and with it you can have whatever you want. Never mind about the thoughts of a grieving family, just wave pound notes at them, it is bound to ease the pain! Thankfully the family will not part with the property thus maintaining a real local element in its rightful place. It must be something about Burnham Market because another former local, this time on Back Street, was faced with the same kind of continual requests. There was general all round unpleasantness and there were deliberate attempts to block his car in. It seemed he had become an unwanted and undesirable local resident.

Burnham Market, Front Street

Locals are also infuriated at how certain estate agents actively promote North Norfolk in London, advertising even the simplest, smallest dwelling place as a desirable country home. Some regularly distribute fliers pleading for local homeowners to sell, such is the demand from potential second home owners and the certainty of quick sales from would-be buyers, many of them cash buyers. While there is no law in the land to say this is wrong, it continues to anger local people who cannot compete against such wealth. The fact that many homes subsequently stand empty for much of the year, it is even more galling not only for those in need of somewhere to live (as opposed to holiday in) but becuse it is leaving villages with a high percentage of empty houses for most of the year, adding further to our dying communities.

The advent of the council tax to fund overstretched local authorities created more ill feelings when a 50% reduction was given to second home owners. It seemed a ridiculous policy although thankfully it has at last been decreased to only a 10% reduction. Many locals quite rightly believe if someone can afford a second home then they are probably quite capable of paying an extra few hundred pounds in tax. The predicament caused by second home owners who limit the housing market for those who wish to live and work here (ultimately depriving the local council of cash for public spending) should be penalised with a tax bill double the size. It would not be very popular but then the incomers are not very popular; so give them some of their own medicine! The problem of second homes dominating the region is often discussed in the local press and at every election, but it is invariably brushed aside by more important issues. The fact is, the tension is starting to reach boiling point. A slogan 'Second home owners are thieving leaches' was painted across the approach road to Burnham Market in July 2004 by some brave soul. Perhaps it is surprising similar incidents have not occurred more regularly.

One venture was deemed as a lifeline; the selling of all the housing at Sculthorpe Airbase, which ceased operations in 1990. With many of the houses in disrepair through standing empty and neglected they were sold quite cheaply. The result was an instant village made up for the most part by a fair proportion of local working class people. With its sombre regimental appearance, derelict hangers and barbed wire topped perimeter fence it was obviously undesirable for many of North Norfolk's higher class incomers and promptly became as close as the area has got to its very own Indian reservation! Although things have improved from that initial sale period, needless to say even here some of the houses are now bought as holiday homes.

If housing is such a problem in North Norfolk why are no houses being built? Well they are, but they are not affordable small houses or council houses. They are half a million pound developments of dwellings suitable for those with plenty of money. Where is the answer? And will it arrive too late?

So with changes created by the lack of employment and housing, what else could alter the character of the region? The incomers themselves of course. They are often deemed as the single biggest factor in the region's altering appearance, some would even say its demise. While the lack of employment and poor wages started the housing problems, it is the incomers who have accelerated it and it is they who in many cases have stamped such a different, almost urbanised, city atmosphere in our once familiar surroundings.

Burnham Market, so often championed as being all that is best in the 'new' North Norfolk, equally epitomises the worst of it. It is often labelled with the horrendous title of 'Chelsea-on-Sea' in the glut of glossy Norfolk magazines (which also seem to be aimed solely at the wealthy incomer). It does however seem to sum it up. Extravagant, top of the range cars with the obligatory personalised number plates and four-wheel drives (that seldom see any off road use), fill the streets. Pompous characters wearing only the best fashionable clothes and speaking in the finest Queen's English proliferate the twee trinket shops, over expensive restaurants and a pub that attracts them in their droves.

You will not hear many Norfolk accents these days. And what 'squit' they utter. The invariable topic of conversation, usually bellowed so loudly anyone within earshot gets to hear, is money or arrogant self-importance. Locals are often looked down upon as an indigenous form of low life. I once overheard someone say how wonderful Burnham Market was, except for the 'awful approach road from the south and the road out to the west, all those ghastly council houses lowering the tone of the place'. Such snobbery can only be laughed at, although perhaps not by those who live there because in many cases these dwellings are homes to some of the last true inhabitants of the village. It often seems if you've got money you are fine, if not then you are either ignored or swept under the carpet. Not all incomers of course come into these broad and scathing statements, but for the most part this is a quite justified, albeit stereo–typed, local view of incomers. Most are definitely viewed with suspicion and mistrust.

North Norfolk was always deemed a friendly place, but today it is becoming anything but. Go for a walk and try saying hello or passing the time of day. It is surprising how often you will be ignored. If you don't get a blank response you might be lucky and receive a perplexed glance. I frequently wonder if the thoughts are along the lines of 'Did that peasant really speak to us?' Is this a product of modern mistrust and city living? Such discourteous behaviour is now also commonplace on our minor roads. Pull up on a narrow lane to give way to an oncoming vehicle and how often is there an acknowledgement of thanks? That is, if the other vehicle does not try to run you off the road. Maybe this is a product of modern driving, but invariably it seems to be a trend instigated by incomers with no time to spare or little thought for others in a rural environment with which they are unfamiliar.

As time has moved on the local view has grown that the majority of incomers are yuppies with too much time and money; that they are unfriendly, insincere and ill mannered; that they have little respect for the lowly strange speaking locals; and that they are all too apt to wangle themselves onto any committee, council or position of minor power where they can influence any number of changes to the area. But then it could be argued do locals show too much apathy and are they too laid back and easy going to bother? What always puzzles me is why do outsiders move here if they want to change it beyond recognition? Presumably they have fallen in love with North Norfolk's unique charm and qualities, so why are they not happy until they have altered them?

I often think of the time when a group of outsiders moved into Burnham Thorpe and after a seemingly short time made waves by trying to stop the cows being milked so early in the morning due to the noise they created and the mud they left on the road. At Wells, fishermen have often been criticised for having smelly crab pots stacked up in their gardens. How pathetic can you get – move to a quaint little fishing town and then complain of the eyesore created by the essential items a fisherman requires for his livelihood! Is it that some people are just not happy until they ruffle the feathers of others or is that certain individuals are on permanent ego trips to make a name for themselves? Then there are the 'five minute wonders', who arrive with great world changing agendas, only to come face to face with the reality of life here and disappear as quickly as they came. Little wonder there is mistrust. It is sadly very obvious that many of them only want to view North Norfolk on their own terms. Why, if they love North Norfolk so much, are they only content to live here in their leisure time instead of in London where the majority of their time is spent? Obviously back to the same problem: lack of opportunities and poor wages although others have said (at least in the past) that its remoteness and inaccessibility were also factors.

With so much gloom and doom created by the modern face of North Norfolk what of the future? Will things improve for the locals or is it too late? In my opinion some aspects will continue on their present course. Many of the previously mentioned problems such as housing and employment need instant action if answers are to be found. Most locals believe the area will continue to be popular and that the abundant wealth of those who are taking over will continue to be the main influence, turning it in to an ever more exclusive place.

So will it eventually be as uninspiring as the south coast of England, completely lacking the character it once possessed? With incomers importing their own social scene and ideas of culture, locals feel increasingly alienated. This has already happened to a degree, pubs with live entertainment are disappearing at an alarming rate. There is a much more lucrative market in serving food to the newer class of inhabitant. Local working class pubs have been forced to change or close. An establishment like the Shipwrights at Wells (to name but one example) is now only a name from the past. Without diversity many others would follow suit. Village shops, garages and post offices forced to close as a result of changes miraculously metamorphose into art galleries and antique shops and manage to survive thanks to incomers with enough money in their pocket to allow them such luxuries.

As much as I detest crime, I think it will increase greatly bearing in mind the abundance of wealth constantly on display and the resentment it creates amongst those with next to nothing in comparison. A while back one lad was committing regular burglaries in the Burnham area to order; such was the number of well-stocked but usually unoccupied holiday homes. Drugs in rural villages have also become more prevalent, something that would have been unthinkable only a few years ago. Crime is increasing because of that too. Unfortunately, with so few active police and laughable punishments dished out if perpetrators are caught, there seems to be no long-term deterrent.

As far as I can see the one saving grace for the region is its wildlife and landscape. While the forces of nature have shaped the latter and will continue to do so in the form of the predicted climatic changes and rising sea levels, no matter who is living here, most of what we see will hopefully not completely alter beyond recognition. For our highly cherished wildlife we have our forefathers to thank very much. They possessed the foresight to preserve our dynamic and charismatic coastal flora and fauna. Had it not have been for their concern and the ability they showed in creating so many acres of protected havens for our special natural history, it is fair to say North Norfolk would undoubtedly have become a far different place.

Their actions prevented unwelcome and unsympathetic developments and ultimately shaped much of what we see today thereby making it one of the richest areas for wildlife in the whole of Britain. Anyone who doubts this will soon realise it if they leave the area having spent any decent amount of time here. Of course, despite its rich diversity of life forms, there are problems. The area's popularity means human intrusion can often be at odds with nature. The large numbers of visitors who come specifically to Norfolk to enjoy its spectacular natural environment present a threat not only because of increased disturbance to many of our important species but also because of the erosion of sensitive and fragile coastal habitats.

Balance is needed. For the most part the conservation bodies on this coast are working both at protection and keeping visitors away from the most vulnerable spots. In the past, conservationists worked hard to preserve dwindling populations, sometimes attracting temporarily lost species back and also creating the right environments for many of our so called specialised coastal species such as terns, avocets and marsh harriers. Today we need to show just as much concern to address the decline of species that once commonly inhabited our farms and woods inland.

Changes in land management, agricultural practices and the use of chemical herbicides and pesticides have all contributed to the decline of many species. There is a need to reverse these trends before it is too late. A dedicated effort from farmers, conservationists and landowners may successfully address the falling numbers of house and tree sparrows, skylarks and English partridges on our farmland, and bitterns in the coastal reed beds, but there is one species that looks certain to become extinct in a quite small time scale. That species is the real old country character of North Norfolk.

Steeped in trades and professions that the modern world is increasingly less reliant upon, he will silently and gradually fade from the public eye until one day he will be no more. With him will go a wonderful language and a deep-rooted sense of pride and tradition. The sad fact is for all the wealth the newer inhabitants of North Norfolk are bringing with them this will be the one thing their money will be unable to buy back. Once that man is gone, he, his kind and the very essence of the region's character will be gone for good.

Field Sports

Andrew Cuthbert

'If you are trying to ban all hunting, are you hoping to make the foxes' lives better? because in fact you will be giving many foxes a life sentence of misery.' To this, the reply of a so called politician was: 'I don't care a * * * * about the fox; all we hope to do is to get those * * * * * * * toffs off of their * * * * * * * horses!'

To introduce the topic of the future of country sports in our area inevitably involves a certain amount of polemic and in my opinion the above exchange puts the whole debate about all types of hunting, with or without dogs, in a nutshell. By hunting I include game and coarse angling, shooting, coursing, falconry and stalking, as well as hunting the fox, deer, hare and, you might argue, the rat. Yes, there are a few genuine thinking people who, through lack of real 'earthy' knowledge, hate the thought of any animal being killed for any reason. The genuine ones in this category are true vegans. If they are not, they should be, otherwise their argument has serious flaws. If only they could put their energy into protecting the horse throughout the world from cruelty and long distance transportation, protecting endangered species of wildlife from annihilation, and supporting the RSPCA for the wonderful work they do (apart from their misguided anti-hunting campaign).

Recently, the powers that be asked the pro-hunting people to produce scientific and veterinary evidence to support the case for hunting. Months of work and proof was handed in. Vets supported hunting as the most humane when compared with other forms of control. True polls showed that public opinion was strongly turning to the pro-hunting side, with 62% saying there should not be a ban. This was a result of hunting people being open about their sport and of many more people taking an unbiased view. Yet government back-benchers forced a vote to literally throw the evidence out of the window to fulfil their desire to do what I outlined in my first paragraph. This is not reasoned thinking; it is bigoted ignorance.

Admittedly, hunters – or field sportsmen and women as I prefer to call them – have a lot to answer for. Years ago they should have opened the doors of all field sports much more widely. They should have freely and proudly told the world that their sport was not only about pest control. It was about a way of life, a livelihood, conservation and an enjoyable recreation for many people from all walks of life.

Andrew Cuthbert

Born in London in 1936 Andrew Cuthbert was educated at Merchant Taylors School, Northwood, did National Service in the Royal Navy and worked briefly in London before meeting his wife Sheelin, who came from Blakeney. They moved to Norfolk in 1960 where Andrew worked in crop spraying until 1982. In his spare time he organised the Binham Pageant and two Son et Lumiere productions (in the ruins of Binham Priory), the Bayfield Game Fair, the first Holkham Country Fair and the Bicentennial celebration of the Holkham Sheep Shearings. In 1980 he formed Andrew Cuthbert Country Fairs to run events at venues such as Fyvie Castle, Castle Howard, Stratfield Saye, Broadlands, Woburn and Chatsworth as well as Holkham, using part of the income to create the Red Socks Charitable Trust. He was the Eastern Regional Chairman of the Countryside Alliance, sails from Morston and is determined to protect the English countryside. Andrew and Sheelin have lived at the Old Vicarage, Binham since 1963.

Andrew Cuthbert would like to thank John Anderson from Hindringham for his contribution on river angling.

Now, seemingly too late, the door is being held wide open. Everyone is being invited to hunt meets and to follow and see what goes on. This should have happened years ago.

That then is the situation as I write – we are faced with a hunting ban and most country people fear that other country sports bans will follow – and in our area shooting vastly predominates. This part of Norfolk is on the fringe of the North Norfolk Harriers and the West Norfolk Foxhounds which killed about 60 hares and 45 foxes respectively each season (August to March). There was a newly formed pack of mink hounds in Norfolk but they mainly hunted in country around south and east Norfolk. Coursing the hare with greyhound, lurcher, whippet and deer hound took place, with landowners' permission, out of the breeding season and seldom accounted for more than half a dozen hares a meeting. The occasional visit of a pack of beagles – which hunt hares – has been known, but there was no official 'country' for one in this part of Norfolk.

In areas where the fox is a real pest, gamekeepers organise fox culls and some estates and groups of farmers team together where the hare population is getting out of hand and hold February hare shoots, accounting in some cases for a large number of hares in a day.

Unfortunately, an annual hare cull is a necessary evil. Overcrowding of any wild animal is not healthy and if you are trying to grow sugar beet, hares love to munch away at rows of new seedlings! However, hunting and coursing the hare, whilst not greatly reducing the hare population, cleans up the old and unfit ones. Certainly, once a hare is caught by the lead hound, it is stone dead within 15 seconds or so. Yes, in its final death throes it sometimes shrieks and this is distressing for the human ear. After death it is eaten by the hounds and they don't wait to be handed a knife and fork or table napkins! But the hare is *dead* at this stage.

Field sports contribute an immense amount to our economy, employment, the cleanliness of our farmland and the survival of our diverse wildlife, woodland and hedgerows. Fishermen look after the cleanliness of our rivers and lakes. And without shooting, the wild grey partridge of this part of North Norfolk – an indicator species of healthy farmland and countryside in its own right – would cease to exist.

In North Norfolk, the Holkham estate and a farm at Snoring have each won the distinguished Laurent Perrier award for the conservation of the grey partridge. A helicopter ride over North Norfolk will show which farms have field sports interests and which farmers are purely activated by cash returns on their land. In the 60s and 70s the farming vogue was to use every inch of land, grub out hedges and turn 1000 acre 30 field holdings into 1000 acre three field ones. Grants encouraged this thinking and so did some agricultural college lecturers. Grey partridge stocks began to dwindle in North Norfolk – the area that had once been famous as their 'homeland'. Sprays were a cheaper option for field cleanliness than good old fashioned husbandry. The result was that insects were never there for young birds; weed seeds were never there for growing birds; and cover was sprayed, burnt and cultivated five minutes after harvest, giving no time for birds to glean. Vermin survived; vermin always seem to.

I have seen some of those same farms being given grants to replant hedges they earned grants to rip out. Those young farmers had come out of college, wet behind the ears but full of 'knowledge' and enthusiasm, and followed the instructions of their college lecturers. They pulled out hedges, bought bigger machinery, burnt stubbles and frequently hedges (by accident) as well. They sprayed paraquat on ditch bottoms so that everything shone like a new pin (it was actually brown and dead) but there was no wildlife in sight. Suddenly, many of the farmers matured or married (I don't quite know which gave a more powerful signal on their Richter scale). Then they stood back and wondered why on say a 500 acre holding they could no longer invite eight friends to shoot a mixed bag of 100 or so birds a day three times a season as their fathers had done. The Game Conservancy Trust, whose logo is a grey partridge, did a wonderful job in bringing back balance. Only in the nick of time did we rescue this lovely little bird, which had come so close to extinction in this, its traditional homeland. Many people who have not had the good fortune to have been part of this partridge story cannot possibly understand how a body can dedicate its work to the survival of a bird and at the same time encourage the responsible sport of shooting the same bird. But this is the problem all field sportsmen have and it goes back to Karen Blixen's much quoted truism: '... hunting is ever a love affair. The hunter is in love with the game; real hunters are the true animal lovers'.

The type of shoot known as the 'put and shoot' type is not to be encouraged. This is a shoot (very few of them around here, thank goodness) which comes into the hands of an uncaring person who kills everything that flies or moves. In the following spring there are no birds to breed, except a few that have strayed off neighbouring land. A re-stock of young birds is bought in and released. Just when they are able to fly in November they are shot each weekend until they have all gone. The same thing is repeated each year. Because these birds arrive in a 'foreign land', they are easy meat for vermin. The whole performance is unnatural, discouraged by proper field sportsmen and will I hope be phased out in the future.

That does not mean one should not improve one's stock of birds year by year, especially after a poor breeding or insect season. But wild birds are always the best stock to survive and to shoot.

In this part of North Norfolk there are opportunities for the game angling community. Two delightful streams, the Stiffkey and the Glaven flow north from the Cromer Ridge. They are quite short, in the order of seven to ten miles from source to mouth, and rise from the chalk. The Wensum, a much bigger river, rises near the Raynhams to eventually flow southwards. Similarly the Nar flows directly south from the area of the Raynhams. The Bure rises in the Edgefield/Briston area and flows away to the southeast. The north flowing rivers support trout throughout their lengths and these fish are also matured in the upper reaches of the Wensum, Nar and Bure.

To maintain the rivers in good order essentially requires the application of the Karen Blixen quote. Without the desire of the fisherman to fish (not necessarily to catch and remove fish) the rivers would succumb to the canalisation of the drainage engineers. To keep the rivers in a near natural state of clean flow with all the variations that become gurgling runs and pools with adequate flora to maintain the insect life that make the river live, requires a great combination of effort. The riparian owners who want their stretches of the river to be in good order are aware of the need to exclude polluting elements. They can be assisted by the fisheries department of the Environment Agency which maintains a constant watch on the rivers and has the means to implement necessary improvements.

The Environment Agency maintains a weed cutting boat and has an active and ongoing involvement in keeping rivers clean and able to support fish. Its involvement includes making grants to those actively working on river improvements as well as carrying out the work in conjunction with others.

A number of recognised improvement works have been carried out in our rivers in recent years. The work done has consisted of improving flow by laying beds of stone and gravel into the rivers, revetting banks to prevent over-widening and establishing five to ten yard wide river bank reserves protected by fencing. This

allows for regeneration of vegetation which significantly checks the run-off of silt and surface drainage waters that may be loaded with nitrates originating from normal agricultural operations. Some of this work has been seen to be of a very high standard and has been recognised as such by the granting of awards. Combined with this work directly within the rivers is the growing participation of the farming community in actions to reduce and control salt laden run off and the nitrate load that such run off may contain. Reserves of five to ten yard strips around cultivated areas have been sown with grasses and other plants to result in soil conservation belts.

Fishery associations made up of active anglers promote river maintenance. They too can rely on guidance and assistance, including active involvement and cash grants, from the Environment Agency. Assistance is also provided by their membership and they have access to support from major conservation associations such as the Wild Trout Trust, the Salmon and Trout Association and the Norfolk Anglers Conservation Association. Additionally, specific to the Glaven is the River Glaven Conservation Group made up of riparian owners, Environment Agency representatives, scientists, fishermen and a others who hold the Glaven dear. The aim of all these groups is to restore and maintain the natural population of self-regenerating wild brown trout whose presence is a marker that points to rivers in good order. This work is ongoing and has been for some years. There has been some stocking of the rivers and this continues but the feelings of all concerned are much the same as those of the shooting community in relation to their wild birds.

The growth of centres of population inevitably brings the need for sewage treatment works that discharge their effluent into water-courses. The standard of cleanliness is generally high. But a cursory inspection of the packets of washing

and dish washing powder found in virtually every home will show that they contain some 5% of phosphates. It is only at sewage treatment works serving major centres of population (10,000 plus) that phosphate stripping plant is installed. Effluent containing high concentrations of phosphates mingled with field drainage water with a high nitrate content can produce massive growth of acquatic plants. This growth can block water flows and remove oxygen from the water to the point at which other life is suffocated. This process of eutrophysication can result in the loss of all green plants and lead to the growth of massive banks of filamentous algae. The installation of phosphate stripping plant at all sewage treatment works is very desirable and is certainly essential to the maintenance of clean healthy rivers. The game fisherman is both the public watchman and instigator in such matters.

The end product of all this effort is that our rivers are kept clean with a reasonable degree of access. The fisherman will see the occasional otter, plenty of kingfishers and the many and varied insect life. Unfortunately he will also see mink which do immense damage and are the result of irresponsible releases from mink farming operations. But if fishing were banned, who would care for and do all the necessary work to preserve the rivers? I suggest it would not be those who free the mink.

Sea fishing is a rather different story because it is the local economy that benefits in the forms of bait digging and boat charters at Brancaster, Wells and Blakeney. Of course it's all declining along with the North Sea fish stocks – 150 people here used to make a living out of bait digging alone! But there are still sea bass, dabs and flounder in summer, codling, and whiting in winter, inshore mackerel from June to October and, further offshore, summer cod, dog-fish and tope. Crab, lobster and other shellfish all support a number of jobs. The future – with sons following fathers – is as bright as fishing policy allows it to be.

Turning to another of our field sports an important feature of the North Norfolk coast is the empathy between local wildfowling organisations, local shell-fish and inshore fishing interests and English Nature. It is a model of mutual understanding and respect. This also includes large estate owners – especially Holkham and the National Trust, both controlling huge areas of saltmarshes and nature reserves.

It is an outstanding area for bird watching and no-one who visits the Wells area in winter can be anything but amazed at the spectacle of up to 100,000 pinkfoot geese flighting in at dawn to their sanctuary roost on the sands of Wells Harbour. A few dedicated wildfowlers, up before dawn, crouching in the creeks to cull a few birds, seem to make no impression on the grey battalions as they head towards the safety of sugar beet tops on the well-keepered estates inland.

In cooperation with the British Association for Shooting and Conservation, the Wells and Blakeney wildfowling clubs are well run, carefully controlled and disciplined. New members are inducted only after stringent interviews and a bird identification test. Even the twitchers, who I'm afraid can be most intolerant of other people's interests, hardly notice this sporting element. Wildfowlers themselves delight in the wildlife on the marshes, help maintain the bridges and access routes and provide eyes and ears to guard against misuse. This is a model of cooperative enjoyment of a fabulous area of unpolluted wild coastline, protected, wardened, yet accessible to the public. Most of the marshes are designated Sites of Special Scientific Interest yet still support cockling, wildfowling and bait digging. This is possibly a unique example in this country of mutual support in action between sporting interests, local commerce and tourist interests. The salt marshes of Wells, Stiffkey and Blakeney have been officially designated as the best, unpolluted, unspoilt salt marshes left in Western Europe. What a glorious accolade!

On Christmas Eve 2004 in Sennowe Park – on the southern fringe of the area covered by this book – the West Norfolk Foxhounds met. There were over 210 mounted followers, of whom at least half were mounted youngsters between the age of three and twenty years. At the end of the day, when the Master, surrounded by at least 50 grinning young faces, said: 'Well, I think we've had enough for today, don't you?' they all shouted: 'No!' with one very loud voice. It is my wish that those youngsters, together with our three grandsons, will, with an overturn of the ban, be hunting well into the next half century.

Because of, not in spite of, our heritage of all field sports, I hope that our patch of North Norfolk will become a leading example of how to preserve the varied beauty of our countryside. Like Teddy Maufe in Chapter 18, I shall do all I can to encourage this and to play my small part in making the area even more attractive.

Two Views on Rural Schools

Catherine Golding

A child's view

Having lived on the North Norfolk coast all my life it was not until I had to spend a year teaching in Leeds as part of my university course that I truly understood how much I loved this place and how much of my very privileged upbringing I took for granted. Ever since the day a four-year-old child asked me questions about what a beach really looked like I knew I wanted to return home and wanted my children to grow up in the same environment. I did not then realise how difficult that would be.

I was the daughter of a Brancaster fisherman and grew up surrounded by the incredibly close knit Southerlands and Looses and the local community of farming and fishing families. From the age of four I attended the local school at Burnham Deepdale. There were two classes (Infant and Junior), a school dog (the headmistress used to bring hers in daily), outside toilets, heating from old coal boilers, woodland at the back, a huge field at the side ...and two wonderful teachers. Everyone knew each other and most of us were actually related in one way or another. On the way to and from school the older people would come out of their houses to speak to us. I found later this was their way of keeping in touch with the village.

Life outside was good. We had more freedoms than are now possible – partly because we knew nearly everyone – to play in the village and on the marshes. Summers were wonderful picnic lunches and days spent wandering, swimming and making mud-slides. We were the envy of cousins who came with us to places we knew that other people didn't. It was like having private beaches.

The whole village was shocked when we learned the Council planned to close the school. I remember being amazed how many people felt strongly enough to get involved: parents, grandparents, aunts, uncles, friends and older people who had been to the school or knew someone who had. Four local schools (Thornham, Ringstead and Old Hunstanton as well as Deepdale) faced closure. At

Catherine Golding

Catherine Golding was born and brought up (surrounded by relatives) in Brancaster Staithe. She went to school in Brancaster, Hunstanton and later King's Lynn and took her degree at University College Scarborough. Her first teaching post was Wells Primary School. She later taught in Hindringham before moving to her current school in Brancaster. She married in 2000 and helps ensure local people have a say in local organisations as a member of the committees of the Deepdale Tennis Club and the Brancaster Housing Society. She is a frequent attender at the Methodist church in New Holkham where members of her family have worshipped for many generations.

a demonstration in King's Lynn our tiny village had nearly four times more support than any of the others.

I clearly remember the day Miss Elsey told us our battle had been lost and the school was going to close. Everyone was very deflated. Unfortunately it was not the end of the battle. The children would be going to Brancaster School but there would be no transport for those over eight because the distance between Deepdale and Brancaster (two miles) was considered too short to justify it. Another campaign; there were many reasons why transport was essential for all ages. The main one was the lack of a footpath between Brancaster Staithe and Brancaster which meant walking would be incredibly dangerous. The parents won and transport was provided.

Burnham Deepdale School closed in July 1985. In September I went to Smithdon High School in Hunstanton and discovered a world outside Staithe and Deepdale. Everything seemed big. I found it very difficult but because I had decided I wanted to become a teacher I knew I had to work. At Primary School and through my family I had discovered a love of music and at the High School found I had an excellent teacher and could spend playtimes in the music room. Towards the end of my time there, geography became a problem. Friends who lived at Hunstanton or just outside the town could stay for after-school clubs and get-togethers at weekends, but the lack of public transport between Hunstanton and Brancaster Staithe limited my opportunities to participate in them. And for a few years my relationship with my village changed.

'A' Levels meant school in King's Lynn, twenty-four miles away. The sixth form college in Fakenham (twelve miles) was closer but transport was not provided. My choices were limited by the fact I wanted to do music. So the school in Lynn was

Brancaster school

my only option because I did not have a grade eight qualification. My years there were the worst I had experienced thus far. As a newcomer I was never accepted and people went out of their way to make sure I knew that. The timetable did not accommodate my subject choices so instead of getting eight hours teaching a week I got six hours in each and the rest of the time worked alone. The school promised that arrangement would only be for the first year. It wasn't.

Transport was still a problem. The bus left Deepdale at 6:45 a.m. for Hunstanton where I transferred to a public service bus that went around the villages, reaching Lynn at about 8:30 a.m. Then came a day in college before the ride home that finished around 5:30 p.m. It was a nightmare. I was tired. A-levels were hard work. After nearly half a year my friend and I decided we could no longer stand it. A teacher listened and for the rest of the year the schedule was put back so we could catch a later bus (7.15 a.m.) from Hunstanton. After a year the Council decided to provide a bus direct to King's Lynn but it was only slightly better because we had to go around all the villages to get there which meant the journey was neither shorter nor quicker.

After a happy year at University College, Scarborough and a less happy year at Leeds I decided Norfolk would be home and aimed to get back there as soon as possible.

A teacher's view

In June 1997 I got my first teaching job at Wells-next-the-Sea Primary and Nursery School and began to see the rural schools of North Norfolk through the realistic eyes of an adult.

I first became aware of one of the many problems when one of my parent helpers at Wells school found she had to pay for transport to get her son, who would soon be eight, to school. The family lived at Warham. The nearest school was in Wells. Free transport had previously been provided for all children. But now those over eight who lived less than three miles from school did not qualify. This change in policy implied that if parents were unable to provide private transport to and from school, children as young as eight would have to walk up to six miles a day in all weathers. The busy road between Wells and Warham had no footpath. The family had only one car (used by the husband whose job did not fit around school hours). In the end a bus pass was obtained and the family had to contribute financially to their child's education because of where they lived. The mother went to see the Head Teacher, who later told the staff that she felt awful about the situation and the fact that there was nothing she could do to reverse the changes or help the family.

To overcome this problem another family purchased a specially adapted bicycle, so the child's mother could tow the younger of her two children whilst her eldest rode her bike. This mother confessed to me she was scared every day as cars rushed past on the narrow winding road, hardly giving them enough space. The eight-year-old daughter was a novice rider and was scared she might wobble into a passing car. I asked the mother why she did not send her younger child on the bus (he was under eight) and she explained she would not then have enough time to put him on the bus and get her daughter to school.

Both sets of parents were able to get or send their children to the school but had, in different ways, to pay to get them there.

It seems the Norfolk County Council has forgotten that the need for school transportation arises from the fact the majority of village schools have been closed. Travelling to school is a necessity not a choice. How then does it dare tell parents that if they live in the wrong place they must pay for their childrens' education? Why do we not hear more outcries? Is this what we should expect because we live where we live?

I keep thinking back to the fuss in my village when our school was closed and how the parents stuck together to demand what was right and fair. Somewhere along the line we have slipped up by not keeping the protests going, allowing the County Council to get away with ridiculous mileage rules and then changing them. I wish I could turn back the clock and advise these parents to stand up for their right to free education for their children and help them in their fight.

A few years back the Government introduced the right to choose where your child should be educated. Great in theory but a completely different matter in practice. For families in cities and large towns where there are alternative schools and reliable and frequent public transport the choice may be real. In rural Norfolk it's a poor joke because any alternative school is outside the local catchment area. For families already challenged by the difficulties of arranging transport to and from schools within the catchment area the prospect of finding schools outside it is ridiculous. Public transport is not available in all areas and in my experience is incredibly unreliable, the only decent timetable being run through the summer months for the benefit of visitors. Unless parents are prepared to spend a good proportion of each day in a car and can fit their work around school hours, their real choices are very limited.

Another problem with 'choice' is that schools with good names have waiting lists so long that many parents are left disappointed. Till recently I worked at Hindringham V.C. Primary School, which works extremely hard to maintain its good reputation. Every year our waiting list is over-subscribed by families from outside our catchment area (including some who live more than ten miles away). They like what the school has to offer. They want their children to be educated there. But it can only take a certain number of children into each year group and the inevitable result is that, every year, some of them are disappointed.

Some parents are now starting to beat the system by putting their child's name down on a number of different school lists. They then accept whatever places are offered and decide later to which school to send their child. This is a nightmare for schools, especially small schools which have worked out their enrolments and planned their budgets assuming a certain number of acceptances and must then contend with a phone calls to say that a family will not, after all, be taking the place that was offered because 'it has had a better offer from another school'. It is then too late to offer the place to another family that was genuinely unlucky not to get in first time around. However, 'playing the system' only works if you are not worried about the length of the school run and how long it takes on a daily basis.

Schools are also incredibly worried about the future. Schools are trying hard to make sure their numbers are up to full capacity because they know the Government will be scrutinising them to see how to save money. The result will almost certainly mean further closures and more families ending up having to pay for transport. It will then be only a matter of time before there are further increases in the number of miles you have to live from your nearest school to get free transport.

Further education is also suffering from transport costs. Most parents now have to pay to send their children to Sixth Form Colleges no matter how many miles they live from the school. In an increasingly competitive job market in which employees are looking for qualifications, young people in Norfolk could be penalised because of where they live. I know a mother who took a job in Hunstanton because she could not afford to pay for transport to get her daughter to and from the Sixth Form College. She has now committed herself to taking her to school and picking her up every day and says these are the sacrifices parents must make if they want to give their children the opportunities they need to achieve their dreams.

It seems to me that many rural parents are now contributing to their children's education from the age they start school at four to when they leave college (now grants have been abolished). What happened to the concept of 'a free education for all'?

For schools to survive they must succeed in recruiting and retaining students and teachers. The growing popularity of North Norfolk for holiday and second homes, the impact on house prices and fact that more and more local families are being forced out of the area has left some schools facing new difficulties. Last year one local school cut down on the size of a class. Next year it may lose a whole class. The result is that children must be taught in mixed age classes.

Recruiting children is not the only difficulty. One local school advertised for a Head Teacher for over six months. Applicants trickled in but not on the scale you need in order to shortlist and interview. Members of staff, parents and friends of the school made enquiries further afield but many potential applicants were put off by the fact they could not afford to relocate to what has become a high cost area and said they would not apply. The County Council has considered the possibility of one Head running two or more schools. I do not see this working very well. Schools need strong management from someone who has that school's best interests at heart. To undertake two schools would be an impossibly pressured job, each set of staff, children and parents demanding you put their school first. This idea needs rethinking.

Every week now the list of vacancies for teaching jobs in Norfolk is increasing. Children have to be taught in larger classes, sometimes by a succession of supply teachers who don't even know their names. High Schools especially are suffering with teachers having to teach aspects of the curriculum for which they have no training. Is this what we expect or want for our children?

I think the provision of education in Norfolk needs reviewing and that people in a position to do something about it must be made aware of the situation. As a teacher I would always like to think that I did the best by every single child in the school where I work. I feel that the County Council should have the same commitment to Norfolk children and their parents. Parents and teachers – always criticised for complaining – now need to make themselves heard.

Christine Abel

Christine Abel's education began at the North Devon preparatory school run by her mother and continued in Sussex, Switzerland and the University of East Anglia where she earned a law degree in 1993. She came to Norfolk in 1970, was Clerk to Wells Harbour Commissioners for twenty years (from 1974 to 1994) and was subsequently the first woman to become a Wells Harbour Commissioner (1993-2003). She became a partner in Hayes and Storr, Solicitors, in 2002 and has lived in Wells since 1970.

The Havens
of North Norfolk

Christine Abel

When I first arrived at the Victoria Hotel at Holkham on a grey spring day in 1968, the North Norfolk landscape seemed flat, wild, windswept and bleak to someone born and brought up on the North Devon coast. Instead of roaring Atlantic rollers breaking against high Devon cliffs there was a new and alien sea that sneaked furtively up the creeks through expanses of marsh and followed me across beaches in flurries of small murky ripples at a remorseless walking speed that seemed slightly menacing. All topped by that vast sky…

By contrast, my first impressions of Wells Harbour were very much of an unexpectedly familiar scene, but somehow reduced as if seen though the wrong end of a telescope. The aspect of familiarity was easy to engage with. Wells is very similar to the small port and harbour of my old home, Bideford, in North Devon, although the port and town of Bideford spreads over both sides of a river, instead of being faced by marshes as at Wells.

This sense of reduction stayed with me as I became more familiar with the harbour and its elements, characters and activities – 'just like a real port only smaller' – a microcosm of ports everywhere, containing all the elements: public responsibilities and private commercial interests, shipping, cargo handling, lifeboat, pilotage, fishing, leisure boating and sailing and, in those days, regatta and power boating; above all, dealing with the elements, and with the forces of nature. Historically, the problems of ports and harbours along the Saltmarsh Coast stem from the actions of man as well as the forces of nature.

In Wells, the quay and harbour are the town's main focus and the Harbour Master and the Clerk to the Wells Harbour Commissioners are key figures. The Commissioners – the port authority – have often been perceived as a shadowy, mysterious body; I shall discuss aspects of the Commissioners' historical and contemporary roles later in this chapter.

In the 1960s, there was, as now, a cast of other characters who populated the quay and harbour and based their lives in and around its activities. This community had a strong sense of its own identity and a vast fund of local knowledge about harbour customs and practices, boundaries, traditions, crafts and skills; essential muscle power; and firmly held views and ready commentaries on events. The cast list was fullest and the 'Quay Theatre' busiest during the peak holiday season – in the 1960s generally confined to July and August – but fishing and shipping carried on more or less throughout the year.

There was a clear sense of coastal community and competition with other North Sea ports. In the 1960s, there were fishermen who had moved up the coast from Whitstable following the sprats and 'roker' or skate, and North Sea coasters would bring news up and down the coast and across the North Sea from Boston, King's Lynn, Yarmouth, Rotterdam, Hamburg and Esbjerg. Many local friendships and relationships were forged through these seaward links as well as through the land-based summer influx of holiday visitors from (typically) Bedford, Cambridge, Northampton and Leicester.

Seamen, both in shipping and fishing were then, as now, hardworking and often hard drinking, competitive individuals, clannish when faced with outsiders but brave and inclusive when fighting the elements. Those I first encountered in the public bar in the Victoria Hotel (just along the coast at Holkham Village) on my arrival in 1968 were tall, broad, weather-beaten men, mostly bearded, one or two wearing one gold earring (before earrings became fashion accessories). Uniformly clad in slops, jeans and sea boots, they looked to my astonished eyes, like a pirate crew, and played that role with gusto, regaling me with stories of Wells pirates and medieval ship-wreckers, plundering wrecks. The medieval pirates were gruesomely known as 'Wells Bite-fingers', because of their way of removing the rings from the bloated fingers of drowned corpses....

As I became more familiar with the people, my impressions were that coastal residents were mainly from the local area and holiday cottages were few. Holidaymakers were mainly summer visitors to the caravan and campsites and hotels. The coastal towns and villages were isolated and the way of life and use of dialect and sayings were noticeably different between settlements as close as Wells, Warham and Walsingham. Retired incomers and second homeowners were rare. Newcomers tended to be those coming to work in hotels, local estates, established businesses and, to a lesser extent, agriculture. Except those who came by sea, there were few people 'just passing through' (on the way to where ...?) and outside the two main summer months Wells and its satellite villages were insular and isolated. After 1964, the nearest main rail links were then, as now, King's Lynn and Norwich. The road system was comparatively rural, consisting of B class roads and traffic lights and roundabouts were unknown within a twenty mile radius. In those days Wells seemed a very long way from ...anywhere.

My first impressions of the geography of North Norfolk rapidly changed as I continued to live and work in the area and the effects of the brilliant skies, never-ending beaches, dunes, marshes, brick-and-flint architecture and gritty living close to nature gradually seeped into my blood, as the muddy tide seeps up the creeks.

I had never lived in a place where I was so aware of the contrast of seasons: the bright warm days of summer peopled with brightly clothed summer visitors engaged in having fun, swimming, sailing and enjoying the outdoors. In winter, when the nor'easterlies blew, Wells Quay emptied and the winter hibernation began: briefer outings warmly wrapped for winter walks and then back to warm firesides where hospitality and resources were shared unstintingly with neighbours and friends. Autumn and spring seemed like brief interludes of blackberries and chestnuts, bulbs growing and planting between the short summer and long winter.

Looking back

The Ports

Many things are – and have been from the earliest times – essential to the development of a successful port: shelter from bad weather; a navigable channel; ease of landing; proximity to a major settlement and good road access, often combined with a river estuary to move cargoes upriver and inland. These do not change.

The Saltmarsh Coast varies from mud flats and salt and freshwater marsh with extensive bird life in the west and central portions to the shingle banks of Salthouse and Cley. There are dunes, pines, marram grass, huge beaches such as Holkham, all beneath that overarching sky. The coast is fluid, changing and evolving with longshore drift and deposition here, accreting coastline and developing marsh there. Man-made changes have been significant, especially the embankment of land 'reclaimed' from the sea – although it has been *claimed* rather than *reclaimed*. Man-made changes also included the creation of 'ports' in natural harbours.

The ports of the Saltmarsh Coast were dependent on retaining adequately deep channels from the sea to natural harbours that dry out between twice-daily tides.

Although there are many ancient settlements in West Norfolk, their coastal villages did not generally develop into 'ports'. Brancaster ('Branodunum') was a Roman defence against Saxon marauders accessed by Roman roads from the South and there were other Roman camps at Thornham, Holkham and Warham. But although Holme, Thornham, Titchwell, the Brancasters and Burnham Overy Staithe have natural havens, they were overshadowed by the larger port of King's Lynn. These villages have nonetheless retained strong sailing and maritime traditions.

In the 16th and 17th centuries, access to North Norfolk from the West was across the Fens, a treacherous water land ruled by tides. The safest trade routes were by sea. Even Holkham and Stiffkey had small staithes (waterside landing-stages) although they were insignificant compared to those of the Glaven Ports and Wells.

The saltmarsh held an enormous amount of water that removed sand, mud and silt and maintained deep, fast-flowing channels and pools. Embankments led to reduced scouring at Wells and Blakeney but had disastrous effects at Wiveton and Cley where estuarial channels and the once navigable River Glaven were eventually lost. Although land reclamation was inspired by the draining of the Fenlands by Vermuyden in the 1620s, the earlier embankment of the Salthouse and Cley Marshes by Sir John Heydon had already caused the 'decay of the haven at Cley' and consequent damage to shipping and fishing.

The Glaven Ports thrived throughout the 14th, 15th and 16th centuries until local landowners, looking to increase their estates at low cost, took the steps that led to their terminal decline. Embankments across the Glaven estuary and at Cley and Wiveton, and the reclamation and drainage of marshland were fought through the Courts by mariners and ship owners but went ahead anyway.

Local mariners pursued the matter through the courts to the Lord Cardinal in the Star Chamber and the first banks were eventually taken down. But the reclamation movement continued and despite local protests, further embankments were built at Salthouse and Cley. In 1637 embankments by Sir Henry Calthorpe and his son Philip blocked the

Cley windmill

48

Glaven estuary at a point close to the present A149 coast road at Cley. This brought an end to shipping up-river to Wiveton and the deep water channel to Cley rapidly silted – allegedly by nearly two feet in a little over a year.

Cley shipping and fishing were very badly affected and trade was lost, some altogether, some to Blakeney and Wells. Mariners and fishermen were angry and resentful and once again they pursued the matter through the Courts. They won their case but did not obtain a remedy until it reached the Privy Council (the highest Court) which ordered the embankments to be removed. But by then it was too late – the silting that had occurred in the intervening two years was not reduced and trade had already moved elsewhere. Wiveton rapidly declined and Cley Newgate (the part of the village near the church) suffered a similar fate when maritime operations moved to Cley Mill. Because ships could no longer reach Cley cargoes for Cley had to be offloaded to lighters in Blakeney Pit and then carted from Blakeney to Cley. The comparatively high cost of overland transport led to a rapid decline in trade and to real hardship in Cley and Wiveton.

Witnesses to an inquiry by the Tidal Harbour's Commission headed by Joseph Hume, MP in 1845, unanimously blamed the silting problems at Wiveton, Cley, Blakeney and Wells on the embankment and reclamation works that had been carried out, against all advice, by land owners keen to acquire land, without regard to the inevitable silting of those harbours. Reclamation and embankment ultimately destroyed the harbours of Wiveton and Cley and the economic problems of these villages were compounded when they were bypassed by the railways in the 19th century.

In contrast, the early 19th century brought improved fortunes to Blakeney. In July 1817 the Blakeney Harbour Company was formed by Act of Parliament on the initiative of local landowners led, ironically, by George, Lord Calthorpe, a descendent of the Henry Calthorpe who had instigated the embankments two centuries earlier. The company directors were very active in building 'the cut' to straighten the Blakeney channel, appointing a harbour master and pilots, drafting bylaws, and collecting harbour and cargo dues.

These activities gave considerable impetus to trade between the 1820s and 1850s and Blakeney could well have developed – as did Wells – as a modern statutory harbour authority. In 1828 the Lynn and Fakenham Railway Company offered to buy the Blakeney Harbour Company for the then considerable sum of £5400. If the purchase had gone ahead it is interesting to speculate about the future for Blakeney as a harbour with a railway link. But it did not happen and from the 1850s onwards Blakeney's shipping trade and population declined. The Blakeney Harbour Company lasted for less than 100 years being wound up around 1914, commercial shipping at Blakeney Quay having ceased before the first World War.

The combination of embankments and enclosures, silting, and the advent of railway links to Wells in 1859, to Melton Constable in 1875, and to Holt in 1884 thus changed Cley and Wiveton from coastal ports to rural villages, and led to the demise of Blakeney as a port. But the purchase of Blakeney Point and its transfer to the National Trust as a Nature Reserve in 1912 rejuvenated Blakeney and the surrounding villages as havens for artists, naturalists, walkers, leisure sailors and bird watchers and led to a different future.

In 1568 the Commissioners for Havens and Creeks appointed five deputies as Harbour Commissioners at Wells. By 1663 the port was considered important enough to have an Act of Parliament passed 'for repairing and better preserving the key of the Port of Wells'. In 1769 Commissioners were appointed to administer the harbour, and harbour 'duties' were increased to six pence per ton, and 'one shilling for any ship or vessel not belonging to the Town of Wells'.

Under the 1769 Act the Commissioners were to meet at 'the house known by the sign of the Fleece …on the first day of January 1769 as thereafter as often as they chose'. The Golden Fleece public house can still be seen today, and an interesting design in plaster relief, many centuries old on the ceiling of the main Commissioners' meeting room in the Golden Fleece demonstrates the link with an early export of the period – the trade in wool and cloth. The whole area and especially some of the fine old parts of Norwich bear witness to the wealth of this time and a local economy based significantly on wool, cloth and links with the Flemish weavers across the North Sea.

Wells harbour records also refer back to a wonderful silt free channel and strong tidal flows in the early 18th century before the then Lord of the Manor, the Earl of Leicester, enclosed tidal lands to the east of Wells and erected the East Bank to enclose and 'reclaim' Warham Slade in 1758. Again, it was argued that the scouring effect of the great volume of 'back' water storage available in the marshes to the

Seals on Blakeney Point

landward side of the present East Bank kept the Quay and channel straight, deep and free flowing. In this respect the history of land 'reclamation' and embankment at Wells closely follows the similar history of the Glaven Ports.

Here too, a case was submitted to the Court (Sergeant Grose's opinion in 1777), which reported that the embankment of Warham Slade was considered 'the most injurious in losing great quantities of back water which had always scoured out the harbour channel'. According to John Smeaton in 1738 the depth of water in the 'Pool' (on the east side of the channel opposite the present Wells Lifeboat House) was such that at low water, two or three tiers of vessels would lie afloat at anchor and swing round.

By 1782 the Pool had filled up so much that at low water there was only six feet of water. Matters reached such a pass that the Harbour Commissioners and townsfolk applied to the Court and were declared to be at liberty to 'throw the bank down' if it were not removed. They apparently did so in 1784 as a meeting minute stated that at spring tides the sea flowed again to the ancient limits of the port.

In 1808 however, the Commissioners of the time eventually agreed that the Lord of the Manor should rebuild the Warham Slade Marsh embankment provided he would, at his own expense, cut out a reservoir and sluice 'to freely admit tide waters in larger quantities and to scour out the harbour'. Evidently, the appointed Commissioners at that time represented the interests of landowners over mariners because the embankment was built but the reservoir and sluice were not.

Cargoes in and out of Wells built up over the centuries and peaked at various periods, notably between 1830 and 1860. The entry for the Port of Wells in *White's Directory* for 1854 shows 484 outward and 672 inward cargoes with vessels averaging 200 tons and 11-foot draft. Outward cargoes included wheat, barley, malt, flour and oysters (fished locally). Imports that year included timber, salt, rape and linseed. Coastal trade in coal, timber and building materials over the 18th and 19th centuries also kept the port busy and in 1756–7, alabaster for the impressive marble hall at Holkham was brought into Wells from quarries in Derbyshire, having been shipped from Gainsborough in Lincolnshire.

There was a subsequent decline in the prosperity of Wells shipping and trade, indicated by the fall in population from a peak of 3675 in 1854 to 2645 in 1881. The busy Customs House at East Quay, built in 1560 and mentioned in *Pepys Diary,* remained operational as the Customs House until the decline in trade lead to its abandonment in 1881, when the Wells Customs area reverted to a creek of the King's Lynn District. Records reported 12 ships' pilots in 1844 but only three in 1890.

At the turn of the 20th century the Port of Wells was continuing to tick over, and between the two World Wars was fairly busy with inward cargoes of potash and coal and outward cargoes of malt, barley and sugar beet. This level of trade

Wells quay

continued until World War II when shipping ceased and the harbour became a base for Air-Sea Rescue. Commercial shipping was started again in a small way in the 1950s by local farming co-operatives whose cargoes included malt barley, wheat, animal feeds and fertilizer, fishmeal and soya. These cargoes increased and the shipping trade grew and thrived through the 1970s and 1980s and peaked in 1985 with 253 vessels, carrying over 100,000 tonnes of cargo. However, the economic case for handling small coasters of under 1000 tonnes which could manage the 10 foot draft limit into Wells was increasingly under pressure, with the added burden of associated increases in road haulage costs.

At the end of the 1980s, the end of commercial shipping at Wells came quite suddenly, being killed off by the failure of the soya crop in South America. Until then, Soya was transported from South America to Rotterdam in bulk carriers before being distributed to North Sea ports in small coasters. When the crop failed, alternative feedstuffs were brought in from other regions to replace it. This tied in with a move towards larger coasters around Britain's coastline. The 600 to 700 tonne cargoes which were regularly shipped into Wells had become uneconomic to ship and transport by road. All of which is a reminder that even relatively small events on the other side of the globe may change our lives.

Thereafter, the 1897 Dutch registered North Sea Klipper *Albatros* continued to bring small cargoes of 126 tonnes into Wells for the local Dalgety depot. Other commercial shipping ceased in 1990 and in 1997 *Albatros* delivered her last cargo bringing an end to a centuries-old tradition.

Shipbuilding and maritime trades

One of the earliest vessels recorded as having been built on the Saltmarsh Coast – earlier ones were not recorded -was the brigantine *Hope* registered at Wells in 1764. From 1801 to 1860 'The Registers and Measures Books' of HM Customs and Excise recorded the construction of more than 60 ships at Wells where seven shipbuilders were active between 1834 and 1883. In 1832 'Coke of Norfolk' and his family embarked on the 80-ton schooner *Holkham* built from oak grown on the Holkham estate, thought to have been built there. Allied trades and crafts: blacksmiths, chandlers and rope makers flourished. The old ropewalks can still be seen running along behind the properties on the west side of the Buttlands.

The last Wells shipbuilder working entirely in wood was the Palmer, Whitaker and Elener yard, the effects of which were sold at auction in May 1905. A model of the shipyard is in the Yarmouth Maritime Museum along with models of the last vessels built at Wells.

Fishing

Men have fished from the ports of the Saltmarsh Coast since time immemorial. The Holkham archives contain early references to whaling from Wells and to 'Blubber Yard'. There are mediaeval cottages in 'Whalebone Yard' off Church Plain in Wells. More recent records show herring, haddock and cod fishing from Iceland Waters in the 16th and 17th centuries. Oysters were prolific from the mid 19th century to the last recorded catches of 1904, and Oyster smacks still figure in early Wells photographs (a modern version of the 'Norfolk Oyster' is still built today at Morston and has proved a most popular leisure craft). In the late 1800s local records show sole, brill and thornback, but declining catches of haddock and cod.

The whelk fishing industry which moved from Sheringham to Wells in the 1930s and 40s brought an influx of fishermen from along the coast to join the local cockle and mussel and longshore fishermen and bait diggers. In the 1950s and 60s skate and sprats were caught in large quantities and the present modern trawler fleet started to develop. The 1970s brought larger catches of pink and brown shrimps, crabs and lobsters, with continuing longshore catches of sea trout and occasional sea bass. Longshoremen, residents and visitors also harvest samphire from the marshes in season, the sophisticated 'sea asparagus' – an acquired taste for visitors.

Wells Harbour Commissioners

My involvement with Wells Harbour began when I became Clerk to the Harbour Commissioners in 1974, a position I held for 20 years and which brought a new perspective to my view of Wells life. The focus and priorities of the Harbour Commissioners, as set out in the Wells Harbour Act of 1835 were the 'repairing, improving, and preserving the harbour and Quay of Wells in the County of Norfolk…'. The unpaid Harbour Commissioners tried to perform their duties as far as was possible with a very low harbour income, mainly derived from shipping and cargo dues. The Harbour has always been a non-profit making, statutory body and income has always been ploughed back into the Harbour.

The challenges the Harbour Commissioners faced then, as now, included a wayward, silting, meandering channel, which could change course drastically with every high wind and spring tide. Their funds would only permit servicing and maintenance of the lights, buoys and beacons (always a priority) and maintenance of the quay wall and surface, and minor channel correction works. The occasional necessary replacement of a single York stone block along the quay edge when damaged would cost in the region of £1000 to £1500 and cripple the spending capability for the rest of a financial year.

Periodically, larger problems would arise in the channel due to excessive meandering or silting, which restricted shipping movements and threatened the 'sacred' 10-foot draft limit. The Harbour Commissioners would periodically commission reports and investigate various channel training works to deepen and widen the channel, reinstate piling at the toe of the West Bank, damming and blocking off channel tributaries which threatened to divert main water flows away from the quay and stabilizing and straightening the east side of the channel.

Some smaller projects were achievable and would always be carried out if funds allowed. However, larger projects were always beyond their slender means. It was therefore necessary to carry out works here and there and to 'work with nature' wherever possible to encourage the channel to flow in the right course for navigation. This required a certain amount of experimentation – and consultation. There were and are increasingly strict constraints on what works may be permitted in an 'Area of Outstanding Natural Beauty' and a 'Site of Special Scientific Interest'. These restrictions further tied the hands of the Harbour Commissioners.

Looking back over my 20 years as Clerk to the Commissioners and my more recent service as a Harbour Commissioner, there are many projects which have been undertaken by the Harbour Commissioners for the benefit of the harbour and the town. Not least the provision of a good, reliable and well maintained navigation system of lights, buoys and beacons, and moorings, the damming of various creeks to protect tidal flows through the quay, the move to the Old Lifeboat House, the rebuilding of the Tug Boat Yard and Jubilee/Anglian Water Quays, the acquisition of the East End boat store and harbour yard, other improvements at East Quay, the provision of a slipway trolley, pontoons and harbour launch, the updating of harbour legislation in 1994 and the comprehensive services provided by the dedicated harbour staff.

There were many other projects that didn't happen – or have not happened to date – as illustrated by a look through old preliminary reports on proposals for new marinas, wind farms and off shore oil and gas exploration, and quay extensions.

The most intractable and enduring problem of Wells Harbour remains the silting and meandering of the channel. These problems date from the land 'reclamations' and remind us of the power that the larger landowners, as well as nature, have had in shaping the Saltmarsh Coast. There have been many expert reports and investigations on these matters over the centuries. The only major works in recent years followed the 1978 floods when the West Bank reinstatement works were carried out. Further channel works on the east side of the channel were proposed and costed. Again however, the Commissioners could not afford the works.

Looking forward

Arthur Purchas attributed the decline of Wells to the arrival of the railway in 1857 and a consequent reduction in shipping. These days a rail link would be considered essential to the operation of a successful port and the present government is trying with no great success to encourage additional port/rail links around the UK. The Wells railway era however did not survive Mr. Beeching's hatchet in 1964, when Wells lost the rail link which connected it to Kings Lynn, South Norfolk, Norwich and places further afield. However, it retains the other advantage – its proximity to Europe through the North Sea ports of Rotterdam, Antwerp, Amsterdam, Ijmuiden and Scheveningen, Bremen and Hamburg. Although appearing to be an estuary port it is, unusually, an estuary without a river except for the egress of fresh water springs and land drainage channels.

Whilst the accessibility of North Norfolk to the continent will continue to play its part in sea traffic across the North Sea, for leisure craft if not for commercial vessels, the ebb and flow of the fortunes of the railways has had its effect, and the cost of long distance road haulage to and from our coast has played a significant part in the recent decline of commercial shipping.

These factors and the channel problems probably preclude the return of commercial shipping to Wells for the time being but all this could change with, say, oil and gas exploration off our Saltmarsh Coast. This possibility has arisen before and could arise again; oil field development, requiring port service facilities and supply boats, based at Wells, would quickly change the emphasis and the economic view of the viability of channel training works. The environmental aspects and assessments would quickly come into play in this specially protected area. Big money talks... one might speculate as to who might win... and whether the local voice would be heard at all. The move now though is to environmentally friendly and sustainable power. Offshore wind farming has been considered and

is being reconsidered. There may be many objectors to its visual impact but would there be the same objections to the harnessing of tide power in strong tidal areas at sea or in channels? It should be possible to construct something much less visually obtrusive offshore.

But without huge changes Wells will probably be limited (and protected) by the fact it is a tidal harbour, drying at low tide and only accessible two hours or so either side of high water for vessels of less than 10 foot draft and 750 tonnes and it is likely that future port activities will be severely controlled, if not curtailed, by the rules and directives controlling environmental risk and impact, linked with the many environmental classifications referred to elsewhere in this book. In future it will be the powerful European Community and environmental bodies which will shape (and protect?) the Saltmarsh Coast. We hope the power of local landowners also will be directed towards conserving and managing their land to retain its special qualities.

Since the 1990s Wells Harbour has undergone a considerable change of emphasis. Still officially categorized as a Fishery Harbour, a Statutory Port Authority and a 'competent harbour authority for pilotage', it retains full port and harbour functions, powers, duties and responsibilities. But the harbour is now used mainly for leisure boats, from small dinghies and tenders through larger sailing vessels, motor cruisers and the occasional historic sailing barge or 'retired lifeboat', and it is clear that this is where a viable future lies. We hope the local fishing industry will always retain a presence, and be supported, but it is difficult to see the way forward for young men coming into fishing today.

Since commercial shipping ceased, car-parking on Wells Quay (which began in the early 1960s when cars were parked on the quay between shipping tides) now provides a significant income to the Harbour Commissioners. Ironically, this income makes it possible to afford much larger harbour improvement projects than were possible in the past although there are now no cargo ships to improve it for. The well maintained lighting and buoyage system is exceptional for the size of port.

In the cargo shipping years the leisure boats were very much a peripheral adjunct to the main activities in the harbour – shipping and fishing. Until recently, the shipping took priority over all other activities and fishing and leisure boats had to move away from the quay to accommodate the ships. Ships needed navigation aids: lights, buoys and beacons as well as pilotage and occasional tug services. Land support from the Harbour Masters, cargo handling crews, transport and shipping agency services, fuel bunkering and provisions was vital. Otherwise, cargo ships were fairly self-contained by way of 'bathroom and laundry' facilities, having all they needed onboard.

Our current visiting harbour users, in smaller boats, yachts and power vessels, all need more accessible shore support by way of such things as showers and washrooms, laundry facilities, waste disposal points and fuel, winter storage and boat repairs and the Harbour Commissioners have been trying for many years to

Old Lifeboat House, Well

raise funds to renovate and protect the Harbour Office in the Old Lifeboat House on West Quay and provide other facilities for harbour users. With recent invaluable assistance they have been successful. The building is Grade II listed and is a local landmark, but is also subject to regular flooding on exceptional tides and is in a poor state of repair.

There are many other pressures on Harbour Commissioners today. In recent years, an increasing number of government initiatives have emanated from the Department of Environment, Trade and the Regions (DETR) under the general heading of 'British Trust Ports Modernisation'. These require the overhaul of most aspects of port and harbour life, from the rewriting of the legislation, constitutions and duties of British Trust Ports to the streamlining of harbour authorities, the introduction of new standards of personal accountability, training and continuing professional development for both harbour officers and Harbour Commissioners alike, the upgrading of procedures, port safety codes and practices, and the introduction of new systems for hazard management, environmental protection, conservation, categorisation of our waters and much else.

These changes add to the many rules and regulations that already apply to the numerous designated categories that apply to our area. Existing and general harbour legislation, health and safety rules and the area's classification as a Site of Special Scientific Interest, an Area of Outstanding Natural Beauty, a National Nature Reserve and a Special Area of Conservation together with habitat directives for wild life and bird protection and other rule based systems and classifications take up time and energy and cause more than a few headaches.

The paperwork, reporting requirements and procedures that are now (seemingly) relevant and necessary to a small port with no ships sometimes seems astonishing. Under new arrangements, there are fewer Harbour Commissioners than in the past and each of them is far more involved in day-to-day management and affairs than were their predecessors.

The move towards openness and accountability, incorporating the 'Nolan' principles and fixed term appointments, advertising Commissioners' positions with applications open to all, can only be a 'good thing'. Particularly, the requirement to consult with and involve all harbour users and local bodies – now of course called stakeholders – is to be welcomed. However, the torrent of paper and regulation sometimes results in our losing sight of the more positive aspects of modernization.

We were recently told by the DETR that Wells was unusual as a small port in having already moved quite a long way down the 'modernization road' of its own volition, before it became compulsory so to do. In this respect Wells compares favourably with many other small ports. In the late 1980s at one early harbour users' public meeting, arranged to improve communication , and consultation with the town and harbour users, a local Wells resident thanked the Harbour

Commissioners for 'coming out into the open'. He said that some had viewed the Harbour Commissioners as a form of 'secret society' because of their closed meetings, and their self-perpetuating nature. They have come a long way since then.

The Harbour Commissioners at the time were taken aback, but they have over the past two decades become far more proactive in disseminating information, consulting and informing local people and harbour users, by open discussions, consultation and regular meetings of liaison and advisory groups. The Commissioners also foresaw problems in finding individuals who complied with the age rules initially imposed by the DETR, those under retirement age, who had time enough to devote to the more demanding role of a modern Harbour Commissioner, which is still of course unpaid. However, a combination of two factors has helped here. The DETR has dropped the age restriction which was objected to as 'ageist', and the recent popularity of the Saltmarsh Coast as a settlement area for 'early retirees' means an available and increasing pool of people with diverse skills to complement the long term residents with their fund of local knowledge and harbour experience.

What are the future threats?

First, without good, navigable channels there are no ports. At Wells, the current constraints on channel maintenance and improvement are adding to the historic problem of lack of funds. The veto powers of the environmental and conservation bodies, which may strongly object to any works which may affect, change or interfere with nature and the environment become ever stronger. Whether navigation is easy or difficult, whether or not the channel banks be cut away by strong currents, or Wells Quay is bypassed altogether (if the channel should redirect itself through the marsh creeks), are not important issues for these powerful environmental bodies, but are the *raison d'être* of the Harbour Commissioners.

The growing, silting sand spits for example at Blakeney Point and Scolt Head could close off further navigation channels at Brancaster, Blakeney, Wells and Burnham Overy. Although it is highly unlikely, in a stretch of accreting coast line and marsh, silting could, in the future as in the past make the difference between harbour channels that are active and viable and those that are defunct and silted. If these harbours should become un-navigable, then the villages they now serve – like the Burnhams and Cley, just a little further away from the North Sea – would simply become rural, holiday and second home settlements.

The future could see a continuing struggle to maintain the viability of these ports and harbours. This is a live issue, which must be kept in the balance between preserving continuing utility and our beautiful environment. For the time being, with our present range of leisure harbour users, there is no great tension between the two.

Second, increasing numbers of harbour users on land and in boats will require strict control of numbers, fuel and sanitation – holding tanks in vessels, the provision of disposal points and careful monitoring to prevent oil spills and sewage pollution will be essential; if the Thames can be kept clean, we can do likewise. On shore, the rubbish generated by visitors and fast food outlets, particularly at Wells, must be tackled.

Third, the risk that our coast could develop, like parts of the South Coast, with acres of marina developments, caravans and waterside dwellings, will call for strong planning controls.

Fourth, the risk that Wells Harbour might be taken over by, say, the Local Authority, Holkham Estates or large commercial enterprises keeping a weather eye on opportunities for developments in moorings, marinas, water side properties and services will require careful vigilance.

Fifth, the risk that the whole area could be spoiled is highly unlikely given the number of conservation categories the Saltmarsh Coast falls into, but it is already recognised that pressure on specific hot spots for tourism could diminish the beauty of these harbours. The fact there are relatively few points of access to the water puts great pressure on the those that exist. Development outside existing settlements is closely controlled but, inevitably, 'the hot spots will get hotter'. The main pressure is during July and August but the coast is busy from May to September. We need improved systems to control numbers of vessels on the water in Brancaster, Burnham Overy, Wells, Morston and Blakeney. It will be particularly important to control certain types of craft such as power boats and jet skis in congested waters and to restrict their use to open beaches away from swimmers at say Hunstanton, Sheringham and Cromer. These controls should not only relate to safety but also to noise pollution. Even sailing dinghies can create a congestion problem. The main problem however is the mix of harbour users competing for limited harbour waters for their own valid uses and the safety issues which arise from the mix.

Sixth, the numbers of moorings are being closely watched by the conservation and environment lobby but are increasing year by year. Morston and Blakeney must be amongst the very few harbours in the country that still offer free moorings. What will happen when they reach saturation; will the overspill try to move to move to Wells, Burnham Overy, or Brancaster? New Sailing Schools and various clubs also create additional pressure with power boats added to existing mix.

Seventh, existing pressures on accommodation, services, road traffic and car parking and the impact of tourism on small coastal villages in the summer months will have to be closely monitored. A project to develop a Maritime Heritage Centre at Wells has been 'hijacked' by the need to provide additional car parking for visitors to the Centre and raises questions about the use of land on the fringes of

Blakeney

the town for car and boat parking.

Eighth, we cannot put the clock back and revert to the small, isolated and independent towns and villages that fill the memories of the oldest local people. Perhaps we can replace the feelings of ownership and community of coastal waters by the seafaring locals – but how? We cannot prevent change but we can and must fight the loss of the special, remote and wild quality of the coast, support or replace traditional coastal livelihoods that are no longer economic and foster feelings of belonging in our children.

Ninth, commercial fishing and related livelihoods are going through very difficult times in the present European political climate and are suffering from many decades of failure to manage and conserve fish stocks. Sustainable local fishing policies are important, and access to waterside land for fishermen's use, must be protected – even if they have to consider visual amenities and clear up from time to time. Boat building has revived and should be encouraged and other maritime skills should not be lost without exploring new ways to train young people in traditional crafts on a sustainable scale.

Tenth, sea defence and environmental strategies can have a dual purpose; improving navigation and providing moorings and keeping the sea out or conserving marshland. The character and appearance of our coast should be considered and where possible, channels, staithes, quays and facilities for vessels should be improved and maintained without sacrificing historical features and natural beauty. We can move or recreate marsh and channels in a natural way even if it means underpinning by heavy engineering works, by moving sand and mud and finishing and replanting appropriately. Conservation and Environmental agencies must liaise more closely with harbour authorities and be prepared to consider how environmental matters can be tied in with the needs of navigation.

Despite actual and potential problems, my vision is that these issues will be managed and the problems dealt with, partly because there is the will to do so and partly because there are sufficient people with money and influence to do so. There is already a great debate about the future of this coast and this book is part of it. The danger is that local people will not have a sufficient say in shaping the future and they must therefore speak out through all the avenues open to them to ensure it benefits both them and visitors as well as the environment. It is essential to give people a voice, to consult widely, to work with nature and to seek excellence and cohesion in new initiatives, buildings and ventures. Our coast has seen many ups and downs in its long history, since records began and before. It must live on by adapting, changing and developing as a haven – for us all.

A Norfolk Life

Dominick Harrod

The Watch House perches on the strand between the sand dunes of Blakeney Point to the west, and the shingle bank of Cley beach to the east. Once a look-out for excise men, it has been for my lifetime a summer resort for campers wanting to sleep under the huge Norfolk sky, with shelter in the square red-brick building against the rain and thunderstorms of July and August. As well as a shelter, the Watch House is a landmark for miles for walkers and sailors in Blakeney Harbour or at sea, where tankers and container ships either pass on their stately courses, or remain at anchor awaiting orders to this berth or that on the North Sea coast.

I often pass that way in the summer, walking at low tide across the mud and and sand to bathe off the sandy shallows, where once were the steeply shelving waters which remain away to the east at Cley. The deposition of sand banks along the shoreline, and in the harbour itself, are likely be a transforming feature extending into the future with which this book is concerned.

Returning across the sand there are two landmarks. Rising above the village to the east are the sails of Cley Mill, most water-coloured of buildings along the Saltmarsh Coast. But if I look to the west of Blakeney, streaming down its hill below the magnificent tower of St Nicholas' Church, I see a low-lying cottage, lime-washed in pale yellow, almost as white as the sails of Cley mill.

These two personal land-marks, perhaps a mile and a half apart, describe my Norfolk life, covering sixty years this season. I have spent three score years experiencing this section of the Saltmarsh Coast, observing what changes, and what remains the same. On the whole, I think what stays the same, or at least remains recognisable, outweighs the superficial changing scene. There are undoubted challenges ahead for those like me who, living a Norfolk life, value what we know but recognise the pressures of 'progress' which are likely to continue to change the scenes we see from our windows or as we go about our business and pleasure along the shore. 'Progress' is perhaps a key word, not least because it sharply divides the population between those who dislike or distrust progress, and those who welcome its very manifestation from intercontinental air travel to the mobile 'phone and i-pod. But there is another division. For those of us who regard progress as inevitable, there is the question whether to ignore it,

Dominick Harrod

Dominick Harrod's Norfolk forbears hail from Aylsham, birthplace of King Harold (killed at the Battle of Hastings in 1066), and include Henry Harrod, c19th archaeologist who first mapped the outline of Binham Priory in his volume *Castles and Convents of Norfolk* (1857). On his mother's side he descends from Elizabeth Fry (née Gurney), the Earlham-born prison reform pioneer now celebrated on the £5 note, and the Ffolkes family of Hillington. In 2000, he published *War Ice and Piracy*, the letters of his King's Lynn forbear, Samuel Gurney Cresswell, a Norfolk naval officer on board HMS *Investigator*, the ship which discovered the North West Passage in an epic voyage, 1850-53. After Oxford, Dominick joined the *Sunday Telegraph* where he worked with both the gossip columnist and the City Editor before spending three years in the late 60s as its Washington Correspondent. Returning to London he worked as the economics correspondent of the *Daily Telegraph* until 1971 when he became the economics correspondent of the BBC for what he describes as 'nearly twenty congenial years'. His Norfolk links have never been broken and he has returned to Blakeney to 'breathe Norfolk air at every chance and to sail a succession of dinghies in Blakeney Harbour'. He now divides his time between Blakeney and London.

and carry on as we were, or to embrace it and continue the time-honoured practice of 'keeping up with the Jones's'.

And for the future Saltmarsh Coast progress is not going to be voluntary. Perhaps this is the moment to pose the most important question about the future of our lives here. Will the evolution of life in North Norfolk continue in the next half century to evolve as slowly as it has in the last?

In normal circumstances, the pace of change speeds up. But no-one who has experienced the pace of change in Norfolk over the last fifty years could say that, on the surface of things, this is so. Norfolk, for instance, has not one mile of motorway in the county. (The M11 looked a threat for a bit, but then veered off to Cambridge, to the muted cheers of proper East Anglians.)

Since I am writing about the experience of life in Norfolk, rather than the strategic discussions of agriculture, infrastructure, etc, elsewhere in this book, I ask the simple question for those who live within sight or sound of the North Sea. Shall we embrace the future on a jet-ski, or be stick-in-the mud?

To some extent the question is different if asked indoors, than out. Indoor life changes with technology. The microwave instead of (or as well as) the Aga. This computer, which will allow me to send this chapter to the editor without moving from my chair, instead of a typewriter, envelope and stamps. All the paraphernalia of TV receiver, video, DVD, and the humble e-mail and Fax. These are the manifestations of progress indoors.

Outdoors is very different; and is the matter with which this chapter is concerned. Perhaps I should give some examples. The humble sailing dinghy was, when I learnt to sail, a wooden, often clinker-built affair, varnished or painted, with heavy spars and sails. Later, tougher fibre-glass boats appeared, some of the best, the Wayfarer and the smaller Gull, from the drawing board of Ian Proctor on the south coast. These are comfortable, as well as performance boats, as are the Norfolk Oyster and Stiffkey Cockle, built respectively by Charlie Ward at Morston and George Hewitt at Stiffkey.

Elsewhere, as I witnessed on west London reservoirs, the latest design in sailing dinghies are outrigged monohulls or catamarans, where comfort is sacrificed to netting support, under huge sails, providing immense speed, but nowhere to put the picnic basket!

Norfolk, especially the western end of the Saltmarsh Coast, has always had its thoroughbred boats. The Sharpie comes to mind. And in more recent years, the range of Lasers and sail-boards has offered everyone brave enough the choice of performance over comfort.

Against this background of hi-tech 'ironing boards' as I have heard them called, it is fascinating to see the success of Charlie Ward and George Hewitt's designs of boats for the 1990s and beyond; for their central message is classic design combined with new materials and technology. It is good to see their choice of wooden spars and brown sails, while the hulls are tough plastic, moulded to resemble the clinker-built boats of the 1940s and before.

What Blakeney, the Burnhams and Brancaster will look like depends on the outdoor choices of future Norfolk sailors. The way may divide between wet-suits and ironing boards, of ever more rarified designs, and a dry place for the sandwiches, with space for the life-jacketed children, getting their early taste for whatever the next generation of dinghies will resemble.

And into the future the matter of noise and other pollution will depend on how our harbour communities react to ever more powerful and adventurous speedboats. So far, for instance, water-skiing has been confined to the western end of Blakeney Harbour, leaving the Pit, and the long eastern reaches relatively free of their noise. It remains to be seen whether such restraint will prevail as more and more people buy more and more expensive motor toys for their pleasure.

For the sailing fraternity speedboats have always been an irritation, not least because their noise swamps the softer natural noise of wind, water and sea-birds. But of course quite a few of the sailors are the same people as the noise polluters, when they decide to take out their motor boats instead of their dinghies.

In my bedroom in Blakeney, the north windows overlook the marsh, the harbour, the Watch House, and on rough days tongues of spray thrown up by the waves crashing on the shore a mile away. The south windows open on a lane with cottage gardens and orchards behind a low wall. In bed one morning, soon after I moved to the coast, I heard to my left – the seaward side – the calls of curlew, red-shank and gull. To my right, thrush and blackbird raising their own dawn chorus.

The Old Lifeboat House, Blakeney Point

For the very fortunate, that blend of sea and land is what makes North Norfolk irreplaceable, but is routinely shattered by noise pollution. It is to be welcomed that the RAF and USAF observe the five-day week. Some of my weekend visitors have never heard the screech of jets flying low over the rooftops and out to sea.

And it's not just noise pollution. The Saltmarsh Coast is falling victim to a more insidious and universal bane: light-pollution. Only a few years ago, the walk along the sea-wall from Morston to Blakeney could be made in almost total darkness. Then, the stars blazed, and as eyes became accustomed to the dark, the ribbon of dried mud that formed the path on the top of the grassy bank showed clear and grey. Now the local council has erected street lamps, and many houses have bright external lights blazing at night. These bulbs may be there for what are deemed good reasons – to deter burglars, or allow the villagers to go to the pub without the torch which used to see them home. The damage to that walk is total. So bright is the glare that the stars vanish, and even the slight contours of the walk itself are made more difficult to read. Now, perversely, you need a torch again to see your way.

I cannot help but fear that modernisations of this sort will be with us in the next decades as in the last. It is not the least of the threats to what we have now, and are in grave danger of losing.

I said that the lights were installed for 'good reasons', and good reasons may often lead to unforeseen consequences.

At the time the wooden footbridges were built down the west side of Morston Creek, spanning the side-creeks, the 'good reason' was to give access to the marshes for those – the elderly, the cautious, or those with prams or push-chairs – who could not be expected to cross the single wooden planks, muddy and covered at high tide, which the bridges replaced. Immediately lost was the not uncommon sight of a local dog trotting across the creek apparently on the water, but actually on a single submerged plank.

A more drastic effect was to allow the ferrymen to build their landing stages well down the creek, making space for more and more who had previously plied from Blakeney quay, two miles to the east. In consequence of these good ideas, Morston creek is suffering acute erosion, becoming shallower and wider. The sailor has to contend with more and more laden motor boats ploughing their paths up and down the creek. It is all very well for the experienced helmsman, but no fun for the beginner, and makes teaching sailing in the creek hazardous if not impossible.

But not all good ideas have damaging side effects. When the Morston ferrymen (I am told John Bean had the bright idea) decided to offer trips down the harbour to see the seal and tern colonies on the far Point, there was one blessing for the self-propelled.

Under the old system of ferries shuttling to and from the Point at Pinchen's creek, the sand dunes of the Point quickly filled up with picknickers, and there arose that other noise pollution of children happily playing on the sand. Now, the boats spend most of the time plying down to the seals, and touch the Point itself, if at all, for just time for the passengers to go to the old Life-boat house a couple of hundred yards along the foreshore. As a result, anyone arriving in their own boat and walking northward finds the dunes empty, and the rich wildlife undisturbed. It is a blessing afforded by the enthusiasm of the paying public for an intimate and charming view of the seal colony and sea-birds nearby.

What is the moral of this long reflection on the evolution of the coastal life?

It may only be that what is certain is further change. What is not certain is how the changes which loom ahead will affect the way we will live in the second and following decades of the twenty-first century. There are some sign-posts to the future which will touch us all, but which we can aspire to influence.

One such is the matter of 'Village Design Statements'. Under these schemes, villagers can put together thoughts on the appearance, and the developments in their own immediate environments. The final papers produced may recommend, for instance, best practice in the use of traditional materials for new or renovated buildings.

Limits of expansion can also be discussed, and Local Authorities may take

Village Design Statements into account in assessing planning applications. The present climate seems on the whole cautious, and less liberal towards new structures than in the past. All of us who live along this coast will know of houses or other structures which, built some years ago, would hardly now be granted planning permission.

But residents trying to improve their properties, or developers hoping to serve incoming visitors, are not the only players in the evolution of the Saltmarsh Coast.

A crucial player since long before Operation Neptune has been the National Trust. I write as a Life Member, and in general a keen supporter of the Trust. (Operation Neptune was a campaign to raise funds to allow the Trust to buy many leagues of coastline round the country.) But I cannot reflect on the evolution of the marshes without one slightly melancholy conclusion.

When Blakeney Point was bequeathed to the National Trust before the Second World War, the intention of the donor, and of the Trust, was to conserve the natural beauty spot and nature reserve. To some extent this object was achieved. But in the ensuing years the Trust's nature has changed, and it is now first and foremost a membership organisation, having more members than any other such in the country, and continuing to try to recruit at every turn, and every Trust site.

Inevitably, this ambition will conflict with that other objective, conservation. We read in the papers of worries about the erosion of pathways and trails across the fells of the Trust's most famous holdings in the Lake District. But we do not have to look to the far west to see the inevitable result of the pressure of numbers. We need only look at the car-parks of Blakeney, Morston and the like.

Naturally, the Trust circularises its growing number of members with Annual Reports and other literature tempting this ever growing army to visit Trust properties. In the battle between conserving the marshland and its delicate ecology, and exploiting the properties in Trust hands, exploitation is winning the day.

Nor is the increase in tourism ('trippers' we used to call them, and an early ferryman from the village was known as Tripper Bean), the only force for change. Nature also plays its inexorable part.

Nature's interventions can be violent or gentle. Most sensational in post-war memory was the great surge of January 31, 1953. A Northerly gale had been blowing for days, and had already claimed a tragic victim in the sinking of the RMS *Princess Victoria* when her hold doors came adrift in the turmoil of the Irish sea, en route from Stranraer to Larne. Many lives were lost.

Still the wind blew; and eye-witnesses said that on the day of the disaster, the tide never went out. Under howling winds, the sea made its cataclysmic assault on the east coast. An aerial photograph taken the following day showed the Glaven valley flooded, the sea having retreated, but the water which had breasted the inner sea-wall beside the coast road was trapped inside the bank. The photograph has an added fascination, for it shows the approximate dimension of the harbour running up past Cley-next-the-Sea to Wiveton, as the sea would have been in the 12th or 13th centuries.

Confirmation of this phenomenon, that in the great flood the sea reclaimed its ancient boundaries, was born out by the fact that only one medieval church was flooded. The placing of the church buildings on the higher ground along the coast arose not so much from caution about floods, as from the fact that the exceptional level in 1953 was where the sea naturally reached 600 years earlier.

To get an idea of the height of the North Sea Surge, the visitor need only go to the quay at Blakeney, and read the metal plaque affixed to the front wall of the hotel marking the level reached. Needless to say, there were hydrographic experts who said that no combination of wind and tide could push the great saucer of water which is the North Sea above mean high tide by more than six feet. They should have been there on the night.

What has happened once (or twice, or three times, counting lesser inundations) can happen again. I sleep easier at night when the wind howls for the knowledge that my cottage at Blakeney, suitably enough for this volume called 'Saltmarsh' was not flooded that night. Metaphorically speaking, I reckon that may give me a hundred years of global warming before I need to get out tide-boards for the back door.

But the sea is out there, and may well be in again, when the wind blows. Oddly enough, the present concern about the water's edge is precisely the opposite. Far from too much water, we are threatened with too little. Over the past fifty years there have been two obvious changes to my local shoreline. These changes are slow moving, the opposite of the violent attacks on the outer defences brought about by gales, one of which recently deposited a large section of shingle bank at Cley into the beach car park.

The two changes have been part of a single tendency. Vast quantities of sand have been deposited at the west end of Blakeney Harbour, and a good deal of it has ended up at the eastern end, silting up the creeks and making the water far shallower for sailors. A small but dramatic instance of this is John Wallace's causeway at Blakeney.

This pathway of rubble, bricks, flints and stones was painstakingly built in the 1950s by John Wallace, local character and benefactor, to allow sailors and

birdwatchers to walk down towards the harbour from the quay. It stood about two feet above the margin of the new cut, as the creek is called, and provided a route avoiding the sticky mud.

Today, the causeway is virtually level with the creek it borders, the deposit of sand and mud in the creek has raised its eastward level by two feet or so. Instead of dropping down into the oozy mud of the old days, the creek bed is now a plateau of firm mud and sand, being colonised by samphire, until the deep channel is reached on the western side; and that deep channel is a good deal narrower than yesteryear.

The second change is part of the same phenomenon, where, at the west end of the harbour, the sandbanks have grown so large, inshore of the Blakeney bar, that they are often exposed at high water on the smaller neap tides.

These shoreline movements will certainly continue into the future, changing the background to, if not the nature of, pastimes and recreation on the Saltmarsh Coast. It may be that the deposition of sand, the silting up of familiar harbours will be as significant as the growth in popularity of sailing and other seaside activities. It looks as though we shall be in for more people in less space.

But there will, I hope, be indestructible elements to life on the Saltmarsh Coast. I bring this chapter to a close with the most important of all elements: food.

It is a delight of living in North Norfolk that the turning of the year brings a variety of treats.

The samphire I have already mentioned as colonising newly deposited mud at Blakeney is a delicacy available only in July and August. By contrast, the sea-spinach which appears among the grass on marshes and margins between land and sea, seems to be about the year round. Not only is it tastier than its garden variety, but it does not shrink so drastically in the pan during cooking.

As wild as the spinach are mushrooms, from puff-balls to field mushrooms and the occasional parasol. But in September and October the fancier needs to be up early to be there before the competition. The same goes for picking crab-apples from the hedgerows, wild sloes and plums.

These delicious wild foods are, of course, threatened in North Norfolk by loss of habitat and by development, as well as by the rise in numbers competing for them. But again, the samphire beds and crab-apple bushes persist where they were fifty years ago, and are treasured by their users.

Then the fish. Summer months find boats, large and small, fishing for mackerel. The mackerel may also, at that time of the year be indicators of the presence of whitebait, needing collection by net, sometimes by teams of children organised by parents, hauling the catch to shore and hoping it will be more whitebait than sand-eel. Both mackerel and whitebait can be taken by amateurs, making the fishing itself as much a mark of North Norfolk life, as the subsequent supper. And for anglers and expert fishermen there is the exceptional sea-trout, a delicacy which

Morston Church

makes salmon taste like cotton-wool.

Finally, shellfish. The turning of the year is simple. In summer, crabs, cockles, and the monarch of all, the lobster; in winter the incomparable mussel. To write about Norfolk life without the taste of these fish, and many other local treats in one's mouth, would be to miss a crucial element of what remains, up to now, a wild coast. Blakeney, of which you've heard a good deal in this chapter, remains a fishing village.

There is the industrious Willie, whose mobile fish bar travels the coast, and who takes his shell-fish as far afield as the Farmers Market behind Marylebone High Street on a Sunday in London. I have seen the lobsters in his holding tanks, ingeniously devised next to his house in the village. Not three hundred yards away is Andy, with a smaller turn-over and a sign on the coast road saying 'Crabs', and on a lucky day 'Lobsters' as well, when his pots off Cley beach have been fruitful.

And in winter the signs are changed to 'Fresh Mussels'. For the future of the Saltmarsh Coast we will not only depend on the succession of fishermen but also the husbanding of the catch which has, and we hope will, populate the sea which above all gives the place its character.

The harvest of the sea is fragile, as one story illustrates. Some years ago an aggregates company sought permission to extract thousands of cubic yards of gravel from an offshore bank well out to sea in the angle between Norfolk and Lincolnshire. This project was subject to Government approval. Opinions were invited.

Among the objectors was the Fishmongers Company, whose experts pointed out that the shingle bank was the spawning ground of the millions of crabs harvested by fishermen's pots all along the Norfolk and Suffolk coasts. The project was blocked. Thus a City Livery company more renowned for its splendid Hall, with the Aningoni portrait of the Queen, and its patronage of Gresham's School in Holt, stepped in to the battle on behalf of the fishing trade. The livery also gave generously to a fund set up to support All Saints Morston, a 13th century church whose brick patched tower is a very special land-mark to walkers, sailors and indeed, fishermen.

Finally, a reflection on the emptiness of tracts of the Saltmarsh Coast. I began this chapter at the Watch House, and will end it there. Having walked across the mud, shingle and sand from the mouth of Blakeney creek to the shingle and sandy beach of the North Sea itself, one may, as often as not, bathe naked in the crystal sea. And that without danger of giving offence to anyone, since walkers are few indeed, the nearest car park being more than a mile away to the east. Perhaps decent separation from the nearest car park is the secret of discovering the special beauty of this treasured coast.

Frank and Margaret Dye

Having sailed 40,000 coastal and offshore miles in their famous Wayfarer dinghy *Wanderer*, now in the National Maritime Museum, Frank and Margaret Dye have been described as 'legends in their own lifetimes'. Born in inland Norfolk, Frank was fascinated by the sea but, busy building up the family firm, did not start sailing until he was 27. Remarkably, he says his fear of the water 'probably prevents him from taking risks'. His first boat was, he says, 'utterly unsuited for cruising', but adds that it and the Saltmarsh Coast 'taught him all he needed to know'. Margaret, also from inland Norfolk, crewed on large yachts before sailing a Broads Half-Decker and met Frank at a sailing course. She taught in Norfolk and Cheshire before retiring to concentrate on her passions of music (she plays violin in several Norfolk orchestras and quartets), dinghy cruising and sailing. Frank and Margaret have written more than 500 articles and many books including *Ocean Crossing Wayfarer*, *Sailing to the Edge of Fear*, *Open Boat Cruising*, *Dinghy Cruising* and *Listen to the Locals*. They live in Wells and Norwich.

Seen from the Sea

Frank and Margaret Dye

Wells-next-the-Sea with its sandy beaches, pine tree belts, picturesque flint-faced cottages, and fishermen's boats lining the quay, gives the visitor a romantic view of this coastal area. True it is beautiful and the fact that the winter population in Wells is about 2000 and more than double that in the summer months testifies to the fact it is a popular place for the visitor and second home owner. But on a winter's day, when the North Sea piles up before an unrelenting northerly, this coast becomes even more beautiful and bracing – and a totally different place.

We sailed *Wanderer,* our 16ft sailing dinghy, along the coast in the seventies, taking a short break from my marina business on the mountainous Macclesfield canal. A Norfolk man of some 40 years I was born and bred 40 miles inland so I knew almost nothing of Wells-next-the-Sea. We planed over the bar, saw the fishing boats at the quay, a coaster loading grain, and whelks being offloaded and transported further up the creek to the sheds where they would be boiled and sold all over the country.

We were deeply impressed by this obviously thriving community. Walking along the quay we said, 'We need a place in Norfolk for when we finish work.' We found a little cottage just off the water and immediately felt at home, for Wells was then a working village bustling with fishermen and farmers, tradesmen, boat builders and farm workers who were proud of their trades and permeated the town with their zest for living, along with the smells of boiling whelks and crabs and dust from ships loading and unloading cargoes that was blown by the wind throughout the town. It was not until a year later that we were able to afford a deposit on the cottage.

Fishermen, almost by definition, are highly skilled people, the last of the 'hunter gatherers', but they are slow to accept those outside their community. Margaret retired early and was always out sailing her dinghy whatever the weather and was soon acknowledged with a 'Morning'; as much as any incomer can expect. Fishermen are interesting characters, hard-working, tough and independent, but they don't talk easily to outsiders, especially women. So I was surprised when she came back one morning from an interview with the ex-harbourmaster. It is such hardy men, thrifty, hardworking and pragmatic, and willing to risk their lives to

help others, who over the years have given (and still give) the inshore waters and harbours of this coast their special character.

A different world

Turning the shoulder of Norfolk at Cromer the East Coast changes dramatically from the deeper water and long picturesque estuaries of the Suffolk and Essex rivers to the low-lying marshes, salt flats and drying creeks of North Norfolk and the Wash. The area is widely considered by deep-water sailors – with some justification – to be dangerous.

A conversation with Frank Taylor

The cobbled yard was saturated in sunshine, its warmth cupped in the sea-grey pebbled floor that had been water worn and smoothed by a succession of tides and generations of fishermen's feet. The vast Norfolk skies hanging over the marshes beyond the yard used to be filled with skylarks' song as the flood tide came in and out of the harbour, reclaiming and releasing its territory: now the harbour, marshes and skies are more empty, more silent.

This view of the harbour of Wells-next-the-Sea, and a thousand other memories of the harbour in its heyday, when often as many as seven trading boats lying double-banked along the quay, bringing fertilizer and animal feed were turned round in just seven hours – are still vivid in Frank's memory, who, in the mid 20th century was fisherman, lifeboat second cox'n, harbour master and pilot of this port. Decades later, now living with his daughter in a bungalow within sight and sound of all these memories, Frank talked to me in a lounge lined with photographs of boats, and R.N.L.I. certificates, vellums and medals.

'I was born in Black Horse Yard in 1903, and had two brothers and two sisters. My father, a seaman, died when I was three years old. I went to the local school and left at fourteen, and went cockling on the beach. They used to be 6d. a peck (2 gallons), now they make £3-£4 a peck. I also used to get mussels and winkles and when the muck cart came out in the roads and the horses put their dung down, I used to go along and bag it up and sell it to people with gardens.'

Frank told me that he first went to sea at the age of nineteen. 'Ted Nielsen taught me how to haul the whelk pots, bag them up, carry them off the boat and put them in the lorries. It was a good life. I enjoyed it.' At the same time he joined the Wells lifeboat. The cox'n was Billy Grimes 1917-1933. 'I'd always wanted to join since I left school. First we had the 'rowing' boat, she was called the 'Baltic', she was about 38ft long with ten foot oars and fourteen oarsmen. She had a loose footed lugsail and a jib and a mizzen sail. When there was a breeze we'd put the sails, they were tan canvas and made by Billy Grimes. When the maroons went up, the crew would stop cockling or leave the granaries, or wherever they were working and get down to the beach as fast as they could; some would bike, others would run.' A team of horses was on the pay role. They were kept on Flint and Wigton farms, and when their gates were opened, they'd be down to the station 'afore the men. Their harnesses were hung up in the boat sheds, and they would pull the boat down the channel if it was a low water launch.

I asked Frank to tell me about his most dramatic rescue. 'It was my first one,' he recalled. 'He was a local chap, skippering an old sailing barge. He got ashore just off Wells loaded with coal. The old boat broke up, we couldn't get her off the bar. There was a smart breeze with wind on the land, so he couldn't tack off. I suppose there is still coal from it buried in the sand. The skipper died some months after his ship got wrecked.'

As I got up to leave, Frank turned back to view the marshes from the window. The sun glinted on the incoming tide and the soft mauve of the sea holly and fresh green of the samphire lining the creeks flashed life back into the salt marshes. Frank was no longer in that room, he was back on the quayside overseeing the unloading of coal or fishmeal from a coaster, or maybe even further back in time in the 'Baltic's day, when women working on the mussel lays on the beach, reporting a boat in trouble, earn't themselves 7/6d, and the men rowing the lifeboat were paid 10 shillings a launch. Perhaps he was pulling on his gloves for a winter launch when it was freezing hard . . . 'We used to wet our mittens so that they'd dry on – that way was a lot better than putting on dry gloves and feeling the cold soak into your bones.'

Or maybe, he was recalling when the 1953 floods devastated Wells. Frank wrote that event up and it was published in a local book.

'We got to the boats, we got the poor old dears in and took them ashore. After that there were bullocks, pigs – everything came floating along the road. There was a poor old woman. She used to take people down the beach in a pony and trap 'cause there were no cars then. She lost her three horses. When we went to get her out there was a great ol' big haystack what had floated off the marshes and got stuck up against her front door. But we knocked her window out and got the woman outa there.'

From Blakeney and into the Wash the shallows extend far offshore with banks and shoals drying out on falling tides; overfalls and strong tides that quickly put up breaking seas in 'wind-against-tide' conditions to trap the unwary several miles out to sea; and drying estuaries with bars that become dangerous with an onshore wind or a left-over sea. It is an area of fierce currents, shallows, sandbanks that dry extensively at low water and strong tides that, running into the wind, quickly build up short, unpleasant seas. An unexpected complication is that the tide turns some two hours before high water so that a boat crossing the bar at high water faces a tide that is setting her down onto the banks at one and a half to two knots. Over the years, shallow sandbanks (known as 'bars'), caused by longshore drift and the strong ebb that deposits silt as it meets the sea and slows, have built up across the harbour mouths All the harbour bars are tricky – Brancaster being the best and Overy Staithe (described by Irving in his *Guide to the Wash & Humber* as 'murderous' in certain conditions – the only time I have seen 'murderous' used in this context) the most dangerous.

Boxing Day afloat
We made a quick, unplanned getaway after one Christmas. Bidding goodbye to our guests after a day's pleasant indulgences, we locked the door on dirty linen, piles of presents, cards and excess food, and escaped to Wanderer. We sailed into Brancaster Staithe, for once peaceful and empty at the weekend. Sailing out through the empty moorings, we gazed delightedly at the empty, flat salt marshes. We have been driven away from the area in high summer, when there is an explosion of weekend yachtsmen, weekenders, and fleets of rubber-suited sailors rushing to catch the tide. Today, however, all was

quiet. The winds were SW force 3, and the offshore breeze was warm. Our destination was Sunk Sand. *Wanderer* lifted to the swell, and we slipped over the bar on the last of the ebb tide. As far as the eye could see there was nothing, seawards was a flat, calm, grey watery waste, the estuarine beaches behind glowed a wet gold as did the stubble fields beyond them. This place is like the very rim of the world; there is no emptier place to visit than the Wash in winter. Deep draught boats shun these dangerous shallows, but centreboard dinghies can find great peace out here. Running about on the drying sand banks to restore the circulation, we picnicked on the hard drying sand.

As the tide returned we carried the last of the flood over a bubbling frothing bar, and the grey, calm afternoon relapsed into a black night. The gulls fell silent, and we later washed down the dinghy in a happy silence, and covered her, tying her securely down in the dinghy park in case the winter gales came before we next visited our boat. It had been a good Boxing Day. Nothing special, just two Norfolk sailors alone in a Norfolk estuary.

The lifeboatmen here admit to different skills to those in other parts. No seaman is happy with a mere foot or two under his keel, where to broach in a following sea is a disaster, and to hit bottom on these hard sands is to capsize and break up, but here it is the norm. So the lifeboat crew have different priorities in equipment, most importantly a drogue for slowing them down when running in the appalling seas that build up over the shallow offshore banks in gale conditions.

Once beyond the harbour bar it is a different world – an area for specialists who enjoy their skill in working the tides and who appreciate the wide skies, the beauty and the loneliness. Even the most enthusiastic dinghy cruiser will expect to keep off the water for some time between November and February. The odd day sail may be snatched even in the depths of winter, but passage making and sleeping afloat are more enjoyable during the spring, summer and autumn.

The North Norfolk coast and the Wash is the finest cruising area in the country bar none but it is certainly not an area for the unwary or careless. I have often heard comments from South Coast sailors such as – 'the temperature drops 10 degrees once round North Foreland'; 'The North Sea is cold and bleak'; 'Shallows and mudflats everywhere'; 'There are no safe harbours to run to in bad weather'; and 'You sail on the North Norfolk coast and Wash area only because you live and work there'. These comments all contain a grain of truth. But come to the area possessed of the right boat and a willingness to learn, and this is a training ground and cruising area without peer.

The coast is indented with numerous small creeks and landing places locally referred to as 'staithes' including those at Blakeney, Morston, Stiffkey, Wells-next-the-Sea, Burnham Overy (Overy Staithe), Brancaster Staithe, Titchwell and Thornham. The Wash beyond Holme Point has an enormous influence on the North Norfolk coast, and to the coastal sailor the two are inseparable. The flood tides pouring down the North Sea are deflected into filling and emptying this large bay, 12 miles across and stretching 16 inland, every twelve hours twenty minutes and there is a great volume of fresh water discharging from the Fen rivers that distorts the times of high water which is why the tidal direction changes two hours before high water. It even distorts the North Norfolk weather. The key navigation marks used to be the light vessels, Lynn Well and Roaring Middle, to which Margaret and I would sail to deliver Sunday newspapers. They have been replaced by efficient but inhuman automatic light floats. From here the channels are buoyed into the four main rivers; the Great Ouse, the Welland, the Witham and the Nene. The area is a myriad of drying sandbanks separated by small swatchways sometimes marked with perches but usually not.

We have often dinghy sailed the North Norfolk coast and the Wash navigating the swatchways, using only chart and compass; estimating 'distance run' by eye and wristwatch and sounding with jibstick or more usually the centreboard. Even in small dinghies a GPS is now considered a piece of essential equipment, and it does make finding the channels between the drying sandbanks much easier. The small hand-held battery-operated type is eminently practical in a cruising dinghy, but estimating speed and distance, using transits, working out tides, laying a course to make a landfall upwind of an unknown and featureless shoreline, are essential basic navigational skills that must never be forgotten; one day the GPS batteries may go flat!

Planning to use the strong tides is essential – sailing with the tide can double boat speed over the ground; stemming it can reduce it to half, sometimes even holding the yacht stationary over the ground while sailing fast. A boat leaving Blakeney, Stiffkey, Morston or Wells, sailing westward for a pleasant day, is faced with four hours of foul ebb tide, and four hours stemming the flood on the return. Brancaster is different, for a yacht heading east has the tide in her favour both ways although all the harbours dry between tides and she will have to anchor off, and the prevailing southwesterly involves tacking back. For those out for a longer period, rounding the shoulder of Norfolk is hard unless blessed with a fair wind; but westward, for those willing to fight the tide initially, there is wonderful cruising. Five of the best North Norfolk cruises are:

- From Brancaster to Skegness on the morning tide and back on the evening flood.
- To Gibraltar Point, carrying the flood tide up Wainfleet Haven, returning next day.
- To Saltfleet on the North Lincolnshire coast with a southwesterly (not to be attempted with an onshore wind).

With a northerly – through the Wash on the morning tide and into Lynn Cut, anchoring to carry the flood through King's Lynn and upriver to Denver Sluice. Not a trip for the fainthearted or inexperienced because the tide races up river and the mast must be dropped on the run for each bridge. Any snarl up and the bridge does the mast lowering for you and a capsize is an added bonus. On big 'spring' tides a 'bore' runs up river bringing the risk of a broach-to as it overtakes the boat from astern. From Denver there is a choice, upriver to Ely and Cambridge – or down-river according to wind direction.

To Boston, locking into the river and Foss Dyke through Lincoln and Gainsborough, locking out into the Trent then down the Humber, over-nighting in one of the havens (see Irvin's guide to the Humber and the Wash), calling at Saltfleet, then across the Wash back to Norfolk. An adventurous seven day cruise – or longer depending on weather.

The tale of the toothbrush

In early November, Frank remarked over supper in Wells that the tides were just right. 'It might be our last chance this year'. Grabbing food, thermal clothes and sleeping bags, we turned off the central heating and just caught the tide. 'Be home tomorrow,' I thought, 'can't stay out long in November, so it won't matter that I've forgotten the toilet bags.'

The coast in winter is a fascinating place to sail: a lonely place of shifting sandbanks and strong tides with little to identify your position. Once you have left the comforting shelter of Hunstanton's red and white cliffs you are very much on your own. Some hours later we picked up a Wash buoy then turned downwind into Lynn Channel. Wrapped up in our oilskins, we were glad not to be beating. Even in settled anti-cyclonic weather, dinghy cruising in November is never warm. We had seen no working boats along the North Norfolk coastline but there were several fishing boats in the channel. 'We haven't much fresh food,' I said, and turning back to a steaming shrimper we asked if we could buy some cooked shrimps. A huge bag was flung into our dinghy, and since they refused payment we threw them our fruit cake. Peeling shrimps as we sailed, lunch was unexpectedly enjoyable. The familiar silhouette of King's Lynn's buildings emerged out of the grey afternoon. As we passed the dock gates the last flicker of wind died. Almost on cue the flood tide picked up, sweeping us through King's Lynn. 'Might as well carry on to Denver Sluice,' said Frank. Shooting road and rail and pipe bridges, the next 14 miles was easy with a fair tide, and by dusk we had floated many miles into the Fenland system. Downham Market bridge was shot in darkness and we only saw the scaffolding stretched across the arches just in time to avoid them. It was very dark by the time we got to Denver Sluice but the obliging lock keeper put on all the lights, and locked us into the non-tidal Ouse. The lights of a riverside pub gave us sufficient illumination to erect our boat tent, and later we ate there royally, being the only customers. It was a lovely meal, the only thing that spoilt it was that I couldn't clean my teeth afterwards.

Next day the mild stern winds encouraged us further. We made Ely just before dark fell. We enjoyed choral evensong in Ely Cathedral and finished off the day watching a fantastic firework display. The next day we planned to reach Cambridge by midday, which would give us time to shop for a toothbrush. However, when we reached Linton Locks, we saw the river full of racing skiffs, and heard that there was a fair at the Meadows where we had intended to camp, so we decided to moor *Wanderer* some way off Cambridge centre where we would be safe and peaceful. We caught the local bus into the city and arrived just in time to enjoy choral evensong at King's College. 'Do you think we're too dirty to go in?' asked Frank at the entrance to the superb chapel.

Ignoring his unshaven face, muddy wellington boots and damp oilskins, forgetting my unwashed face and teeth, I was deeply moved by the glorious singing of the King's College Choir. It was when we were walking out at the end that I realised everybody else was dressed as befits a solemn Remembrance Day service, in silk blouses, smart suits and elegant hats. We walked tall and tried to feel clean!

We had left *Wanderer* at the friendly Cambridge SC, and when we returned found the remains of a huge bonfire still burning. They had been clearing up after the October gale. We cooked a chicken leg in the embers and enjoyed our supper in the mild darkness. Owls hooted in the nearby copses A mini-cruise in November is a great treat but I was glad to get home, where I had left my toothbrush'.

There is another side to this unique area of shallows, sands, shoals, mud-flats, marshes, wide skies, often grey, occasionally sunlit, and unfrequented. The mystic!

It is flat, desolate and enormously lonely. It is not the scenery that would appeal to the average sailing man. But when the tide ebbs into the North Sea the whole scene changes dramatically. The banks lift above the water, and soon there are hills, sunken valleys, shallow lakes and headlands of sand. It is an extraordinary experience to see this area at low water in mid-winter under grey, lowering skies when it has a primeval quality, unchanged since the world was young.

Even in summer there is an eerie and uncanny feeling to the place. It is very difficult to describe and it was only when I began sailing single-handed from Brancaster Staithe that I began to realise this presence was the ghost of an ancient man.

The Ancient Man

We first met during the hard winter of '63 when there was some wonderful winter sailing, for it was so dry it was possible to sail in normal summer clothing in spite of the intense cold. This was the first time in living memory that sea ice sufficiently heavy to break mooring chains in Brancaster Harbour and carry away attached boats had formed on the Norfolk coast.

I had sailed on the morning tide and pulled the boat ashore on Holme Beach. I was standing with my back to the wind when I felt a presence close by. For some time we stood quietly looking at the unusual condition, ice everywhere, sea birds and waders starving and trying to find food in the frozen ground, the air so clear it seemed possible to see even beyond the horizon. After half an hour I sailed back along the coast. We had said nothing and neither of us looked back.

This is one of the few times the Ancient Man has been seen at high water or on a Norfolk beach. But conditions were so unusual he must have been tempted to visit the mainland. At low water he is always somewhere among the drying sandbanks and it is possible, if he is in the mood, to walk the banks and hear him talk of this remote place that he has made his own and which he so obviously loves.

Sometimes, when I have eaten lunch on Middle Bank or Sunk Sand he has directed my attention to the soft black contours of the Norfolk hills beyond the lonely beaches. On occasion I have watched the sun drop below the horizon while the dusk crept silently in from the east to swallow the area and I have known I was not alone. At other times he has shown me the intricate channels, and the lonely beauty of this area on a still night, the loneliness somehow emphasised by the lights of Skegness and Hunstanton in the far distance reflected in the still water between the sandbanks. We have watched the violence of the race over the Dog's Head as broken water flooded violently over the sand with the incoming tide. He tells me boats have been wrecked on these hard sands and that this is inevitable.

On one occasion I was returning across the Wash from Skegness with the flood tide and deliberately took my boat across the Outer Dog's Head Sand to give my crew some experience of broken water. As we got nearer I could see conditions were far worse than I had expected and dearly wished to beat back. But the tide swept us on. For several minutes it was doubtful we would survive in the appalling cross sea, but I knew the old man was watching us fighting for our lives with some amusement. Had we drowned he would have said we deserved our fate and have told me I was a fool to take such risks.

His age is indeterminate for he is never more than a vague shadow but I think he is an old man, for he has the collected wisdom of the Ages.

Sometimes he has looked beyond the Northern horizon and across the open sea towards the Arctic ice and I have thought he was a man of the sea. Now I realise I was misled for he is a landsman and his interest stops at the edge of deep water. He seems to be East Anglian, and certainly has the East Anglian's intolerance of strangers in full measure; 'foreigners' he calls them. His talk is of Norfolk and Suffolk, Cambridge and Kesteven, but he does not know Fenland was drained by Vermuyden in the Middle Ages and is now the most fertile land in England. He has no interest in the Fens and dismisses them contemptuously as 'marshland'. The only other areas of which he speaks are the shoals of the German Bight and it seems this knowledge was part of his tribal history. Perhaps he was a Saxon and it was handed down to him from the time the Saxons spread across the North Sea from Germany.

Now windfarms are being built and there is talk of building many more to generate electricity whenever the wind blows. The need is self-evident, but I wonder what will happen to the Old Man? I feel sure he will not remain, for he is a solitary person who enjoys the loneliness and beauty of the area. Only sailing men and fishermen from local harbours who sail here regularly can appreciate his attachment to the area. I have never asked if they have met him but I think they must have done, for he is an integral part of this bleak and little-known place . .

I have often been grateful for the knowledge this coast has given me – when sailing *Wanderer* through a tide race in the dark off Portland (Iceland), in the maelstroms of Arctic Norway, in the ferocious ebb tides of the Bay of Fundy (Canada) or trying to beat out to sea off Utsire to ride out an onshore gale rather than run into a coast I didn't know in the dark. We return to the Saltmarsh Coast and the Wash with never ending fascination, because they are always changing.

You can never know it all; each time you leave the shoreline the huge skies, the light, the shifting sands, and the wildlife give pleasure and adventure – particularly in a shoal draft boat. Approaching the bars of the drying harbours is always a new lesson in seamanship because they change continuously, sculpted by the ebb and flow of strong tides twice daily.

In Margaret's book *Listen to the Locals*, fishermen like David Cox, Tony Jordan and the Frary brothers describe the seamanship required to take the lifeboat and their fishing boats in and out of North Norfolk harbours to catch fish or rescue boats in trouble. The bars of the Saltmarsh Coast have my undying respect, as they had for the old skipper recollected in Margaret's mardle with Frank Taylor. My log book records an early learning cruise. I never made the same arrogant mistakes again…

An Early Learning cruise

The second weekend in December 1959 was a date we selected as ideal (full moon, morning and evening tide) for a cruise to Yarmouth and next day to Norwich to race on the Norfolk Broads during winter. All that week gales raged in the North Sea causing the loss of 22 lives and culminating in the loss of the Broughty Ferry lifeboat. A gale forecast was issued 'SE Iceland force 15' which I could not believe but was true.

On Friday the wind died to force 4 with a next day forecast of force 5 easterly, and we decided 'to have a go' and prepared for frost and snow with gloves and a spare set of clothing. We launched at first light. At Blakeney bar a big sea was running but Alan took *Wanderer* through nicely, meeting each breaker bows on, and I was glad of the extra weight of stores and spare clothing to give us sufficient momentum to drive through or we'd have driven astern and capsized. Out at sea conditions were bad with a heavy sea from the gales of last week running into the wind; we made little progress. At 11.00hrs we abandoned Yarmouth as there is no shelter from an easterly wind on this coast until Yarmouth Roads. Benefiting from previous bad weather experience we lowered the mainsail and sailed on jib alone and ran for Brancaster Staithe well under control. Further out, tremendous seas were marching west that, we realised later, were caused by the stronger tide in deeper water running into the wind. We took turns to stand by the mast to watch these steep waves marching rank on rank endlessly to the west – an awesome demonstration of the power and menace of the sea.

As we worked gradually offshore to clear Bob Halls sands off Wells we suddenly found ourselves in the heavy seas we had been watching all morning. A wave of 12ft came at us from windward and I immediately put *Wanderer* before it for no dinghy could be expected to luff a wave of that size. As the brute overtook we climbed until the jib filled and *Wanderer* began to plane. I had great difficulty in persuading *Wanderer* to drop back particularly as the wave face was becoming steeper on the approach of shoal water. As the wave passed Alan hoisted the mainsail deep reefed and, with no hope of safely passing Wells bar, we left this dangerous patch as smartly as possible beating back for Blakeney. (We discovered later that Alan had rolled two sail battens round the boom and they came out looking like corkscrews – we came to the conclusion that he was either very strong or like me was very scared).

Blakeney bar looked bad – bad but not dangerous; and as Alan had no experience of sailing through breakers I suggested he sailed in warning him to keep square before the waves. Our first attempt went well, planing in at terrific speed on the front face of a roller. There wasn't sufficent depth and after baling out we went out to sea and tried again further along where it was deeper although rougher. *Wanderer* had almost crossed safely when a larger wave came up astern and *Wanderer* wasn't square, and 'broached to' under it and capsized. I hung onto the shroud, righted the dinghy before the mast touched the water and looked for Alan. He had been thrown clear and the next breaking wave swept him back and he managed to grab the tiller extension and hang on.

By the time he was aboard we had been carried into calmer water in a waterlogged condition. Things were in a shambles with two thermos, gloves, one of my wellington boots, stores, baler and a haversack floating about. Baling out with a saucepan and a bowl did not take long and we anchored against a sandbank while Alan changed, and after a hot meal we returned to Blakeney quay in the dark. My log sums it up: 'This was a most interesting days sail. We gained a great deal of bad weather experience. One is inclined to forget the shocking sea that occurs as the tide turns against the wind. I feel that it will pay to experiment with a small drogue to be used when crossing a bar. Alan regarded the capsize philosophically. He discovered later that he had a tremendous bruise on one thigh extending from hip to knee received when he was thrown overboard.'

The marshes

The marshes are different again, a halfway world between the solid, warm, predictable land and the cold, restless, bleak North Sea. They are harvested by locals – for shellfish and edible samphire, the gullies are dug over by bait diggers and until World War II they were grazed by sheep and cattle which must have been hardy breeds, for 'sheep samphire' was their feed. Gulls' eggs were a welcome addition for the house.

Lost on Morston Marshes

It was a beautiful clear night walking over the marsh, the stars shining in the velvet sky, the heat of the day rising from the ground to warm the air. This clear night was a surprising contrast to the fog inland which had so delayed me on the drive down to the coast that I did not arrive until late evening.

Two weeks earlier when sailing along the coast from Brancaster Staithe shortage of time had prevented us beating up against the ebb tide to Blakeney Quay and we had been forced to leave the boat anchored on the mud in the lower part of Morston creek. Now I was walking across the marsh to spend Saturday night aboard.

These Norfolk marshes are a lonely and attractive area but treacherous to those who do not know them. They are criss-crossed by deep drains and hidden gullies but I was confident of my ability to find the boat even though the moon had now set. In the stillness of the night the voices of two men carried clearly across the marsh, and I could hear the engine of an incoming boat and the murmur of the sea on Blakeney bar in the far distance.

Ten minutes later I was completely and utterly lost! How I strayed away from the edge of the main creek and missed the plank bridges over the side creeks remains a mystery, but I was not worried. I looked up for guidance but overhead a dull black overcast had hidden the stars. I was alone; the voices had gone and there was utter silence except for the whisper of the wind in the tops of the marsh vegetation. Outside the yellow circle of light from my hurricane lantern, the marsh had become frighteningly hostile and I could feel the evening tide silently filling the creeks all round me. A long way behind me were the lights of the village, but they gave me no idea of my position on the marshes and whichever way I went, I risked slipping into one of the drains which would already be half full of water.

Suddenly I realised how easy it is to be trapped and drowned on these coastal salt marshes for they flood completely when the moon is full. I have always been cursed with a vivid imagination and I could visualise the lonely fearful death – the sudden fall through the dark into the mud, the panic scramble to climb up the slippery side of the creek, then falling back exhausted and, held knee-deep by the suction of the mud, watching death approach slowly and quietly with the incoming tide, and finally the chill bite of the cold North Sea as the water rose up my body…!

It took a conscious effort to remind myself that I was quite safe provided I was careful where I walked, for it was a neap tide and the marshes would not be flooded this night. I even had a sleeping bag with me for warmth and a boat tent for cover in case I had to spend the night on the marshes. I walked for another hour before I found the seawall and followed it back to my car – a much wiser man.

Geese and duck are still shot 'for the pot'. Wildfowling must be the most extreme and skilled sport; cold and wet in a bitter east wind, hiding in a muddy gulley before dawn hoping for a shot at the most alert and observant of all birds, more often than not returning empty handed. One of the most magnificent sights is that of thousands of geese flighting across the sky just before dusk in mid-winter after a day feeding inland. But the marshes are no longer harvested to the same extent and the wooden bridges have decayed leaving only rotten stumps to show their positions. They have a beauty all their own but they can be hazardous with hidden gullies to trap the unwary, deep mud and overgrown insecure vegetation that gives no handhold as you try to scramble out..

The future

Offshore there is a different world that people can enjoy with little interference, relying on their own knowledge and skills. Sail-training and regulation is voluntary and comprehensively managed and standards are maintained by the Royal Yachting Association (RYA) which sensibly resists Government interference.

It used to be said the sea is unchanging. Maybe that is true of the deep ocean but the coastal waters of North Norfolk and the Wash are visibly changing. When, in the past, we landed on one of the banks, there were always masts of work boats beyond the sands, and sometimes we were called alongside and given a half bucket of freshly boiled shrimps for lunch.

Now there are few working boats. Only fifteen or twenty years ago, more than one hundred men from Lynn were getting a living harvesting cockles for twelve months. Now there are thirty men working six weeks. There is no market for whitebait and sprats. If it doesn't come out of a can or a freezer bag, the modern person doesn't want to know. Longshore netting is almost a thing of the past, seals ruining the catch by taking bites out of fish in the nets. Parts of the North Sea are infertile deserts because offshore dredging has created a blanket of silt on feeding and spawning areas over vast areas of the sea bed. Much of the aggregate goes to Holland, the Dutch having wisely banned dredging in their sensitive coastal zones. A study by the European Community has established that offshore dredging increases coastal erosion a hundred kilometres away (contrary to our government's denials) and there is a suspicion that the increasing deposit of sharp sand now spoiling the bait digging grounds may be accelerated by dredging.

The harbours are crowded at weekends and moored boats have almost reached saturation point. Inevitably too, many tourists spoil what they come to enjoy because of their sheer numbers. The competition for space on the water has made me give up sailing at weekends. The growth of boat ownership has however created an excuse for the Government to attempt to licence all yachts and boats to increase tax revenue and that would also fit its obsession with regulation.

The sea gives perspective on what goes on ashore. For centuries, the land, the marshes and the sea were interdependent. Coal, timber and fertilisers were imported. Grain from local farms, fish and shellfish harvested by the inshore fishing fleet, and duck and geese from the marshes were exported. All by ship. These connections have broken down as coastal towns and villages have turned their backs on the sea, losing parts of their souls in the process. And when local small boat sailors look back at the marshes and the land behind them it now seems as though the future of the Saltmarsh Coast is being shaped by short-term planning and threatened by urban values.

As long as anyone can remember there has been no long-term planning for rural coastal areas. Everything has been short-term and often short-sighted. Short-term ministers with short-term ideas for solving long-term problems run departments of which they often have little prior knowledge; when the minister changes, so does the policy. Ministers are not efficient administrators; they are politicians and their interest – often to the detriment of the sparsely populated countryside – is in the next election. It is time to change the system; there are much better democratic systems than our antiquated one.

A good example of how urban values are affecting the countryside of the Saltmarsh Coast is the way bureaucrats are dealing with animal rights and animal rights activists. A countryman will take a lot of trouble to put a suffering animal out of its misery. But urban dwellers have been brought up to believe animals are furry, friendly and self-regulating. In reality, life in the wild is brutal and always will be. Bodies are usually devoured within hours. Break a leg or a wing and there are plenty of takers for an easy meal. Gamekeepers and those who grow up in the country work on the principle that as the dominant animal man has a responsibility to manage nature. This concept seems to be beyond the understanding of animal rights activists.

Urban values in the countryside

Boat trips to see the seals at Blakeney Point are a popular attraction of this fragile coast. But there are too many seals. Overcrowding results in fighting, injuries, crushed pups, stripping the coast and tidal inlets of fish, and eventually seal virus (similar to dog distemper) that leads to hundreds of rotting bodies. But suggest that culling is essential rather than wicked and the animal rights lobby is roused to fury; even intelligent people who grew up in urban areas view culling with distaste.

In Cornwall, seagulls have learned they can mob holidaymakers and snatch sandwiches and some of them have discovered that if they draw blood they can take the lot. So local District Councils have asked people not to feed gulls, to put waste food in metal containers, and to prick eggs. This approach is taking a long time to work. Meanwhile the Cornish gulls will be copied by other gulls and it is not hard to imagine the impact on tourism when the habit reaches our area. Will our District Councils react more sensibly, taking advice from the countryman who could tell them the only effective measures are shooting (dangerous in peak season), netting and ringing their necks, and giving local boys sticks and a 50p bounty to solve the problem? In nearby Southwold rabbits were digging up turf on Gun Hill and raiding gardens. Pest control officers were called in but had to be called off after protests about killing the rabbits. The protesters called in an expert who recommended birth control pills! But a recent plague of rabbits in Wells was quickly dealt with without reference to anyone. Wild rabbit, fed on slightly salt-tangy grass and the best garden vegetables, in a stew or rabbit pie with crust and a couple of rashers of salt bacon is a great delight. Norfolk wildlife sanctuaries take in large number of oiled-seabirds and virus-affected seals, a large proportion of which die before or after release. But to suggest it might be kinder to wring their necks or shoot them is politically incorrect. Then there are the cormorants (cormorants being protected birds). The Department for the Environment, Food & Rural Affairs (DEFRA) reacted to wide-scale concerns that cormorant numbers are out of control by calling a meeting of interested parties. The Department said emphatically that culling would never solve the problem and that the solution was to provide 'Refuges for Fish' by extending reed beds and netting over the water to turn the cormorants off!

A quiet unassuming marshman and bait digger, chatting to me, said, 'I love it out there. It's clean!' If you don't know what he meant stay away from the North Norfolk Coast; it is not for you. Forget your 'Weekend Place in the Country' which is so rarely occupied and contributes nothing-to the area except to force property prices and rents beyond the reach of local people who of necessity have to move inland where prices are lower. Forget your expensive, aggressive-looking four-wheel drive vehicles, your designer dogs and your expensive extensions to convince the neighbours of your importance; they cause resentment.

For those who have made their home here it is a different and rewarding world. Mix with the locals who, admittedly, are slow to accept strangers and may take a few years to say more than ... ' Mornin'. There are the same proportion of good and bad people here as anywhere else. The difference is that these people are highly skilled, knowledgeable and proud of their independence. So learn to understand the coast and the countryside from them.

Learn to sail and you'll learn about the tidal waters, and the detrimental effect that man, with his ill-conceived ideas, has on this fragile environment. If you have a boat make it a small one you can enjoy sailing, for the area is not suitable for large yachts. Go out and learn. RYA Courses and Certificates are useful because the knowledge required to gain them gives you a good basis. Yachting clothes have greatly improved since we taught ourselves to sail; they are more efficient, lighter and stylish, but they aren't essential. Sail – instead of using the outboard. You will get muddy and wet and there will be times you will be scared, but with common sense there will be nothing you can't handle. Don't go near the harbour bar when the tide is ebbing and the seas are breaking; learn to reduce sail quickly and efficiently when the wind blows; carry oars, an anchor and compass at all times. The worst that can happen in normal conditions is that you run out of water as the creeks dry. Never panic. Anchor the boat and wait for the next tide – with adequate clothing and a sail for cover, you may have a cold night aboard but it won't kill you. Only walk back if you are certain that you can reach the shore; the creeks wind tortuously and it is only too easy to take a wrong turn and head seaward. Don't walk back across the marsh; the gullies are dangerous, sometimes hidden, and difficult to climb out of. Fog is still the most dangerous weather phenomenon. Only the compass can be trusted. Even with GPS it is disorientating. The great danger is being run down; fortunately, the shallow draft boat can anchor in the shallows out of reach of bigger vessels but there may be a long wait until the fog clears. Seals can be useful – they give a good indication of deepwater as they only haul out alongside deep water channels.

Local inshore fishing can be sustained with careful management, as it takes only a small proportion of the total catch from the North Sea and if bureaucrats, politicians, ministers and government agencies have the will and moral fibre to resist pressures for an increased share of the catch from big offshore vessels – which with their efficient equipment have brought fish stocks so dangerously low and some species almost to the point of collapse – at the expense of the inshore boats.

Hopefully the bureaucrats, politicians, ministers and government agencies will even begin to understand the countryside. If so this area will retain much of its character and colour with a vibrant working population of knowledgeable and well informed fishermen, boat-builders, farmers, gamekeepers, marshmen and their families. With more tolerance and understanding between those who live in the area, they will hopefully speak with a more powerful voice and will be heard by an Establishment that seems to distrust self reliance, common sense and independence as triple evils to be regulated out of existence.

But they will not survive here unless a solution is found to the problems arising from the lack of affordable accommodation. With property prices escalating beyond reach, even a small cottage is above the threshold for inheritance tax. Why not exclude all property from inheritance tax provided it is left to a Housing Trust to manage? It would have little effect on Government finances as even the Chancellor cannot have anticipated such an increase in value or made plans to spend it. If the traditional trades and tradespeople do not survive the area will be increasingly dependent on tourism. But without the local families that make this place what it is, the visitor can only look forward to a pleasant walk through a landscape of wide skies, sand dunes and windswept fields looking at raucous seagulls – and small waders along the shoreline.

From Meat to Millinery

Gloria Hurn

I've spent my whole life in business in North Norfolk and I've loved every minute of it. I never want to give up and I hope I never have to retire. I'd miss the excitement of thinking of an idea or grasping an opportunity. I've had all the opportunities I needed right here; the thought of leaving never crossed my mind.

My father bought a butcher's shop in Staithe Street, Wells, when he came back from the war and it was there in the family business that I grew up and learnt the trade. As a small child I once asked my father why he was always sweeping the shop floor, keeping busy although there were no customers.

'You've got to keep busy,' he replied, 'customers only come into a busy shop.' It was my first business lesson.

I also learnt from other shop-keepers. Jeff Cooper, the baker, was a neighbour and his bread and cakes were wonderful. So much so that sometimes his wife sold

Gloria Hurn

Gloria Hurn was born, schooled and grew up in Wells. Following in her father's footsteps she first trained and worked as a butcher. Then following her mother's interest in hats she opened her highly successful millinery business, Pentney House, Burnham Market. In 2004 she was one of six finalists in a national competition to choose 'Women Entrepreneurs of the Year'. She lives in Burnham Market.

out early in the day, even using up the 'special orders'. So Jeff would send her round to some of their regular customers to 'borrow' back what they had just bought and then Jeff would bake replacements.

My first personal business venture came when I was about ten or eleven. I used to pluck pigeons and pheasants bought from local gamekeepers. Dad would sell them for me, displaying them right in the middle of his shop window, decorated with parsley to attract shoppers. I was too young then to pluck chickens since they had to be plucked while still warm and I wasn't fast enough.

I also helped make chitterlings out of pigs' bellies or intestines. When I came home from school I'd have the job of taking these bellies from the abattoir at the back of the shop and washing them thoroughly under the tap. Just one pig's belly filled a pail. They were very slimy and it was a messy job to clean them thoroughly. It involved stretching each piece and washing it out with lots of cold running water. If a customer bought a whole raw pig's belly to cook at home, I got the money – half a crown each. Dad also cooked bellies and made them into chitterlings which he cut up and sold. Customers could season them with vinegar, salt and pepper and eat them with brown bread and butter. Very tasty!

Pork cheese, or pork brawn as they call it in Norfolk, was something else I helped prepare. Dad would boil up the cheeks, hocks and bones from the pig, and when they had cooled I would pick the small remaining pieces of meat and fat from the bones. We'd season the brawn with pepper and gravy salt and put it into moulds to set. Nowadays brawn is sold in plastic molds, but after the war the moulds were aluminum, so we turned out the brawn for the customer and sold it on a piece of greaseproof paper.

I also made quite a bit of money from pheasant tail feathers, cockerel hackles – the brightly coloured neck feathers – and from rabbit skins. When I came home from school I'd find the skins laid out flat for me to salt, to preserve them. When they were ready I used to send them, with the feathers, to Horace Friend, who had a business in Wisbech. The feathers were used for hats and the skins for coats, gloves and scarves. By the time I was twelve I was getting a postal order for eight or nine pounds every few weeks: quite a lot of money for a child in the mid 1950s! It was also a lesson in the art of making money from things that other people would just throw away.

There were special highlights in the year which were also business opportunities. I loved the annual Wells Carnival held on a Saturday in August (as it still is today) when we worked extremely hard to put on a good show. I was even allowed to stay up all night to help decorate. Days before we would collect greenery from Cuckoo Lodge (a mile or two above Wells) which my aunt Blanche would make into long swags with a wire base. Then from about 8pm on the Friday evening the whole family would set to work twisting the swags around the posts outside the shop and adding flowers as a finishing touch. Mum cooked us something to eat about midnight – usually bacon and eggs – and then, in the morning, I would go off on a trade bike to see what the other shop keepers had done. Most businesses dressed up for the occasion but we often won the best-dressed shop competition, not to mention the best trade van in the carnival parade.

Christmas was also tremendous fun. Our shop was especially smart – and extremely busy! The floor was covered in straw a foot deep and it used to get everywhere in the house; upstairs, downstairs, even in the beds! We had sides of meat and turkeys hanging in the shop and it all looked very festive. It's a sight we'll never see again because nowadays meat has to kept refrigerated and you're not allowed to display it in that way. Dad would put a pair of antlers on our van and hire a Father Christmas (usually Horrie Webdale), who gave away small presents (purchased by Dad) to children. At the time it seemed magical to me.

From my parents – Arthur and Harriet Howell – I learnt to make that little extra effort in order to be successful. Times were hard right after the war, meat was still rationed and there was a lot of competition from other butchers in the town. (Now there are no others!). Mum and Dad made sure that if customers couldn't come to us, then we would go to them. So Mum would drive our van down to the Pinewood Caravan Park at Wells Beach and I would sit in the back ringing a bell. Then the caravan occupants came out to buy from us because we literally brought the meat right to their doors. We rarely went to the beach other than for business – even though it was a holiday resort. My parents didn't think it was safe and they wouldn't let me go. But I was happy enough playing with my cousins in the town in my grandparents' orchard.

I didn't enjoy school much because I wasn't very academic, except for arithmetic at which I excelled. So after secondary school I took a two year commercial course at what was then King's Lynn Technical College, in shorthand, typing and bookkeeping. Then I went straight into the family business. I never really thought of doing anything else. Dad taught me how to cut meat and prepare it attractively and Mum showed me how they did the books. My parents never took holidays (they've only had one in their lives!) and always worked until late at night. They're both still working (in their eighties) but not at night!

Soon Dad began to expand, buying up butchers' shops in other villages. I was useful since I could cut meat, do the books and drive the van. This meant I could fill in for employees who were sick or on holiday. Then I married Peter Hurn and at the same time Dad bought a business in Walsingham. So rightaway Peter and I went to live there and run it. We didn't even have time for a honeymoon. Two years later our daughter Vicki was born and we seemed settled.

But Dad bought another butcher's shop in Wells – Ramms in High Street – which had been the biggest butcher's in Wells when Dad's was the smallest. He asked me to come over and manage it so I did. There was a small addition to the shop with a window on to the street and mother decided to put sheepskins there. One day, quite out of the blue, she said to me, 'Why don't we put a few hats in there?' Why not? So we went up to London, bought half a dozen very smart hats and displayed them. I can't say it was great business but it brought in a little pin money and we enjoyed it. The *Eastern Daily Press* did a story on mother's venture in which she was quoted as saying that she 'wasn't going into the general millinery trade', which we thought was very funny.

Dad's next venture was to buy a butcher's shop on The Green in Burnham Market, together with a large house, Pentney House, next door. When Mrs. Barker, who had lived in the house, died, we had to decide what to do with it. At first we let it as a holiday home, but that's not a good investment for a prime location right in the centre of the village. It seemed we could do more with it. There were quite a lot of antiques in the house, some inherited from Peter's grandmother. They fitted in the house and looked very attractive. I decided it should be a shop of some kind but distinct from others in the village. To be successful you need to do something different – be unique!

So I went back into the millinery trade and scattered hats all over the beds upstairs. Then I filled the downstairs rooms with things I bought at auctions: framed pictures, kitchenware, and particularly plates, thousands of them. At that time I had a huge dining table at home in Walsingham but we could never use it

because it was always piled high with plates, since I took everything home to wash, sort and price. It was a frantic time, I was rushing backwards and forwards between auctions, home and the business, but it took off. I looked for things that were pretty and cheap. By that time Burnham Market was becoming popular as a holiday destination, people were coming up for weekends, buying cottages and needing plates and pictures to decorate them. Pentney House seemed to fill that need and find its niche. The shop has been busy ever since.

As auction sources began to dry up and become too time consuming I switched to going to gift fairs and expanding the range of items in the shop. While we still lived in Walsingham I'd been offered the run of a little drug store/gift shop and later I acquired – through my father's persistence (he bought it then rented it to me!) – a house in Wells to use as a gift shop. (My father was shocked when I told him I was going off to my first gift fair – in Birmingham – in the company of two male friends!) Now Peter comes and we make a mini-break of it.

In fact it was on a real holiday, in Florida, USA, that I thought of another idea for my shops. We were in a shopping mall where I noticed a '$2:00 Store': every item was $2.00 and the place was crowded. I said to Peter that we should try it in Norfolk. He thought that two pounds wouldn't work, but we decided one pound would be perfect. I just had to find the items when we returned! It worked splendidly in Walsingham with the pilgrim trade and in Wells with the holidaymakers too.

The growth of North Norfolk as a holiday area and the particular popularity of Burnham Market as a busy shopping centre has obviously helped my businesses expand without the need to advertise. I now have 5000 hats at Pentney House and stock thousands of different items in my gift shops. We're busier than ever. Customers who want to buy a hat have the convenience of the Hoste Arms across The Green if they're not renting a place or staying with friends; visitors to the Hoste frequently discover the hats. Paul Whittome and I often joke that we're very good for each other's business.

I'm sometimes asked to explain why my business has grown. After all, if you think of all the things that might sell in a rural area a long way from any city, hats might not be near the top of your list.

First, you have to focus on what's missing. Where are the gaps? What could you sell that you can't buy now?

Second, you have to know your market. There's no point trying to sell something that is not available if nobody wants it. So you have to be realistic. It turned out that hats were realistic. And not just for the people you might think buy hats but young women too, provided you have what they really want. I employ a girl – she's been with me since she was a teenager – who buys all my jewellery for young women. She knows what they want much better than I could and I give her full responsibility. In business, you need to know when to let go and give responsibility to a younger person.

Third, I realised that to sell hats I had to create a special setting for them. When I started out by scattering hats on furniture in Pentney House I created something different. Ordinary hat shops are not like that. But my customers liked it and they told their friends about it and then they came back, bringing their friends with them, or sometimes the friends came alone. Pentney House has become a shopping experience and in some ways a tourist attraction. People have heard about it and they come to look and then they buy. Of course, being in Burnham Market has helped but I think I could have done the same thing in Wells if I'd had a shop with as much space.

Fourth, once you've made up your mind to go for something, go for it all out. Work at it all the time. Keep thinking about what else you can do to build the business, even when you're not there. I often sit at home in the evening watching television with one eye and working with the other, doing something like drawing a graph of this years's sales against last year's and how they're related to the weather or to special events or ups and downs in peoples' feelings about the economy.

Fifth, although Burnham Market is sometimes called 'Burnham Upmarket' – and it's true we get lots of well-off people here – I cater to everyone. I have hats that cost £250 and others that are as low as £25, including accessories. If this shop was very exclusive I'd be missing opportunities, and the fact that it's not doesn't put off the women who want the best. The other day I sold a customer from Colchester eleven hats for Ascot and she spent over £1000 on them. People come 200 or 300 miles to buy here because they know I've got the goods. And I know that if I can't give them what they want they won't come back.

Sixth, I don't think you have to spend a lot on advertising. I don't. It's word of mouth and reputation that does it and once you've got the ball rolling it keeps on rolling as long as you keep working hard to make it grow.

I don't know if these are secrets or not. What I do know is that anybody, and I mean anybody, can make a business grow here in North Norfolk provided they've got an idea and are willing to work and work at it to make it happen. People tend to say there's no future here except for tourism. As I've said, my business has certainly been helped by the fact we get lots of visitors. But I'm quite sure that if I'd gone for something else, something more dependent on local people, I could have made it work if the idea had been good and I had been willing to persevere and to keep trying. At the end of the day there's no substitute for vision and effort.

I get a bit sick when I hear people around here complaining that there's no future, no jobs, no opportunities. It's no good sitting back and moaning. You have to find something and go for it. We can't stand still; we have to go forward. This place, like any other place can never become what it was. It has changed and it will go on changing. And that means people have to adjust to the way things are now instead of wanting to put the clock back.

I realise that some of the changes that have happened here recently, say in the last twenty years, have made things harder for some local people, particularly young people. House prices have risen so high it's no longer possible for them to buy houses on the coast. But there are houses inland that are much cheaper and maybe that's where people should be looking. It's a fact of life, a new reality, and the important thing is to adjust to it and make the most of it.

Bear in mind too that the fact so many houses, particularly in places like Burnham Market, have been bought by wealthier people who use them as second homes, means there are lots of new opportunities. They want plumbers and painters and electricians. If someone wants to start a business and make it grow there are all sorts of possibilities that didn't exist thirty years ago. They have to grab them.

If a young person wants to make a go of a new business here they have to be very practical. All too often they go out and get expensive business cards and put advertisements in the Yellow Pages and then wait for customers. That's wrong. They would do much better printing flyers, getting on their bikes and putting the flyers through letter boxes. And they should call people who also started with nothing and ask for advice. Nobody seems to do that but they should. And those of us with experience should be willing to act as mentors to those who are just starting. Not a big organisation, just a group of people like me who have succeeded in growing businesses and would be only too happy to help them. I think I'll do something about that.

I was lucky to have been born in North Norfolk and to have grown up and established myself in such a desirable place. I'm a firm believer in making the most of what you've got – and here we have everything. If I hadn't lived here I would certainly have wanted to retire here! People with ambition and energy have ample opportunities to create new businesses or expand existing ones in the recreational boom of this area. I've gone from meat to millinery and who knows what next– I'm still getting ideas. I just hope that my grandson, my only grandchild, will one day marry a girl who loves hats!

Landscape, Seascape, Mindscape

Godfrey Sayers

First contact

It was in the spring of 1946 that I came to Blakeney for the first time. All that I saw was strange and different, enduring images that are clear in my mind to this day. Far more powerful, however, than what I saw was what I could smell. Wall flowers and washing in my grandmother's yard, her outhouse and cottage; inside it was a rich, almost indecipherable mix of scents. A blend of substances – few of them in general use today – that had had ages to soak into the fabric of that little place. Coal, candles and paraffin oil fuels for softer warmer lights that were only then going out in favour of brighter, instant electricity. Later I discovered that all the cottages I went in smelled the same. It was a composite smell, like flower shops and tobacconists.

The most powerful new scent of all though was still to come when I wandered down to the bottom of West Gate Street and looked on the quay for the first time. The breath of sea, sand, mud and marsh; sea-weed and the last tide-line and, lingering still as part of an older alchemy, tar. The ships and smacks that had been sealed with it were gone, but just enough tar-encrusted detritus remained rotting into the mud to offer my keen four-year-old senses the chance, just once, to touch directly a world that had gone, like seeing that elusive green flash as the limb of the sun drops below the horizon. I am in no doubt it was that brief touch that gave me my subsequent fascination with Blakeney's character and history.

I have remembered that visit often, usually when returning from an extended period away. By extended I mean months rather than weeks; because it is only after those stretches of cold turkey that the smells come back with the same familiar potency, although usually only for a day. After that the background smells of sea, marsh and mud are absorbed unconsciously.

It was another world; a tranquil unspoiled place that during those impressionable years laid the foundation of a worldview that would grow to become the model against which I would set my experience and view of the changes I would witness during my life living on this coast.

Godfrey Sayers

Although Godfrey Sayers's love of painting and drawing was encouraged at school in Blakeney, Langham and Wells, he became a longshore fisherman and owned wholesale fish and shellfish and furniture removal and road haulage businesses before becoming a full time painter. He has had considerable success with one-man exhibitions and for many years exhibited in London. Now content to sell his work from the back of a lorry on Blakeney Carnser, he says his work is most appreciated by those who really know this place and adds that if you have not had Morston mud under your nails you're probably unqualified to judge it. He is irritated by incomer artists who, claiming they have come in search of space, light and sky, produce abstract interiors and by their habit of denigrating local artists. His other consuming passion – the protection of what is most special about North Norfolk – began to develop in the late 1960s with the formation of the Blakeney Preservation Society. He says that although some of his battles to save important elements of village and landscape character from urban development have been won, there is little to show for his efforts apart from a few trees and an odd path or two. But he measures success not by what is there, but by what is not there...

To each is own

As a landscape painter I am grateful that since 1968 the status of 'Area of Outstanding Natural Beauty' has done much to protect the landscape and inform the design and character of new development on the North Norfolk coast. Although the use of 'Natural' to describe a coast shaped so much by the hand of man may be questioned, it is hard to think of anything better; I am more concerned with the concept of 'beauty'.

Can 'beauty' have an objective and specific meaning? Is one person's idea of what is beautiful the same as another's? The old saw has it that 'beauty is in the eye of the beholder'. But of course it is really 'in the *mind* of the beholder'. We look with our eyes but see with our minds. The world is not the same for all of us. We each see a different version and each of us lives in a universe of our own creation shaped by where we are born, grew up, developed our beliefs and have spent the greater part of our time. As this model takes shape it can, in turn, shape what we see and experience.

The landscape can have as many forms as there are people who look at it. This passage from a book by Professor Paul Davis entitled *Other Worlds* attempts to explain this rather difficult concept:

> The act of experience requires two components: the observer and the observed. It is the mutual interaction between them that supplies our sensations of surrounding reality. It is equally obvious that our versions of this reality will be coloured by our model of the world as constructed by previous experience, emotional pre-disposition, expectation and so on. Clearly then in daily life we do not experience an objective reality at all but a sort of cocktail of internal and external perspectives.

So when I look across Blakeney Harbour, over the marshes and creeks to the beach and sea beyond, what lies before me is folded over an intellectual template formed of countless earlier images and experiences. A construction begun with my first childhood wanderings into a landscape so vast it seemed to go on forever. As the daily backdrop to my working life as a longshore fisherman it became the subject of continual observation and re-invention – as I later attempted to capture in two dimensions what I experienced in four.

I think it is beyond question that we see landscape in very individual and personal ways. But among people who are themselves products of the landscape there is a remarkably complex and concise consensus as to what is valuable in it. It is no longer a surprise when at a planning meeting or in a landscape debate a local stands up and says exactly what I am thinking, or that the reverse occurs when someone else, usually an ex-town or city dweller, expresses an opposite view.

I believe this consistent and ever more evident dichotomy of world views is a major driving force in the difficulties now faced by country people. Whereas the rural world- view offers some consensus as to how the countryside should look, the urban world-view does not, because it aspires to an infinitely varying and non-existent idyll based on second-hand preconceptions and urbane idealism.

Country people who have lived in the same landscape all their lives experience it four-dimensionally. They have seen it change and have an intimate and intuitive relationship with it, which is expressed in a strong feeling of ownership, particularly if their families go back many generations. Then it is their heritage.

Holt Country Park offers an good example of the urban world-view. When my children were small it was a wild place of thick, sometimes impenetrable undergrowth, threaded with mysterious winding paths that, if they led to a clearing, would invariably prompt one of the children to say, 'Daddy, do you think we are the first people to ever come here?'

No child is likely to say that today. Notice boards display maps and instructions; posts with coloured arrows illustrate an almost infinite number of ways for you to become lost; steps and railings mitigate imagined risks; your interest is maintained by a variety of wooden constructions, including some very large trolls. A failed attempt perhaps to put back the lost mystery and magic? This stuff is the product of an urban psyche. No country person would do it. They would just take the gate off.

In other parts of Norfolk, wandering into a woodland clearing, you may encounter 'art'. A couple of years ago, cycling with friends, we discovered that 'art' is appearing along the Peddar's Way in the form of large stone monoliths etched with urbane and romantic alliteration. We met two Americans standing bewildered before one of them. 'Did somebody famous die here?' they asked. 'No,' I said, 'nobody famous, just another small part of the countryside.'

Two more examples: a young lady who felt Kelling Heath could be improved by planting a forest of red sticks; and a large and unfortunately very heavy sculpture dedicated to Benjamin Britten on the beach at Aldeburgh. Both provoked public debate but in each case the arguments were clouded by the credibility of the objects themselves as works of art – as though they would have been OK if they had been 'good art'. The real issue is the appropriateness of artifice in an otherwise natural scene and the gulf between those who think it improves nature's handiwork and those who are appalled by it. The Chrysler Building is also very beautiful but would it still be so if it were situated in Holt; would the statue of Liberty look right towering over the entrance to Wells Harbour? Of course not – scale, space, and context are vital elements of both art and design.

The beauty of open landscape is its openness and the feeling of looking into the past, at a place that is as it always was. Renowned beaches like Holkham are special because they have this four-dimensional space. Aldeburgh Beach is the same, so why put a huge stainless steel structure in the middle of it? I have no doubt that Benjamin Brittain would be appalled. Even in the bleak fastness of the Scottish Highlands the cairn builders are at work. I am totally puzzled why people do such things. My only explanation is that people who have always lived in places where open space is the width of a road or at best the distance across a park, are uncomfortable in huge open spaces and subconsciously need to fill them – just as a child needs to run over fresh snow.

Affectation destroys naturalness more effectively than a bomb; this stuff represents the gradual but escalating erasure of the most vital elements of rural character. Every bit of semi-natural landscape left in North Norfolk has garden style infrastructure scattered over it. I appreciate it is being done with the best of intentions. Public art is ubiquitous in the townscape – on buildings, public spaces and city parks. What could be more natural from that perspective than to extend it into the big park outside? But from the perspective of those who have always lived here it symbolizes the assumption by urban man that he has dominion over everything and that the countryside is just an adjunct to the city. Irksome as they may be, they are ultimately only small things, ornaments, and if it were about no more than that, they would although irritating, be tolerable. They are, however, the vanguard for intrusion on a far greater scale.

Ghosts

Twenty years ago I had a powerful dream that left me more than usually moved. Its theme was a day of celebration in Blakeney. It was centred on the Blakeney Hotel and the quay. The cast were from my early life; some were almost forgotten, others were friends. It was a hot summer's day and people were coming from the hotel to cool in the light sea breeze. I was standing with a group by the quayside, five of us, all but me, dead. We had been reminiscing about earlier times and their eccentric characters. The layers of memory were extraordinarily fresh and clear.

As I awoke, the sadness as so many loved and once familiar faces retreated to their graves was tangible as grief. There were so many, it was more than just lost friends and acquaintances, it was an entire community, a whole village gone, leaving, in their going, so many unfilled spaces. Not because they had no successors, but because they had so few successors here. The houses and cottages that would have held them were now empty.

Picture a walk down Blakeney High Street on a winter's night in the 1970s. The windows are dark and but for the miracle of the Blakeney Neighbourhood Housing Society the entire heart of the village would have ceased to beat. Coming out of the British Legion Club I look at the row of cottages opposite. Not a single light to be seen.

The successors of those in my dream had gone, scattered by the explosion in house values that began in the sixties. The community I mourned was robust and cohesive, held together by bonds of friendship and ties of blood going back to the days of Blakeney Haven, Doomsday, even the Saxon Shore. Such a loss ought to have been felt more deeply. That it was not can only be explained by the fact few now remembered it. Like most of the characters in my dream, the community seemed to have died. Its demise was not sudden. Its life had just slowly ebbed away. In a process not unlike petrifaction, incomers had gradually replaced the original inhabitants. The physical fabric of Blakeney remained but it had a different heart.

But was village life really so much better?

In a material sense clearly not. My childhood, rich as it was, would have been considered deprived. In a world where, for the great majority, material considerations were paramount, it is unlikely I would have touched a common cord by saying we were poorer in the 70s than thirty years before. Yet village life had undoubtedly become less connected; people to people and people to place.

In the village of my childhood an impending tidal surge would have been anticipated by most of the population likely to be affected by it and they would have taken the measures necessary to protect life and property. By the 70s, far fewer people in any community could predict those events and their consequences. By then (as now) it was the responsibility of the Environment Agency to warn people of impending risks. But the new system was designed to respond to prescribed factors that could not be adequately applied to the 'chaos' nature of the weather. Even with modern communications, wardens, sirens, and the enormous resources of the Meteorological Office, dangerous events (as the later events of 1996 showed) were not always predicted. Some people were even more irritated when the system reacted blindly to quite normal wind-driven big tides and local people – usually those who were most aware of what was happening – were forced unnecessarily and 'under protest' from their homes.

What impoverished us most at that time was the loss of connectedness between people. The personal intimacy between those who lived here when I was a child was, by the 1970s, only paralleled within the family, and even there it seemed to be disappearing. The old village social structure was, like an onion, composed of layers of personal relationships legitimate and otherwise, family ties and feuds, internecine squabbles and inter-village differences, personal acts of heroism and disgrace, and at its centre was the collective heart of the community.

By the 1970s all that was left were the diluted remnants of the old community where it came together at parties, on shoots, or in places like the British Legion Club. Those who had recently come to live here were generally unaware of it. All they saw of the onion was its shiny outer skin. They may have realised something existed underneath but did not really understand what it was. As a consequence, they were often quite baffled by events that, like earth tremors, occasionally came to the surface as a result of more than usually violent disturbances of the lower layers.

The community evolved and had remained in existence because it served a purpose. But it no longer functioned as it had because there were no longer enough people to form the judiciary. The terrible cases of child abuse and of old people being robbed and beaten in their homes that were by then occurring around the country could never have happened in the old village, yet they flourished in a disconnected world in which (as in the Environment Agency's response to flooding) problems were addressed by policies and strategies rather than common sense.

In my childhood, nobody who fell on hard times, became ill, or was bereaved, would go unobserved. A person could not die at home unnoticed until, weeks later, neighbours found the smell intolerable. It was a shared life, a community with coherence, tolerance and a common purpose, even if, for much of the time, the purpose was just to survive.

One of the first and most often expressed resentments I remember hearing as a young man was that most of the relatively small amounts of petty crime then beginning to occur were almost entirely put down to new families who had moved from towns – although 'crime' is almost too strong a word to apply to what were usually no more than small deceits and petty thefts. The resentment came because those doing it were breaking the rules. They had failed to understand

how it all worked and their behaviour threatened the stability of a culture that helped sustain the quality of village life. To someone unaware or unconcerned about village opinion it had no meaning so there were very good reasons to integrate newcomers as quickly as possible.

These feelings and resentments, the first small dark clouds racing across a previously clear sky , 'pageboys' the old fishermen would have called them, were the precursors of change. But we could not have imagined the extent of change or how fast it would come.

Blakeney had grown steadily century upon century with the same architectural patterns of cottages and houses clustered round yards and lokes. Suddenly, in the 60s and 70s, it doubled in size in just a few years in an explosion of growth totally out of scale and character with its setting. Wonderful opportunities to add constructively to what had gone before were squandered to tacky brick boxes of the worst and most homogenous kind, thrown together on every available bit of land within easy reach of the quay. A mindless and occasionally cynical sacrifice of history, character, and community heritage to a bland suburban newness that had no regard for its surroundings, vernacular or history.

Even the old names that had come into being over time were sacrificed. Village names like 'West Corner' for the row of cottages that, when given that name, marked the west corner of the old village. The Old School House because it once was the school house. Names chosen quite prosaically out of function, origin or position, each telling a small part of the village story.

Those names have mostly disappeared now and have been replaced with some quite startlingly original and irrelevant nomenclature like 'Woodpecker Cottage', 'Ladybird Cottage', 'Bobbin Cottage', 'Twitchers' and 'Marsh Haven'. These names too tell a story because there is no clearer window into the minds of the new Norfolkians. You can almost imagine how they were arrived at. 'Oh Bollocks! A ladybird just fell into my Martini'. 'Darling! What an absolutely super name for our new little cottage.' 'What, Bollocks Cottage?' 'No dear, don't be silly, Ladybird Cottage. Isn't it just perfect?'

In themselves, such names were harmless, little more than irrelevant embellishments to the bright clean outer skin of the onion. But they suggest that any real knowledge of the underlying layers will probably remain forever out of reach of the 'Ladybird' and 'Woodpecker' cottagers.

Friction

With views of rural life so totally out of kilter with reality, friction was inevitable. Complaints about smells off the fields, of mud on the roads and cockerels crowing at unsocial hours are the stuff of the *Eastern Daily Press*. But irritating as they may have been to the farmers concerned, they were really only symptoms of the much wider gulf of ignorance between incomers and local people.

The traditional occupations of the coast are unselfconscious and unused to spectators, so fishermen and others were nonplussed by the critically outspoken incomers who protested about many aspects of what they did, the local authority not least among them. Their seeming indifference to complaints, interpreted by some as unwillingness to respond, was simply utter bewilderment. Fishermen had been doing these things for generations. They were (and are) inseparable from what they do. 'What,' they might reply, 'are they asking us to do: become invisible?'

Fishing families who had processed their catches at home for generations suddenly had newcomer neighbours protesting about smells. Fishermen launching boats in the early hours of the morning found new owners of nearby properties protesting about noise. Others complained that the fishermen's scruffy tractors and gear cluttered an otherwise beautiful beach scene, a scene of course that existed only in their heads and which they brought here with them.

Like misplaced art, these things would have been no more than minor irritants to men whose jobs involve struggles of a far more arduous and life-threatening kind, if only planning law and local authority policies had been on their side. North Norfolk District Council, instead of saying to complainants, 'Look, fishermen have always been here and have an inalienable right to do what they do,' attempted to placate them. Often with farcical results, such as the idea that all fishermen on this coast should store their gear in one place – which turned out to be North Walsham!

Many of those who came to live here in the 70s remained fixated by the shiny outer skin. Exerting a pressure to polish, tidy, gentrify and sanitise. In places like Blakeney where they became the majority, they effected real change. Demands for pavements, street lighting, traffic islands, even traffic lights (they didn't get them) almost transformed the village and surrounded it with a new one, leaving the old one like a lifeless museum from which most shops had gone, and that, like a museum provided opportunities for those with dusters.

I do not see any of this as a deliberate premeditated attack. The polishing was carried out with the best intentions. It was seen as progress and improvement and those involved genuinely did not see what they were destroying. But that does not excuse it. While the motives may not have been explicit, what happened was too consistent to be anything but an expression of deeper subconscious desire.

I am convinced, and for me the evidence is everywhere, that many of these 'New North Norfolkians' would have been happier if they had colonised an empty land. With clearances no longer an option they had to settle for indifference. It was easier for them to have their own rather superficial sense of ownership if they could pretend the locals didn't exist. So to them locals came to have an occasional existence, invisible most of the time but springing into being when some menial job needed doing. They were convenient for those tasks and also qualified as a part of the background. They added 'simple' charm to the place but lacked the sensibilities to really value the subtleties around them.

North Norfolk was not alone. Throughout rural England (parts of Northumbria perhaps being an exception) the same things happened inevitably and inexorably. Everywhere, the richness and complexity of rural life, centuries in the making, was rolled flat to be replaced by a social make-up that paralleled the landscape transition from historic countryside to featureless prairie.

There was probably never very much rural people could have done to prevent it, although at the very beginning there might have been a chance. It is clear from many accounts, notably those of Lillias Rider-Haggard, that many mid-19th century incomers were well aware of the mutually sustaining social benefits of rural life. They even sought to capture and relocate them in towns like Bournville and Port Sunlight. But that period, with a steady trickle of newcomers, was not when the damage was done. The villages of this coast have been points of arrival and departure throughout history. The real change came with the motorcar, which gave Joe Urban the key to the door of the countryside.

Renaissance

In the last few years it has become increasingly apparent – at public meetings, at the supper table and on the ground – that we may now be moving in to a new, more promising era.

More and more cottages and houses are being sympathetically restored. Old render has been stripped and hidden flints cleaned and re-pointed in what could be a material expression of a wish to get under the skin of the place. It is hard to explain why, but recent incomers are unlike their predecessors.

The staggering increase in house prices has undoubtedly had something to do with it. The people who are now able to settle here tend to value the place as they find it, appreciate its unspoiled qualities, are not offended by the odd rotting tractor or boat and seem less tempted to try to resurrect the world they left behind. As a result, the ranks of North Norfolk's guardians are growing and a unique place is finally getting the protectors it deserves. An ever-decreasing amount of land is available for development and this, coupled with (and partly responsible for) increased property prices, has made it much more worthwhile to restore old cottages, even quite small ones. Stricter planning controls, bigger money and bigger imaginations are producing a steady renaissance.

Hungry developers still prowl the perimeter looking for opportunities such as social housing, to take a quick and profitable bite. But so far, largely due to an increasingly vigilant local authority, this has not happened although it has come close and could still happen.

Blakeney

The extent to which things have changed has been brought home to me quite forcefully by recent incidents. The unanimous support and effort in Wiveton, Blakeney, Morston and now Langham for preparing Village Design Statements took me quite by surprise. So did the following incident. I am one of three trustees for the area at the west end of Blakeney Quay, called Red House Land where boats and other maritime detritus accumulate from time to time. It is a bit muddy in places. There is an area of grass where people can sit and a place for cars to park. It has little that is special except the view – which is timeless.

Norfolk County Council looked at it through the eyes of urban engineers and saw an eyesore that could benefit from tidying up: a new pavement, smart new railings, clear modern signs, more yellow lines. A meeting was called to discuss their proposals and explore what might be done. It was very well attended, the majority, as is now the norm, incomers, some long-standing, some more recent. Many of them lived close to Red House Land. As the meeting progressed they all made it absolutely clear they wished no change. They liked it as it was and wanted it left that way. Twenty years ago that could not have happened. The idea of a new pavement then would have been almost irresistible.

So we have come a long way. But I have come much further. Even the 1970s development that offended me so much when it was built, now seems much less intrusive, shrouded as it is by all the trees and shrubs of its verdant gardens. More important however, is the change in me arising from the fact that many of those who have chosen to live here I now count among my most loved and valued friends. Good people who care as passionately about this place and what happens to it as I do, some in a better position to do something about it. These changes are not confined to the village fabric. New communities have emerged, different from those I knew as a child, but nonetheless real and energetic.

Even in Blakeney, people stop and talk in the street again – the most obvious sign of a real community in which people have time for one another. Wiveton, where I live, is small, with a very eclectic social mix, but come Harvest Supper they are packed into our little Parish Room like sardines. It is a village that turns out. For the Queen's Golden Jubilee, the entire village spent the day on the 'Green', from the youngest to the oldest, wholly involved with each other and the day's activities. It was a completely happy day.

Wiveton is undoubtedly special and being small might be seen to have rediscovered community more easily. But I do not believe that is the explanation. Blakeney too is vibrant with new life. Groups like the British Legion, the Blakeney Players, the Glaven Caring Committee and the Blakeney Area Historical Society bring people together. The historical society in particular brings together incomers and locals alike. The locals can tell it as it was and the members can combine their talents and energies to uncover not just a better understanding of Blakeney but of each other. Altogether it seems a very positive state of affairs.

It is therefore ironic that the forces of renewal that are reviving the affluence and fabric of the place are at the same time disassembling the last remnants of the indigenous community. Locals are being incidentally disadvantaged in many ways. By the huge wealth gap between them and incomers. And by the cost of property to rent or buy. The first rung on the property ladder is now so high local youngsters need another ladder to reach it and the likelihood of most of them ever owning a home is almost nil.

The first property price increases in the 1970s forced many locals to buy inland where prices were slightly lower. That is why so many Blakeney people now live in Langham and other villages back from the coast. Now, however, even that option has been priced out and if this were not enough the situation is exacerbated by the lack of rentable accommodation. The area's popularity as a holiday destination means that holiday rents can be up to ten times the going rate.

The result is that very few youngsters who work in North Norfolk can now afford to live there. They can neither afford to buy nor rent a home, a particularly bitter irony considering their forbears built them. A single boy or girl working in a local hotel earning the minimum wage can be paying £450 per month rent plus £130 per month Council Tax. It is not difficult to see how little a working person, who in most cases cannot get to work without a car, is left to live on.

The local authority's poor grasp of how rural communities function produces social housing policies that do little to help because they see rural villages as groups of buildings rather than living, working communities. A fisherman working out of Blakeney Harbour might be offered a house in Fakenham. A local council house that might at one time have been available to him is given to a family from Manchester that, having spent the winter in Social Security accommodation in Cromer, refuses to return to Manchester when summer comes, and it gets the house because the family has become a responsibility of the local authority.

If the housing officers of the District Council reflect the new population mix and the predominant urban world-view, then part of the explanation for decisions such as these lies with the fact that most if not all of them will be town or city-born.

Existing council housing estates, built mostly in the 1940s and 50s, now represent some of the most inappropriate (ugly is better) parts of North Norfolk's built environment. To follow that path again, tacking cheaply designed brick estates onto the edges of villages, would be disastrous because it would conflict with North Norfolk's greatest strength – its unspoiled character. Compared to Cornwall or Cumbria, its assets are small and its open landscape is particularly vulnerable to built intrusion. Its wide skies and undeveloped landscape underwrite its economy. And if the appeal of the area were thus ruined the property and tourism markets would collapse and the local economy would be wrecked.

The problem is difficult but not intractable. With imagination, and with give-

Blakeney High Street

and-take on both sides (those who want development no matter what the price, and those who would keep the place the way it is) much could be done. Most villages have some space into which one or two, in some cases more, cottage-type developments could be successfully integrated. They would have to be designed and built in sympathy with their surroundings and this would increase the costs. But the twofold goal of reinstating buildings and local people to live in their rightful place, at the heart, rather than at the edge of their communities, is all the justification needed. Planning means preparing for the future, not holding up templates of inflexible rules against which developers tilt their plans and deceptions.

There is no doubt in my mind that many of the resentments I experienced back in the seventies are being perpetuated by the underlying resentment generated by such conspicuous wrongness. I find it difficult to believe that the many fair-minded people now living here will be able to live happily with their consciences much longer knowing the price others are having to pay for their privilege. It has to change and when it does those who profess to care about North Norfolk and its character will have to realize that you cannot divorce the landscape from its people. They service its economy but, much more than that, they are its heart, its creators and its maintainers; it has no real identity without them. They have given it, and continue to give it the most precious thing it has; its distinctiveness.

Green destroying green

The North Norfolk coast, unique in Britain, remains basically unspoiled. It is a place of vistas, not often high but very wide, the lack of height compensated by towering skies and wonderful unbroken sweeps of fields, woods and hedges in which occasional splashes of terracotta indicate a village or farm, and the flint finger of a Church points towards heaven. Modernity rarely intrudes. We can still admire the views of our forefathers – which may be why we often take our surroundings for granted. But we can no longer afford to take things for granted because we stand on the verge of a new landscape.

Three current threats serve to illustrate the fact that, although things have improved, the future of this place is far from assured: the spread of wind-farms and telecommunications equipment; agricultural diversification; and housing encroachment on village perimeters.

First, under existing government plans and incentives, wind-farms could soon be marching across the most empty and unspoiled parts of North Norfolk and lining the offshore horizon. I am not denying the merits of wind power but having been an active environmentalist all my adult life, I learned at an early stage that balance is one of life's fundamentals. And the balance achieved by nature offers a perfect lesson in how success is achieved. I am baffled by the fact that those who

profess to love the planet seem to do so in such an arbitrary way; how can they be 'Friends of the Earth' but not friends of the landscape?

The case for wind power lacks balance. Its very poor economic efficiency compared with those of other forms of renewable energy is being distorted by those with vested interests. Government incentives are attracting those who want to make money rather than those who want to save the planet. Here, the urban mindset that scatters unnecessary art across the countryside is set to destroy it altogether.

Wind-farms change the character of their immediate surroundings and that of every other place from which they can be seen. They also change the scale of everything in the same field of view. One of their effects would be that the magnificent churches of North Norfolk would appear small and insignificant when seen in the same space.

I believe most thinking people now accept global warming as a reality with consequences that are serious beyond prediction. I believe it would be folly to squander any opportunity to mitigate its frightening potential. But wind power is just one option and in the long term probably the least realistic, unless of course the whole country becomes a huge wind engine. I believe an all-encompassing bottom up approach starting with generation at the home and workplace would provide renewable energy with minimum environment costs and spare those who, as things stand, are going to have to live under or near these enormous machines. It would also preserve the landscape and seascape. In any case, renewables apart, I think a pragmatist would accept the notion that against the predicted scale and rate of climate change the only clean power that offers any real chance of success [apart from carbon dioxide removal during energy generation] is nuclear.

Second, the pressure for wind-farms and much else comes from outside. Decisions made in London and Brussels affect the overall shape of the land by dictating how it is or is not to be farmed. Farmers are being told they must diversify if they are to survive. All those I have spoken to believe major changes in land use are both inevitable and imminent.

Third, solutions to the problems of housing for locally dispossessed young people could result in central government policies sweeping away hard won planning controls to produce unimaginative social house building programmes. These programmes could destroy vitally important areas of countryside not to mention some of its most important economic strengths.

The Government has abolished county plans, replacing them with a regional quango, the make-up of which does not reflect the largely rural nature of the area. Its brief is to produce a twenty-year master plan [RPG14]. Using the most suspect extrapolations they have estimated the regional housing requirement for Norfolk up to the year 2021 to be more than 72,000 homes. Out of that total one might expect North Norfolk's share to be the equivalent of another village every ten years.

Economic development, telecommunications, transport links all pose threats to the conventional view of how our countryside should look. The Countryside Agency, the East of England Development Agency, the Norfolk County Council, are all scuttling down a tunnel toward the light of Economic Development, creating policies and structures that the ordinary man in the country lane can only tilt at, Don Quixote-like, with little hope of making a dent.

Outside rural Norfolk we rush ever faster into the realms of the European Community's perfect world where everyone is safe, suffers no disabilities or discrimination, has perfect health and will eventually live forever. Apart from those who are afraid of their own shadows, these initiatives are driven first and foremost by business power that is shaping government policy toward the single objective of profit, leaving the true values of the countryside as a closed and unimportant book. There may be arguments for why we may need these things, but they are not taking place here. In a democracy, one would think change on this scale merits a debate that includes those affected.

When discussing these issues I have more than once been told that many more people live in the towns and cities than in the countryside and asked why, in a democracy, the majority view should not prevail? If this is how the majority is happy for the countryside to look, then who are we, a diminishing rural minority, to take issue? That is of course too simplistic. If democracy worked that way we would almost certainly have capital punishment, vigilantes would roam the streets at night and there might even be special days when we could declare war on France.

Fortunately, democracy is more complex and has mechanisms that 'occasionally' allow the enlightened view to prevail. In the case of the countryside the enlightened view resides mostly with country people. Do not assume that those who have always lived here are backward or behind the times because they resist street lighting, pavements, traffic lights, wind farms and major road schemes. Wait and you too will realise that country life is better and has a more secure future without them. They are sops to the urban world view and the false dream that all Norfolk's problems can be solved by economic development.

James McCallum

James McCallum was born in Wells, went to school there and earned a Masters Degree from the Royal College of Art in 1996. Painting, writing and bird surveying have taken him to places as far apart as Namibia, West Africa, the Middle East, Lapland, Siberia and Alaska. He has illustrated numerous books. He has also written and illustrated three books of his own about North Norfolk wildlife, the most recent being *Wild Goose Winter* and *North Norfolk Summer Sketchbook* (www.jamesmccallum.co.uk)

Natural History in the Future

Something to be revered or simply another resource?

James McCallum

The North Norfolk in which I grew up in the 1970s and 80s was a very different place to the North Norfolk of today. My interests were centred on the bird life around my birthplace of Wells. Outside the busy summer holiday period the area was very much deserted, leaving me to watch with relative freedom the bird and other wildlife of the beach, coast, marsh, woods and farmland. Looking back, it seems almost dream-like, along with a couple of friends, to have spent days wandering around Holkham beach, the neighbouring woods and marshes, barely meeting a soul, particularly in the spring, autumn and winter. Today's picture is very different. Over the last decade the area's popularity has escalated beyond our wildest comprehension. The holiday season continues virtually throughout the year and more people with much more leisure time have, of course, had a much greater impact on the area, its wildlife and its habitats. In an attempt to cope with the increasing number of visitors and the impact of their activities, much more careful thought must be given and measures taken if the area is to remain one of the richest places for wildlife, particularly birdlife, in the British Isles.

Essentially, the entire coastal strip falls under the jurisdiction and control of a network of local and national conservation bodies. The remaining land is either farmed or managed by estate owners. Within this area are some rare and threatened plant and bird species which need protection. Protection of the coast and its various fragile ecosystems is a huge and complicated issue. This, coupled with the added pressures of more people with more leisure time visiting and using the area, makes managing and protecting the wildlife and habitats of this coastline a far from enviable task. In common with many areas of the British Isles, its economic prosperity has now come to rely on tourism. As every piece of the coast is scoured for its economic potential, the challenge of protecting the more sensitive and vulnerable species and habitats becomes even more crucial.

Conservation bodies and landowners already have management policies in place, but the purpose of this chapter is to consider some of the issues which may threaten the natural history of this coast in the future. Although chords may be struck or objections raised by some of the views that follow, they are offered as food for thought and as a possible focus for debate.

Firstly, an important point to remember is that the natural history of the coast, particularly its extremely rich birdlife, only prospers because large areas are out of bounds or are difficult for the general public to reach and are therefore left undisturbed. It is a fundamental requirement of the wildlife here that it is allowed to have undisturbed breeding, roosting, feeding, loafing, washing and preening areas. If just one of these basic components is removed the whole chain can be put under pressure or even break down. Many nature reserves, particularly the larger ones such as Cley, Holkham and Titchwell have large areas without public access and so are totally protected. Other areas such as the huge tidal saltmarshes of Thornham, Brancaster, Burnham Overy, Wells and Stiffkey have vast spaces that are dangerous and difficult to visit.

Sudden unregulated changes in use, promotion or access could have profound negative effects on the wildlife; therefore any changes must be carefully considered. The effect of disturbance by increasing numbers of people is difficult to quantify but people should, within reason, have the right to pursue their chosen

interests in the area. Unfortunately, certain leisure activities are too demanding for some sensitive locations. The scene at Holkham beach on a hot, busy August day has changed dramatically since my childhood. How can several thousand people, a dozen horses, mountain bikers, kite buggies and surfers, dog walkers, nudists, families and birdwatchers – not to mention several dozen pairs of little terns, ringed plovers and oyster-catchers – coexist harmoniously? Put simply, they don't.

The kite buggies and surfboards are difficult to control in strong winds and need too large an area of beach, so their use has been banned. Where can leisure activities such as these be accommodated? Has this coast large enough beach areas that could justifiably be dedicated to minority needs? Or would they be better catered for further inland, away from specialist wildlife areas?

Mountain-bike riding is restricted to paths away from fragile and easily damaged sand dunes. Nudists, with their minority requirements have their own fenced-off area of beach, as do the terns and waders. Unfortunately, these birds are very susceptible to disturbance and frequently suffer poor breeding success here. They do far better on the less disturbed, constantly wardened reserves such as that on Scolt Head Island, further to the west. Here, these species, along with other specialist breeders, have a much better chance of prospering in the future. We need therefore to accept that areas such as Holkham beach have become popular with people and now cater for their needs and the more inaccessible habitats and wildlife reserves such as Scolt Head should not be allowed to develop in the same way. But already in this new economy, dominated by tourism, there are trips by sailing boat to explore the 'remote, undisturbed beaches of Scolt Head Island' and other sensitive areas. Of course people need to earn a living but surely this should not be at the expense of wildlife, the very thing that brings people here.

It is interesting to compare the situation at Blakeney Point with that at Scolt Head since they are, superficially at least, similar in terms of wildlife and habitats. The National Trust, which owns and manages Blakeney Point, operates a much broader access policy and each year the Point is visited by 60,000 people, more than 10 times the number visiting Scolt Head. The general public is allowed much more access to the Point and is able to explore it with greater ease and freedom. The results of this heavier usage are clearly evident in the erosion of the dune system and the plant life that grows there. Its nationally important colonies of terns and waders are however more strictly wardened. Looking at the coast as a complete unit, Blakeney Point and its habitats can largely be experienced by large numbers of people but there is an element of habitat damage. Scolt Head, on the other hand, is far more pristine and therefore should not be opened to greater access or promotion if we wish to retain these unique examples of specialist habitat.

The same must be said of the intertidal marshes between Wells and Stiffkey. These are large, inaccessible areas, dangerous for people without local knowledge. They are essentially a continuation of some of the best examples of salt marshes in Northwestern Europe. They hold a vast abundance of salt tolerant plant communities – the most readily evident and therefore most well known being the carpets of light purple sea lavender seen in the summer months.

Again, looking at the coast as a whole, these vast open areas are the breathing spaces for lots of birds. Outside the breeding season they provide night-time and tidal roosting and daytime loafing areas for huge numbers of waders and wildfowl. Additionally, they are used by small but significant numbers of our wintering birds of prey. The marshes are breeding grounds for vulnerable numbers of redshanks, oystercatchers, ringed plovers, terns, including the rare and protected little tern, and passerines such as reed buntings, meadow pipits and skylarks that have become scarce elsewhere.

In contrast, the reserves of Titchwell, Holkham and Cley are able to cater much more for visiting groups. They also boast much larger numbers of a greater variety of species, which are easy to observe and they are safe places for groups of people to watch wildlife compared with the dangerous tidal areas.

There are some good examples of how tourism and wildlife can function harmoniously, causing minimal impact to the natural environment. There is no better example than that of seal trips to Blakeney Point where colonies of both common and grey seals are a popular attraction, particularly in the summer months. At this time of year the common seals haul out to moult and give birth to their pups, frequently using the tip of the Point at high-tide. This is exactly where the bulk of the nesting birds breed and is therefore out of bounds to the general public. The seals are easily observed from the boat; neither the terns nor the seals perceive a boat full of people as a potential threat. In fact, they are so used to the daily tidal routines of the ferries they hardly bat an eyelid. Some of the dozing seals don't even bother to stir and the terns, gulls and waders carry on incubating or brooding their young. However, if a boat were to land and a human form emerged from it then chaos and panic would break out in the colonies. The seals would lumber into the water and all the birds would take to the air. Seal pups would become separated from their mothers and nests would be left unattended with the eggs and young becoming easy pickings for opportunist gulls.

The ferry operators' skill and knowledge of the harbour's wildlife enable visitors to obtain great views of the seals and birds without causing them any disturbance.

Passengers sometimes have the option of landing for up to an hour on less sensitive areas of the Point, near the old lifeboat house. This allows enough time for them to experience the area but not to penetrate the more sensitive areas. A single boat landing in the wrong place, or a walker coming up from Cley and ignoring the signs or requests from the wardens, can cause far more damage than the thousands of ferry passengers put together.

Elsewhere, different considerations apply and so far, the conflicts between people and wildlife have not been satisfactorily resolved. The last decade has seen a dramatic change in the number of pink-footed geese wintering in the area. The species has had a chequered history here. They were much famed in the early 1900s in the writings and paintings of people like Peter Scott, Frank Southgate, W. M Hudson and Pat Cringle. But during the Second World War, bombing ranges on the saltmarshes at Wells and Warham bordering the traditional goose roost sites resulted in their abandoning the area until the early 1960s when small numbers began to appear irregularly.

This pattern continued throughout the 1970s but more than a couple of hundred were seldom seen. In 1983, a group of 300 settled here for the entire winter and since then numbers have increased dramatically to the present record of just over 100,000. Their vast skeins have become a huge attraction, with spectacular daily flights to and from their roost sites on the tidal sands of Wells and Warham and Scolt Head Island. Their now familiar presence has come to epitomise the winter and is proving to be a great attraction to visitors. Many people all too quickly take it for granted and forget that this is a surprisingly recent development. It is one that could quickly be reversed and if the area is to remain attractive to the geese it must provide them with several basic needs: food, safe and undisturbed roost sites and feeding areas.

When the geese returned in the 1980s, local wildfowlers were quick to recognise the importance of protecting the roost sites if they were to continue to return to the area. Shooting on the roost sites was banned, and more recently bag limits have been introduced. Recently harvested sugar beet fields are the main feeding grounds where they seek out the beet tops that are mechanically chopped off and discarded when the root is lifted. The continuing farming of sugar beet is of paramount importance if we are to continue to enjoy this spectacle. However, as if the local farming industry were not under enough pressure already there is talk of the government gradually phasing out sugar beet production. Sugar beet quotas have already dropped and some sugar beet factories, which took locally grown beet, have closed down. The pinkfeet's plight is further complicated by recent requests from the remaining factories for beet to be left in the ground and harvested when required instead of beginning the harvest in the autumn and storing the beet on large concrete pads. The geese are suddenly finding large acreages of unharvested beet, where there would normally have been fields of

left-over sugar beet tops. They have recently begun to eat unharvested crops and are therefore not popular with some farmers. These issues need to be quickly addressed by government and major conservation bodies whilst the situation is still rectifiable.

Undisturbed feeding grounds are essential to pinkfeet. As long distance migrants from Iceland and Greenland, and being gregarious birds by habit, various other species of geese frequently become lost and mixed up with our hordes. Once a rare species of goose is found and the news of its discovery broadcast, large numbers of birdwatchers head to these inland feeding areas. Flocks of geese feeding inland are extremely wary and quick to take to the wing if disturbed so a good deal of careful fieldcraft is needed.

They are very tolerant of cars as they don't associate them with a threat, but the sudden appearance of a human form will put them to flight. Carefully moving along hedges without breaking the skyline or not walking past gateways and gaps in the hedges is fine but one careless move will disturb them, so it is best to remain in the car. Visiting observers seem unable to understand this point. Perhaps the task of educating birdwatchers should be one for the commercial bird information services that supply constantly updated news of the whereabouts of such rarities.

Repeated disturbance is unacceptable to these wild geese and unfair to careful observers. It is also unfair to the farms that happily tolerate the geese on their land provided they are feeding on left-over beet tops. Once disturbed, the geese may move onto other areas such as cereals where they won't be tolerated and farm workers will have to waste their working hours scaring them back onto the beet tops. Repeated problems with birdwatchers frightening geese combined with inconsiderate parking and verbal abuse when politely asked to allow space for farm machinery to pass have, not surprisingly, left some farms less tolerant of the geese. They like the geese but not what comes with them.

There are a couple of other factors that could have more serious implications for pinkfeet in the future. One is the larger scale inland shooting of geese. Here geese, attracted by decoys on the feeding grounds, are shot from concealed positions. This style of shooting is not to be confused with traditional wildfowling which, when carried out responsibly, has a relatively low impact on the overall wintering populations. As mentioned earlier, the local clubs have introduced measures to protect the roosts and to limit daily bags.

By comparison, inland shooting, which is more prevalent in areas of Scotland, is a far less skilful pursuit and large numbers of geese can be shot at close range as they drop in to feed. This has so far been largely outlawed in this part of the world and the estate owners on whose land the geese feed and the tenant farmers' work should be applauded for it. Although not a shooting person myself, I can appreciate the differences between this method of shooting and traditional wildfowling, which requires local knowledge and fieldcraft.

When considering the well being of migrant birds it is essential to remember that they spend a large proportion of their time elsewhere in the world. It is not enough to safeguard religiously their winter quarters in Norfolk if they are under threat on other parts of their range. An American aluminium smelter project in Iceland could potentially have major implications for our pinkfeet. There are plans to build dams and flood large, remote, wild and virtually inaccessible areas of Iceland's interior – right in the heart of the pinkfeet's breeding grounds. This project has been off and on for many years but in spite of Iceland's promotion of green tourism the project has currently been given the go ahead. So it seems that sometimes no matter what safeguards are introduced for migrants on the doorstep, some wildlife needs to be protected globally and 'our birds' are, in fact, winter or summer migrants which may need help and protection elsewhere.

The long-term protection and overall improvements made for wildlife and habitats over vast areas of this coastline by various landowners and conservation bodies should be applauded. Lots of hard work and management goes into maintaining what is so easily taken for granted. The area has become increasingly recognised as not only a nationally but also internationally important one for wildlife. The combined area is ever changing and evolving and new management approaches and decisions are constantly being looked at.

Some topics can be very difficult to address and can cause much debate and create moral dilemmas not only for individuals and conservation bodies who have to make the decisions but also for the public who support their work.

There is no better example than the highly emotive topic of predators and their potential control. Their impact, particularly on ground nesting bird populations, is evident and although not a pleasant subject, it is one that people who are interested in the wildlife of the area should give some thought to and try to understand, even if they can't come to a definite decision. Ultimately the decisions that are made will have a major long-term effect on the future of the area's breeding birds.

Survey work and observations by local people show frequent high levels of pre-dation of breeding birds on nature reserves. Whereas much farmland has become a super efficient and increasingly sterile place for wildlife, huge improvements have been made on some of the nature reserves. This is particularly obvious on the fresh water grazing marshes of the coastal strip, where the balance of the countryside has changed dramatically. Nesting lapwings are a good way to illustrate this. Only twenty years ago their dramatic breeding displays were a familiar sight over much local farmland. Forty years ago they were very common arable nesting birds. In the early 20th century, while the railways were still in operation here, large numbers of bird's eggs, including 'plovers eggs', which at that time were not protected, were shipped to London markets. This abun-dance was a national rather than a regional trend. However, in recent years, as farm-land has become increasingly unsuitable for wildlife, the carefully managed grazing marshes have become more attractive and important. These areas have quickly become focus points for predators.

In recent summers, in some areas, very few young birds have fledged – a trend which can only spell long-term decline for some rare species. This requires difficult ethical decisions to be made such as whether to control the numbers of predators or to sacrifice some of our highly-prized bird populations such as lapwings. Predator control does not provide a long-term solution to the problem, it merely gives us time to develop viable alternative measures. A step in the right direction might be the development of a network of smaller pockets of suitable breeding habitats dotted all over the countryside rather than large isolated areas of relative richness.

As mentioned earlier, in this part of the world man has had and continues to have so much influence on the use and appearance of the land that any notion of nature finding its own 'natural balance' is unrealistic. It is important to recognise that, in the past, agriculture and gamekeeping probably had a far greater influence on the bird populations of the area as a whole than the relatively recent improvements made by nature reserves.

The subject of shooting, hunting and gamekeeping raises so many extreme reactions and heated debates that in many ways it would be sensible to ignore it. However, it is so much part of local life that it is difficult to avoid. As I have said, I am not a shooting person but have friends and colleagues who are. The comments which follow reflect the thoughts and fears of myself, local observers and genuine country people. I believe that it is important to put aside some personal feelings and consider the topic from a broader wildlife perspective.

The way the countryside and its wildlife have evolved in this area is very complicated – sometimes surprisingly so. North Norfolk has a long history of wildfowling and game shooting, and therefore, gamekeeping is significant when considering the numbers and variety of birdlife. Natural predators that prey on game birds and their young have been controlled for hundreds of years. The numbers of crows, foxes, stoats and weasels, and in former years birds of prey, were much reduced by a continuous network of gamekeepers. This control of predators had, of course, some benefits for wild birds and it is impossible to look at their history in the area without bearing this in mind.

The grey or English partridge is a native wild species that has a British stronghold here and it is true that gamekeeping has played a major role in its preservation. As farming has intensified, the use of machinery, herbicides and pesticides has become more widespread and effective and increasing areas of the countryside have become sterile for much wildlife and declining numbers of farmland birds. Whether we like it or not, the provision, albeit not always intentionally, of game strips, cover, seed bins and headlands has become a lifeline for farmland birds. This provision was particularly important before certain set aside schemes were introduced. Until longer-term changes in government and conservation approaches to managing farmland and its wildlife take place, game strips and cover, along with set asides will remain important lifelines in this area.

Shooting in the past has largely fallen into two categories: sport for the wealthy and food for the table for the working classes. In my grandparents' time, shooting ducks and rabbits was essential both for food and survival. For the working classes in modern times shooting is more about personal choice than necessity. However, as we look to the future, several ethical issues are being voiced by a surprisingly broad cross-section of true country folk.

Gamebirds can be conveniently separated into two main groups: sedentary birds such as pheasants and partridges; and birds that migrate through or come to winter here. The gap between them is bridged by species such as the woodcock that have a small declining breeding population here but whose numbers are boosted in the autumn and winter months by migrants from Scandinavia and western Russia. Pheasants and red-legged partridges are introduced birds. Their naturalised popula-tions are maintained and encouraged by gamekeepers and their numbers are being boosted by hand-reared and released birds. Their presence here is now very much part of the local landscape and these sustain-able populations, brought here as game-birds, form the backbone of the local commercial shooting economy. The native

population of English partridges is declining and is currently on the whole unshot. Much work is being done to try to reverse the decline.

The numbers of wild migrating quarry species – wild ducks, geese and waders – are less easy to assess. Relatively large numbers of these migrating and wintering species are dispersed over huge areas of northern and eastern Europe and large parts of the Arctic. Waterfowl such as teal, widgeon, pintail, gadwall and pink-footed geese often winter in the region in internationally important num- bers. Waders such as wood- cock and golden plover, often by their nature difficult to count accurately, winter here in at least nationally important numbers. Some potentially worrying developments need to be addressed if we are to respect the future of these birds. Firstly, there is the con- troversial topic of shooting-related tourism. What to wear, where to go and what to do 'in the country' seem to be almost obsessive topics in many of the 'in vogue' glossy magazines, aimed at the more affluent visitor and potential new North Norfolk resident. Stereotypical country looks and culture, prevalent both here and elsewhere, are so incredibly false and far removed from the real lives and ways of country people. They nevertheless bring with them a notion that it is fashionable to be seen shooting in the countryside.

Shooting has largely been an activity for those with a shooting background and consequent knowledge of the subject. Is it acceptable to promote such pursuits to a wider range of people who may have limited understanding of the subject? If a shooting based tourist economy is to be developed there is a need for more concrete information on international migrant bird populations and their ability to withstand it. The increasing revenue generated by intensive dusk shooting of duck at flight ponds is a good example of this issue and one that causes huge debate within the shooting world itself. Traditionally, the majority of flight pools in this area were well maintained and grain was put down for ducks throughout the winter. They would often only be shot as a special event on a handful of occasions. Now, shooting them has become a lucrative business and large numbers, particularly teal, are being killed. During an entire season the cumulative total shot of this species alone is estimated to run well into four figures. In the long-term this level is not sustainable and some form of voluntary restriction must be put in place. The introduction of bag limits is a step closer to sustainable shooting.

During a recent trip to Alaska to survey waterfowl and waders it was interesting to note the close ties between wildfowlers and conservation bodies. The findings of surveys made on both breeding and winter quarters are used as a tool to establish how the populations of these birds are faring, and therefore which species and in what numbers can legally be shot. Admittedly the Americans have the advantage of complete control over their birds' breeding grounds, wintering grounds and migration routes. However their approach to wild bird populations and the coming together of conservationists, hunters and native subsistence hunters has brought many waterfowl back from steep declines and the measures imposed have helped to ensure their continued survival for all to enjoy.

Another situation which is causing more than a few mutterings locally is the popularisation of various quarry species by several well known and well-advertised eating establishments. Game is very much part of the local heritage and pheasants, red-legged partridge, rabbit, deer and pigeons do have sustainable populations to cater for these requirements. The question must be posed as to whether the shooting and eating, although legal, of some of the wild migratory birds should be popularised in this way. Should the names of pintail, wigeon, gadwall, teal and woodcock appear on menus of places visited by continually growing numbers of tourists who may not always understand the nature and origins of what they are ordering? These are not locally bred, they are wild, long distance migrants whose populations we know little about. It is worth remembering that a significant proportion of tourists come to North Norfolk specifically to see the hordes of wildfowl and waders.

Woodcock, notoriously difficult to survey accurately due to their elusive ways and mysterious lifestyles, are known to be declining over parts of their Scandinavian forest breeding grounds. Recent surveys have shown that the small local breeding populations are also in decline. Fashion is a peculiar human phenomenon and if a trend is generated for eating these wild birds the demand for them could be great. One has to ask whether tourism, so important to the area, should be developed in this way. How long will it be before other declining quarry species such as snipe and golden plover are promoted here as quirky lunches or starters?

Some thought must also be given to the regional harvesting of native wildlife such as cockles and samphire which have long been gathered in vary-ing quantities. In recent times small-scale commercial harvests have helped to provide income to local families and small amounts are gathered for personal con-sumption. These harvests are sustainable and long may they remain so. What we must ensure is that small-scale local indus-tries and traditions are safeguarded because in other parts of the country larg-er scale, sometimes illegal, cockle har-vesting is reaching unsustainable levels and in other regions of East Anglia organised gangs of samphire pickers filling vans destined for London markets are beginning to have a huge impact.

The saltmarshes of East Anglia are the national stronghold for this plant, and being a regional speciality it requires extra consideration. It is an important autumn and winter food source for large numbers of waterfowl and specialist shore-feeding passerines such as twite, snowbuntings and shorelarks. In common with all wild plants it is fully protected and therefore it is technically illegal to pick, but while the local harvests have remained at sustainable levels these laws have not been enforced. However, we must be careful that such local fares are not over exploited or over popularised in the local and national press and media. The gathering of samphire or cockles for supper has long been a special day out or summer tradition for many people and it would be nice to see this continue to be enjoyed in the future. Not only this, the picking of samphire has provided an annual source of local amusement when visitors, new to the area, return from the marsh with bundles of the superficially similar annual sea-blight. No doubt this is in preparation for an evening of local culture, but heaven knows what this 'local delicacy' must taste like.

Rising sea levels, coupled with the gradual natural subsidence of the East Anglian coastline is an obvious cause for concern in both the immediate and long-term future. The impact on the human and natural world could be enormous and ways of coping with it are another source of mixed feelings and heated debate.

Conservation and environmental organisations have concluded that large areas of low lying, coastal grazing marshes and wetlands will not, in the long-term, be protected from rising sea levels. So famous coastal nature reserves such as Cley and Titchwell will be at the mercy of natural elements. The topic of Cley is a particularly emotive one within the birdwatching world. In the past Cley has played a major role in building foundations for the evolution of the British birdwatching movement. This small parish is shrouded in ornithological history. However, in the greater scheme of things, its life-span is but a tiny moment in the history of the area's geography and wildlife. The reserve was created largely by the sea and it seems likely it will soon be reclaimed by it. So if this is to be its future we must put sentiment aside and quickly start to look at the future requirements of the wildlife that lives there and in similarly threatened habitats along this coastline.

The logical move is to create new habitats or enable low lying land, previously reclaimed from the sea for agriculture, to revert back to a more natural state. This policy of not maintaining the coastal defences of vulnerable nature reserves and duplicating similar areas in safe locations further inland comes under the label of Managed Retreat and it is beginning to be adopted both nationally and regionally. Locally, if this is to be the case new areas have to be created rapidly before the sea invades and some of the specialist wildlife is left without a home. Such work is beginning to be carried out locally, but whether the Cley Reserve can be recreated further inland and a new chapter added to its famous bird watching history remains to be seen. Judging by its much depleted shingle sea-defences, the current chapter is fast coming to a close.

Of course the future for the wildlife of this coast is not all doom and gloom; many of the topics I have covered are included to generate awareness and debate. In the last decade we have seen some dramatic changes in our coastal visitors, most notably in the arrival of little egrets. These small herons have begun to colonise the area and their distinctive white forms are now regularly dotted over the saltmarshes and in the saltwater creeks and harbours. Other birds are gradually beginning to gain a foothold on the coast. Mediterranean gulls – our birds originate from Eastern Europe rather than the Mediterranean – are an increasingly common sight and several pairs have begun to breed. Cettis warblers, although shy and unobtrusive, have very loud, rich, abrupt songs which are starting to ring out from fresh-water marshes. They are very susceptible to hard winters so our current mild climate seems to suit their spread.

It is impossible for me to consider the area's natural history and voice thoughts and fears concerning its future without looking at the threats facing the lives of the local people who have grown up amongst it. This region, its wildlife and the people who live here are an integral part of my life and interests and cannot be viewed in isolation.

The future for the younger generations of the North Norfolk people is as threatened as that of any of the area's wildlife. It would be easy to write at length on this topic as it gives rise to so much anger, despair and frustration locally that it alone produces enough material to fill this book. However, due to the confines of this chapter it must be kept as short and direct as possible. The lack of affordable accommodation for either sale or rent is the fundamental problem for the area's young working residents. Rent and property prices here are dictated largely by London and the south-east.

In such a small island it seems incredible that whole generations of young people, born, growing up and later working in an area of the country they

consider home can't afford to live there. While others, simply because they work in another area of the country, are able to move here and readily buy property. It seems totally unjustified that entire local communities, their traditional culture and local dialects, not just in North Norfolk but in other areas of the United Kingdom, are being eroded away in this manner by seemingly disproportionate wage levels unevenly distributed throughout the country. Surely, young people here who are prepared to, and indeed do work hard should have the opportunity of building a future or starting a family in an area where they were born and have deep roots. Frustration is compounded by the fact that some people are able to buy second homes while local wages do not even enable the purchase of a first one. These problems are further complicated when council housing is sold yet not replaced. The properties available for rent by local councils and many housing societies are largely awarded on a points system. Incredibly, workers, whether single or couples, are regarded as having low priority needs and are therefore constantly relegated to the bottom of extremely long waiting lists. Unfortunately, no matter how the current situation is viewed, the future looks pretty bleak for young local workers.

This chapter must conclude with a wider look at the region's future development and appearance in relation to its move towards a more tourist based local economy. Decisions affecting the future use and look of the region will increasingly be made by individuals or people new to the area. There are frequent pleas and suggestions for improving the appearance of the area. Sometimes people should stand back and remind themselves of why they moved here in the first place or why tourists choose to visit. People frequently talk of the area's special charm; much of that charm is that it has not been altered greatly over the last century. The factors which make up this charm are subtle, elusive and very fragile but are certainly worth recognising before they are changed. Of course we need to move with the times and some areas may need improvements and tidying up if they are to become attractive to the new tourist industry. But we need to recognise the area's true assets before they are replaced by thoughtless, universal, 'kit form' flower beds, landscaped seating areas, cream tea parlours, etc. Do we really want to develop theme villages, further small replicas of 'fashionable' London regions or soulless anonymous landscaped sea fronts? Surely it is possible to adapt to a changing, more tourist-based industry without creating a false image? Much of our true history and heritage is deeply rooted in the sea and agriculture. The agriculture is particularly well-represented and is known to many from school textbooks – most notably the Agricultural Revolution.

The history of the coast is equally rich but we need to acknowledge its true roots rather than create a false heritage. Wells for example was traditionally a working port and a small fishing town. It was a hard working community and its appearance was simply that of a very real place, frequently dirty and smelly, as many working ports are, but full of character and tradition. This is what people have come to love and expect from the area as it has retained a genuine feel, free from the pretence of many other coastal areas of the country, which have been so overly manicured and prettified that they have lost their identity and heritage.

Wells should be recognised for its true and fascinating history, a working quay with fishing boats, boiling sheds and coasters unloading their cargo and catches onto carts, vans, lorries and at one time railways. A heritage recorded and documented in wonderful photographs. This is the true and real past and surely if we are looking to develop the area's history for a tourist economy we should concentrate on these facts rather than create some romantic myth of past life. But why should we be looking to turn this place into a museum bringing in old redundant boats that have no connection to the area when we have an existing real life, working fishing fleet that, when unloading catches on the quay, brings people here in droves?

It may be an everyday occurrence here but we need to remember that this is what visitors find fascinating and actually come here for. The same phenomenon is hardly likely to be expected when a large yacht arrives and is being moored. Ultimately the most important point for people to think about and keep at the forefront of their minds when making decisions is that, once places are changed and tidied up too much, the irreplaceable charm and authenticity is lost forever. Just take a look at the long, anonymous and almost uniform looking seafronts of the south coast of England or the rather soulless cream tea invasion of the south west. Do we really want to head that way when we have such a unique history and living charm? Sometimes decision makers miss the obvious, that the attractiveness of an area to visitors is simply that it hasn't been overly changed or thoughtlessly developed.

The future of North Norfolk is changing rapidly. A lot of careful thought and planning must go in to how the region, its people and its wildlife are able to cope with these changes. The future economic prosperity of the region comes largely in the form of tourism. Hopefully the area can adapt to this industry without losing too much of its charm, its traditions, and its natural beauty. Protection of the area's wildlife and habitats will continue to be of great importance. Some new ideas, however, may need to be formulated if the wildlife of the region as a whole is to flourish. Certain aspects, for example migratory birds, may need more global thought and help. What deeply saddens me is that unless drastic changes are made to address the current lack of affordable housing for local residents, many Norfolk people of my generation and younger will not be able to continue to live here,and be unable to play a role in future decision - making concerning a place many will always regard as home.

A Sense of Community

Janet Beckett

Y ou don't have to be an artist to be struck by the vibrant colours of barns, cottages, fieldscapes, heaths and woodlands that have attracted artists to this area for centuries. But its unique quality does not come from beauty alone. There is also a sense of community that many parts of the country have lost.

As a child I lived in several different parts of England and after the age of twenty moved from county to county but rarely experienced the sense of belonging and of being cared about I have experienced here.

It is generally accepted that East Anglians resist change and have an almost pathological distrust of new fangled ideas they know are likely to be ephemeral and are probably worthless. This mistrust of fashion and of change for change's sake accounts for the preservation of the landscape and of many sound standards and social and family values. There are likely to be as many people in North Norfolk who are computer literate and make full use of modern technology as in any other part of the British Isles. But there are also many who make great efforts to pass on the timeless traditions of work and society to new generations.

Areas not on main routes to somewhere else have strong individuality. This part of Norfolk has been off the track of marching armies and travellers for centuries. Traders made great use of routes from King's Lynn, Norwich and the East Coast ports but this windswept and dangerous north-facing coast was not part of the network of free flowing communications radiating to and from London. Its inhabitants battled with the coast and weather adapting their own philosophy and passing wisdom and knowledge of their environment to their successors.

These 'end of the world' places often allow individualism to develop and are tolerant of eccentricities. Those who have revelled in the rainbow decorated houses of Provincetown, Cape Cod and accepted the gay and lesbian communities there will know that differences can enrich the population. The shipping that came to this coast until the last century brought contact with other cultures and countries, broadening the ideas of the people in the ports.

Despite these outgoing contacts, people in this area tended to stay put and to make a living out of the land or the sea. On the 1668-9 map of the Manor of Wells the names of the owners of the ships and the land are the familiar ones of Frary,

Janet Beckett

Janet Beckett was born in Kent and lived in six other counties before coming to Wells in 1972 where she taught English at the Alderman Peel School (to, among others, two other contributors to this book). She began to paint in her spare time, becoming a full-time artist twelve years later. Her paintings are very popular with local people as well as visitors and now hang in many parts of the world. Reviewing one of her exhibitions, the critic reported a remark he'd overheard from a Norfolk sage who said, 'When you look at one of her paintings you don't think "That might be Wells". You say "Blast, that is Wells".' She rates it as her highest tribute.

Janet's drawings decorate the book – along with those of Keith McDougall.

King, Dobbs, Tidd, Leech, whose descendents are still found in the current telephone directory.

This continuity of families through generations means that many people are related to each other, sharing characteristics and memories which bind them together. It pays to think before you criticise someone local as you are bound to be speaking about a relative of your listener who will soon put you right on your facts.

A tremendous contribution to the community bond in this area is the link with the sea. Despite the visual beauty of pale gold beaches, windswept marram grass, slaty grey creeks and the haze of sea lavender, it remains, always, powerful.

Jack Cox, Wells fisherman and renowned artist, summed up his deep association with the sea when interviewed by Sally Festing (*Fishermen*):

> I respect the sea... you've certainly got to respect it. You're only a puny thing, only a small thing you know. It's much bigger than you are. There's an old saying the fishermen used to have in Sheringham, 'You watch and pray.' I think a lot of people go through life and they don't have anything that brings them down to size do they? It's the job that counts. If you're a coal miner, I think that brings you down to size in the same way. Quite a lot, I should imagine. In a storm you get more or less excited. You're like a dog running about in rough weather. The sea is glorious. But it's like a woman isn't it? Full of moods.

Jack's words about the sea bringing you down to size are meaningful. No one can be arrogant about their own self-importance when faced with the power of the sea. This has always been a dangerous stretch of coast with shifting sand-banks and ever changing channels. Several ports have dangerous bars across their harbour mouths. It is often subject to fierce on-shore winds as the twisted trees, shorn on their seaward side, so clearly witness. Scouring tides and dramatic erosion also bring constant change. The only certainty is that nothing will stay the same. This is why the sea and its moods affects the whole mentality of the community. It gets under your skin. You're always aware of it, reading its mood. Like a love affair it gives you the best and the worst but it always matters.

The fierce independence and self-reliance of those who work at sea or on the

marsh was put into words by Philip Green of Stiffkey when talking to Sally Festing:

> If you go inland to any little village or any little town how much room have you got to manouvre? It might be a little park, a little bit of green, a couple of square yards and you're on someone else's property. Here what you've got is right of way from Wells East Hills through to Blakeney, h'aint you? All that ground that you can call your own. I can use it just as my own. I can shoot on it, wander about on it, sit down on it, take whoever I like on it. There's no restrictions. And there's so many things to see and explore and find, each day is different. You see, being next the sea, the whole damn thing is changing.

This strong-minded sense of freedom makes the locals obstinate but intensely loyal. They value quality of life as well as outward show. They are often unimpressed by worldly wealth and can cut through pretence or pomposity with ruthless wit. Anyone who dismisses the local people as rustics had better beware the oblique but deadly put-down which often dents an inflated ego. This well developed sense of humour and ability to get through to essential values helps the bulk of local people to accept and welcome the incomers. Before I moved to Norfolk I was warned to expect deep reserve from the natives. This was far from the reality. Within days we were shown amazing kindness. My children made friends at school. I met other mums at the school gates. Shopkeepers trusted us to have goods on approval and we were helped in our search for somewhere to live.

I have heard a few people complain about the abrupt manners and hostile attitudes of local people. But the complainers invariably turn out to be harking back to some virtue of their home area, comparing Norfolk unfavourably. We who live locally can bewail the lack of petrol stations, civic amenities, banks, cheap food and transport but bitterly resent being told, 'The prices here are a rip-off. I can buy that at half the price in Leicester.' The response is usually, 'Go back to Leicester then.'

Local clubs and organisations are almost exclusively organised and run by incomers. The mutterings about newcomers taking over the town stem from the evidence that they run the social life and are represented on the councils and committees. A local friend who takes an intelligent and lively interest in everything that happens in Wells often criticises the incomers who 'organise everything'. When asked, 'You've got some really good ideas why don't you get on the Council?' he replied, 'Well you just don't do that do you?' This self-effacement or apathy creates a gulf between locals and incomers that takes some bridging. This is certainly an area where more active participation by locals could benefit themselves and the incomers.

In this place there is very little chance of anyone being alone and friendless as is often the case in cities and urban environments. Within a day or two your face is recognised by shopkeepers, postal workers, dog walkers and the jungle drums will ensure that the jigsaw of fragments of information is put together. If you respond with friendliness acceptance will follow easily. There are strong family bonds and relationships here and establishing a friendship with someone often means you are quickly accepted by their friends and families.

This network of information does cause gossip. And misinformation travels like a bush fire. My late husband died twice according to the town. Everyone was deeply sympathetic when told he had been diagnosed with terminal cancer. A few weeks later some other unfortunate person lost their battle against cancer and probably because my husband was in so many peoples' minds it was assumed he had died. This information was announced at the school where he had been a much-respected teacher and a collection was instigated. It was only when my telephone began to ring and the first sympathy cards plopped on the doormat that I could go out in to town to correct the story.

In that incident it is easy to understand how the rumour began but in many cases there is scarcely a link to connect the story with reality. When a friend disappeared from the town with the utmost secrecy I knew she was fleeing to a refuge for battered wives. Within a day or two I had heard several stories to account for the fact she was missing. 'Her mother is ill and she's gone to look after her'… 'She's gone on holiday with a disabled friend'.…'Her brother had a serious operation on his eye and she's gone to help him organise his home better so he can manage independently.'

These notions seemed to have been plucked out of the air but each was told with tremendous conviction. It certainly pays to wait a while before believing or passing on what you have heard. A year or so ago, a new housing development was started on the site of a former garage and petrol station in Wells. The old buildings were cleared, footings were dug and cement was poured. Bricklayers began working and the first houses began to rise. Then suddenly, the work stopped. The town was full of rumours that the work had uncovered the remains of an early Saxon church and settlement. The reality – as usual – was that the cash flow had temporarily stopped flowing.

This sort of gossip is not of the malicious variety that sometimes mars the lives of people in small villages where everyone is almost too aware of their neighbours' lives. It is no more than lively speculation and an embroidery of facts that enriches rather than damages. And even if you have behaved scandalously you will not be in the forefront of everyone's attention for long. Your story will fade as soon as another one comes along. Like a family we can discuss each other's inadequacies but become tight lipped and reserved when strangers criticise us or try to winkle stories from us.

Also like a family, we are aware of each other's grief and unlike the scandal the support given is not short lived. When my deeply loved partner Lionel Fortescue and his younger friend William Cracknell were drowned in December 1999, the whole town was shaken to its core. William was recovered from the sea on the evening of the day they set off to bring a dinghy round to Wells from Burnham Overy Staithe. Lionel's body was found still held up by his lifejacket six days later on December 22nd.

Visitors to Wells could hardly credit the difference in the town. Everyone was quiet and withdrawn and the sense of loss affected the whole community. I know that William's family and mine were helped through this awful period by the sure and certain knowledge that everyone was caring about our loss and would do anything to ease the pain. We in turn have been able to put ourselves in the shoes of others who have had more recent tragedies to bear. It is because we know each other and are unselfconscious about showing that we care that this unique sense of community exists.

It is marvellous to be accepted as part of this fellowship but it is not enough to merely absorb its benefits without wondering why it works here but is dying elsewhere. I have mentioned several characteristics like the essential values brought about by harsh but simple life in this area, its tolerance of newcomers as long as they are not pompous and pretentious and the willingness to be involved in other people's lives.

These aspects of society have continued for centuries. They remain strong despite the influx of newcomers. Men of this coastal area will continue to fish, worm-dig, use the marsh and shore. As Philip Green said, 'I can shoot on it,

wander about on it, sit down, take whoever I like on it.'

It is vital that this great wilderness of saltmarsh retains this openness so that its freedom can be enjoyed by those who appreciate it. But it must be protected from pollution and other destructive forces. We must be prepared not to merely defend but actually participate in protecting what we value in the environment. Those who have grown up here and have a lifetime's knowledge of the area are the experts whose practical knowledge should be blended with the scientific viewpoint of the professional environmentalists.

Change will come. You can't stay with the old ways while life around you is moving on. We all know that house prices have escalated so that young couples find it harder to find a property they can afford. The other side of the coin is that all the householders in this area have benefited from the increased value of their properties. Those from the South where property values are high cannot be barred from coming to live here. Perhaps their increased spending power will eventually raise the average wage in East Anglia a little nearer that of some of the areas from which incomers come. We must work to use the talents and skills of newcomers so that they are motivated to protect the best of this locality. It's no good backing off and moaning about their presence and their 'take over' of this desirable coastal strip. I apologise for speaking of newcomers when I have only lived here for thirty years – which makes me a newcomer too and means that when I am asked if I am local I always say, 'I'm not locally born but I do live here.'

There are many places in England, particularly in scenic rural areas, where young people struggle to gain a foothold in the housing market. A second home bought for whatever reason has to be classed as a luxury. Many of these properties stand empty for the bulk of the year. Having been on the verge of homelessness myself, unable to scrape together a deposit or raise a mortgage and drawing a blank on houses to rent, I can sympathise with the aggressive feelings of the 'have nots'.

I would not be keen on legislation like that being mooted in the New Forest National Park where newcomers must have family connections with the area and must establish residency for a period of years before being able to purchase or build a property. That would not fit in with the sense of freedom and independence that is so strong in this area. I would rather see a heavy tax levied on second homes and the money raised spent on affordable housing for local youngsters. No doubt a fairly hefty tax burden would persuade some second property owners to cut their losses and sell, thus releasing a few more houses which might then be bought by some of the local people who have ambitions to own their homes.

Luckily, most of the new building and any alterations which require planning permission are being constructed to fit in with and enhance the environment. Our planning officers and the conservationists are doing their utmost to keep the 'infilling' of villages and towns here as harmonious as possible. The mushrooming of so many towns in other areas is alarming: Poole, Market Harborough, Swindon, Reading….the examples are endless.

Nearer to home we all notice the estates at King's Lynn marching relentlessly towards the bypass. In the main, much of our local development has been infilling. A part of the Wells school playing field has been built on. The old railway yard is an industrial estate. A garage becomes the site for several new houses. We can look at the town from any angle as we approach it and see the clean-cut boundaries with which we are all familiar. We are also looking, in the main, at boundaries that have stayed the same within most peoples' memories.

Part of the closeness locally is that we all shop in the same area. We know and are known by the staff. We meet constantly and find almost all our requirements are met by the family-run businesses in the main street. We have so far resisted having a large supermarket built here. It may create some employment but would also cause unemployment because some of the existing shops would not be able to compete. The luxury of having your groceries delivered promptly and willingly is an asset not frequently found in this bustling modern world. The staff training schemes for supermarket employees teaching them how to project a friendly and caring relationship with the customer is unnecessary here. We already know each other and benefit from affection that is genuine.

I find this area scenically captivating. But even more important it is an area where people know and care for each other. I can go out every day with my paper and paints and try to create an image of this place but its elusive magic is as much in the people as in large and dramatic skies and windswept marshes. Some change, we must accept, is as inevitable as the ebb and flow of the tide. But we must fight to defend the uniqueness of this locality. We cannot and should not 'raise the drawbridge' against newcomers but should encourage and instil in them the love we all have for this area. Locals must not sit back and moan about change but must be actively involved so that their knowledge and expertise can benefit the future. We owe it to the people who have lived here in the past and we must preserve it so that our children and grandchildren can benefit from living in or visiting this place.

The Story of the Golden Goose

Jim Ring

This precious stone set in a silver sea,
Which serves it in the office of a wall,
Or as a moat defensive to a house,
Against the envy of less happier lands....

Richard II

Transport was the making of the Saltmarsh Coast and will likewise be its undoing. The wealth created by the ability to move goods and people relatively easily generated many of the qualities that draw visitors to the coast and keep its residents transfixed by its subtle beauties; yet as communications improve they destroy much that makes the coast unique. 'It is important that Norfolk's beautiful coastline, historic towns and villages and wide empty landscapes are not spoilt by the very people who come to see them', wrote Susanna Wade Martins twenty years ago in *A History of Norfolk*. This is the conundrum that has to be solved if our children and grandchildren are to have the inheritance they demand and – when they behave – deserve.

Transport is the enhancement of human movement. It began in pre-history with the saddling of the horse and the camel, and has so far progressed – via the miracles of the steam age – to space flight. It promotes the development of social, political and commercial links, paves the way for the glories of trade, and lets each particular area produce whatever it produces best. Yet there is more to transport than this. As George Stephenson's biographer L.T.C. Rolt wrote of the advent of railways:

No other invention had such an overwhelming effect on society as this first form of mechanical transport...we have since conquered the road and the air with newer forms of power...but no subsequent development has equalled in significance or in sheer impact on the imagination this first mighty stride which took man from a secure and settled environment hallowed by centuries into a new, exciting yet disturbing world which at once opened up

Jim Ring

Jim Ring's first book, the *Financial Times*'s standard textbook on the advertising industry (*Advertising on Trial,* 1993) was translated into Spanish, Italian and Turkish. *Erskine Childers*, a biography of the author of the classic thriller, *The Riddle of the Sands*, followed in 1996 and won the Marsh Prize. *How the English Made the Alps* appeared in 2000 and in paperback in 2001 which also saw *We Come Unseen*, a study of Britain's Cold War submariners which won the Mountbatten Prize and formed the basis for Anglia TV's critically acclaimed documentary *Submarine*. *Riviera*, a history of the Cote d'Azur was published in 2004. Married with two children, Jim learned to sail on the Norfolk Broads and first visited North Norfolk in the early 'sixties. He bought a cottage in the Burnhams in 1989 and has lived there with his family for the last seven years.

limitless possibilities. The railway train was the harbinger of this brave new world.

Transport is one the stepping-stones of civilisation, moving men's hearts and minds as well as their dusty bodies. Who knows where it will take man a century hence?

Transport has shaped much of the coast visible today. In the Middle Ages, Norfolk derived its prosperity principally from wool and cloth, produce that was taken by road and coaster to markets elsewhere in England, and by sea going craft to the Continent. This wealth enabled communities dating back to Roman times to replace dwellings of wood or wattle & daub with those of brick, flint and chalk that now characterise the area. It is not for nothing that the phrase 'wool churches' was coined. The towers of Cley, Wiveton, Brancaster and many besides are testimonies to wool as much as to faith; and it was the sheep magnates who likewise built great houses like East Barsham Hall. The agricultural revolution in which Norfolk played such a part would have been still-born if the fruits of Townshend's and Coke's labours had not been able to reach the Smithfield markets. It is to this that we owe Holkham Hall, the enclosure of acre after acre of common land, the draining of the marshes, and the transformation of a place like Burnham Market from a rabble of thatched cottages into an elegant Georgian village. By the end of the 18th century the coast's ports were exporting to Holland more grain than the whole of the rest of England. This gave us the maltings of Thornham, Brancaster, Overy, Wells and Blakeney, pantiled roofs and crow-stepped gables. The development of turnpike roads and the era of the stage-coach saw the building or enlargement of coaching inns like the Hoste in Burnham Market and the Crown in Fakenham. It was the coming of the railway to the coast in the 1860s that opened up a national market for perishables, enabling Wells to exploit the shellfish beds along the coast, leading to a vogue in London for 'Stiffkey Blues'. Later, milk was steamed into the fast-developing urban markets; and it was rail that facilitated the development of the Holkham brick kilns and the local sugar beet industry. The railway enabled Yarmouth and Cromer to flourish as holiday resorts, their visitors spilling into the coast. Sheringham and new Hunstanton were virtually creations of the railway; the railway engineering works of Melton Constable entirely so. It was the railway that permitted the development of the coast between the wars, particularly the Midland and Great Northern line, which brought visitors in substantial numbers from the Black Country. During the last thirty years, the national and local road network has enabled visitors to continue to reach the coast with relative ease. It is – in short – to transport that the coast owes much of its appearance and most of its wealth.

The coast would still exist if the sail, the wheel, the steam and internal combustion engines had never been invented, yet it would not look, feel, or be the same. Without transport, we would not have Felbrigg, Blakeney church, Overy boathouse or Cley mill; the uplands would still be yellow gorse heaths like Kelling or Brancaster; Burnham Market, Cley, Stiffkey, Blakeney, Walsingham, Wells, the Creakes and Brancaster would not be the gems of colloquial architecture that their hearts remain. This matters because the qualities many find so appealing in the coast don't lie simply in the wilderness of the marshes, in the shrill cry of the oyster-catcher, in the beat of sea on shingle, in the big skies and the rolling landscapes. It lies also in those features that evince the hand of man: the flint churches and chalk cottages, the great barns, maltings and fragile windmills, the footpaths, tracks and roads, the hedges, holts and coppices; fields of wheat, barley, rape and rye: in a flourishing rural community that dates back more than a millennium, where each generation has left traces of its passing.

Yet if the character of the coast has been shaped by the existence of transport to and within the area, it's also been affected by the very limitations of that system. It used to be said that Norfolk was isolated from the rest of England on three sides by the sea and on the fourth by its railways. Certainly in the absence of any major centres of population, there was no demand for a dense railway network. It's significant that the railway ran along the coast not at all, and touched it only at Wells and Sheringham. The line from the Midlands – nicknamed the Muddle and Go-Nowhere – was notoriously badly run. Norfolk has no motorways and the roads serving the coast should be designated second or even third class. Calling the A149 along the coast an A road is a misnomer. This has been fortunate. It has been very difficult for large numbers of people to descend simultaneously on the coast in the way that they engulf the Lake District on bank holiday weekends; and there has been little need to develop an infrastructure to cope with them by way of the hotels, restaurants, car parks, supermarkets, fast food chains and amusement arcades that characterise many coastal resorts. Think Great Yarmouth or Skegness. Particularly over the last few years, this wonderful coast has been saved from itself by the very deficiencies of the transport system.

This won't last. Even in the quarter of a century since I first visited the coast, it has changed considerably in terms of its inhabitants, its homes, the shops, in the number and nature of visitors, indeed in the economy as a whole. I have seen it change from a small working class agricultural community distinctly linked to its past to one dominated by tourism and tourists, second-home owners (of whom I was one), and the cosmopolitan upper middle-classes. These developments are dealt with elsewhere in this book. What concerns me here is the way in which the North Norfolk coast is now being destroyed by lorries and cars, and what we should do about it.

Seventy-five years ago Evelyn Waugh wrote, 'There are very few roads in Europe now where one can walk without a furtive circumspection; one may sing away for a mile or so, then there is a roar at ones heels and one is forced to leap for the gutter in a cloud of dust.' Then there were something like 2 million private cars in Great Britain; today there are close to ten times that figure. Like the country as a whole, the coast is being slowly strangled by the tentacles of the road network, and by the car itself.

Take two of the roads that form the ultimate boundaries of the coast, the stretch of the A149 from Lynn to Hunstanton, and the A148 from Lynn to Cromer, the roads that enclose the magic triangle. Once, these were pleasant examples of county highways, narrow carriageways roaming the undulating countryside of high Norfolk, following the contours of the land, twisting and turning with the idiosyncrasies of streams, land ownership, the pull of a village here, another there. They could carry relatively few cars, and those cars – Morris Minors and Austin Cambridges – could be driven only slowly. The roads had character, they blended in with the landscape and, like almost all roads – with the exception of motorways – they had the promise of the infinite:

One road leads to London
One road leads to Wales
My road leads me seawards
To the white dipping sails.

Then they were improved; or, as it so turned out, worsened. They were widened, some of the kinks were taken out, and in some places on the A149 an additional

carriageway was introduced. As anyone who has tried to drive back from the coast to Lynn on a Sunday afternoon will testify, the result has not been the elimination of traffic jams; as the police remark, neither has it seen the elimination of accidents. Over short stretches cars can be driven faster and more people can pile into Hunstanton and Cromer more rapidly than could otherwise have been the case. This is progress.

An ever-increasing number of these cars then find their way onto the coast road and heading for Thornham, Brancaster, Burnham Market, Wells, the Creakes, Stiffkey, Blakeney and Cley. The coast is lucky that the stretch of A149 from Hunstanton to Weybourne has seen so little of the highways authority's attention. It is narrow, unobtrusive, in parts positively attractive, and generally of a standard to restrict drivers who possess any common sense to an absolute maximum of 50 mph. Nevertheless, the weight of traffic it carries on summer weekends means that you sometimes think it needs traffic lights, sleeping policemen and pedestrian crossings: on a typical summer's day at least 4000 cars go through Morston, 5000 through Brancaster, forcing pedestrians and cyclists into the gutter. A very fair number of those cars end up in Burnham Market, quite a few in Wells, Blakeney and Cley. In summer, and increasingly at other times of the year, these places are being drowned in traffic. According to Nikolaus Pevsner, Burnham Market boasted 'a handsome broad village street leading from the Church to the Hall....several notable Georgian houses and not a cottage that does serious damage'. Today it is little more than a car park for BMWs and Mercedes on day-release from the Boltons. Wells, with far greater space at its disposal, has managed the problem slightly better. The car-park by the Ark Royal pub keeps a fair number of cars away from the more attractive parts of the town, but car-parking on the quay and the Buttlands is grotesque. In Blakeney, the park by the British Legion is a model in so far as it is virtually unnoticeable, but the east end of the quay which doubles as a car park in the summer brings all the joys of a visit to Tesco to the prospect of the marshes out to Blakeney Point. Then there are the lorries. The booming sugar-beet industry sees roads intended for driving sheep given over for six months of the year to monstrous 38 tonne sixteen-wheelers taking the crop down for processing at Wissington. The drivers are clearly paid by the load.

As the county council observed six years ago in its transport strategy for the coast, 'There are clearly severe and growing traffic problems, largely associated with the seasonal influx of visitors to the area.' Cars, motorbikes and lorries bring visual, aural and chemical pollution, they bring widespread unease, occasional fear, and periodic mutilation and death. It's inaccurate to say that – at present – they dominate the coast; but they dominate certain parts of it at certain times, and they are far more intrusive than ten or even five years ago. At best they detract from, at worst they destroy the place. Precisely what Susanna Wade Martins feared twenty years ago has come to pass: the coast is being destroyed by the very people who come to enjoy its charms – or if not the people, their cars. As a littoral, in 1968 it was rightly designated an Area of Outstanding Natural Beauty (AONB). Its subsequent destruction at the hands of the internal combustion engine is a disgrace, a reproach to a county and country that presumably regards itself as civilized.

Mere recognition of the problem is not enough. The challenges posed to the coast by the car were obvious enough when the AONB was established, and it required no Galileo or Einstein to spot them. When I moved here ten years ago as a more or less permanent resident, there was plenty of talk about the problem. The talking has continued, the roads get busier and busier, and almost nothing is done: by the local council, the highways' authority; the local amenity societies, the police, community leaders, public benefactors, those actually supposed to be managing the AONB, the lot of them. Worthy documents like the transport strategy and the AONB management plan are generated at public expense, 30 mph signs erected on grass tracks (at Burnham Overy Town two years ago), and the local bus service somewhat improved. That's about it. Nothing will come of nothing.

Actually, it's arguable that the policy of doing nothing is a policy in its own right and it may be quite a tenable one. Some years ago academic studies showed very clearly that the widening of roads, improvement of junctions, provision of motorways and so on did little to 'solve' traffic congestion. For a short time after a new road was opened, it provided a degree of local relief to congestion; then the new road simply filled up. Roads create traffic. As organisations like Friends of the Earth have repeatedly pointed out, schemes like the widening of the M25 would improve traffic flow if the numbers of cars using it remained constant; but as the roads 'improve', the number of cars using them increases. The same argument applies to the A149. The stretch from Lynn to Hunstanton was a very busy road before it was widened. It now carries more cars but it is still a very busy road. The stretch from Hunstanton to Weybourne along the coast is busy at times and in places; if it was 'improved' it would still be busy at times and in places, though more cars would use it. Such expenditure of public money would not very clearly benefit the individual motorist, nor would it enhance the amenities of the coast. In fact, it would do precisely the reverse – as the county council has belatedly recognised.

Likewise Burnham Market, at the heart of the coast. There is no reason to suppose that the provision of a proper car park would solve its traffic problems. At present the congestion in the summer presumably discourages people from driving into the village and attempting to park there. If they could do so easily, then more of them doubtless would, and the place would become even more like Bluewater. The traffic 'system', as it stands, is effectively self-regulating. The capacity of the coast's roads and car parks is close to its peak, and once that peak has been reached the number of visitors will flatten off and the traffic problem, though very considerable, will become not significantly worse than it is today.

This is a tenable but courageous argument. Leaving aside macro-economic factors like a slump, bubonic plague or nuclear war, it is reasonable to expect visitor numbers to the coast to continue to grow both during and outside the summer season, and those visitors – the vast majority of whom arrive in their own cars – are putting increasing pressure on the environment. Which means that – as well as money – they bring noise, litter, petrol fumes, traffic jams and dogs' mess to the coast. The limitations of the road system may keep this growth down to manageable levels, but it may not. If it doesn't, then the coast will undoubtedly be destroyed.

In which case a more radical solution to the transport problem than the policies of the county council and those nominally responsible for the AONB needs be developed.

In the past, transport systems have been developed in response to demand: the requirement to move goods more cheaply from Liverpool to Manchester, the desire of the travelling public to cross the Atlantic in five hours rather than five days, or to bypass the centre of King's Lynn. Just such wants and needs are to be found on the coast because plenty of people either want or need to visit it. The provision of a transport system meeting these needs has generally been seen as socially and economically desirable in itself. If the road's too busy, widen it. However, where the system and its users have a patently damaging effect, when the economically desirable becomes the socially undesirable, it's time to call a halt. Rather, we should create a transport system not intended to service demand to whatever level it grows, but only to a level acceptable or – in fashionable parlance – sustainable. There can be few objective measure of what *is* sustainable, but as the Norfolk Coast Project discovered in 1997, there are plenty of people who think the levels of tourism on the coast are no longer so. In particular they feel that the 'peace and tranquility' they recognise as the area's chief attraction is being threatened, principally – they say – by the traffic.

Now the council's so-called Visitor Management Strategy has not chosen to tackle this problem by attempting to reduce the number of visitors. 'It is recognised,' it states, 'that the tourism industry is of very great value, in terms of jobs and income, to the economy of the AONB and its adjacent towns.' Rather, it has chosen to try to get people out of their cars and onto public transport, horses, bicycles or their own two feet. Has it got it right? Who would benefit from there being more visitors? Not the residents in general, who seem to feel that there are enough already. Certainly not the locals, whose children discover when they want to leave home that they can no longer afford to buy a house around here. Not the visitors themselves, who are finding it increasingly difficult to find a place to park, buy their ice-creams, watch the lapwings, and walk their retrievers in peace. In fact the only people who would benefit are those directly or indirectly dependent on tourism: hoteliers, publicans, restaurateurs and some of the builders and retailers. Even for them, the issue should lie as much in what visitors spend as how many of them there are. In the late 'seventies the city of Nice on the Cote d'Azur decided to attract business travellers on the grounds that they spent several times more on their visits than tourists. Today the argument would also be that fewer – richer – visitors put less pressure on the environment. On our own coast, fewer tourists – and fewer cars – means a better place to live, to work, and even to visit. More visitors and more cars means nothing less than ending up with a coast that's not worth living in, working in, or anybody taking the trouble to visit. It's time to curb visitor numbers, time to come clean about the cholera, marsh fever, and the other endemic, ineradicable and often fatal diseases that plague the coast.

And as the council actually does recognise, it's also time to get visitors (and locals) out of their cars. Principally – it thinks – by improving public transport. The evidence suggests, though, that this is only a partial solution. Despite the provision of community bus services and the heavily subsidized coast service, the vast majority of visitors prefer the convenience of their own cars, in which padded cells they can come and go as they please, listening to Meat Loaf. It would be desirable if they abandoned their cars on the fringes of the coastal area, but I don't believe they are going to do so voluntarily in significant numbers. Neither, as it turns out, does the council. In 1998 it set a tentative target for a mere 10% fall in peak (August) traffic along the coast road between 1997 and – wait for it – 2010. To date, traffic levels have of course grown. The solution to our increasingly dire problems has to be much more draconian. We should simply ban visitors' cars entirely from the AONB.

The coast is fortunate in that it is a relatively discrete, well-defined area, bounded by the sea to the North, the stretch of A149 from Lynn to Hunstanton to the east and the A148 from Lynn to Cromer to the south. All the roads east of the A149 and North of the A148 should be closed to visitors, similarly the A149 itself from Hunstanton to Cromer. This would effectively seal off the coast – much as it was during the Second World War. Visitors would be allowed into what would amount to an *enclave* as pedestrians, cyclists, and users of public transport in the form of an improved bus services, a re-introduced rail network, and by boat.

Buses need no further explanation, although the road system itself does. No 'improvement' schemes – new roads, junctions, roundabouts, etc. – would be countenanced; those less frequented roads in the immediate interior should be allowed to revert to cart-tracks and banned to vehicular traffic; certain roads should be restricted to pedestrians and bicycles, augmenting the 'green roads' already instituted; there would be a blanket speed limit throughout the area of 50 mph, 20 mph in all villages. Much of this, curiously enough, the council already has in hand. Second, rail. Currently the coast is not serviced directly at all by the

national rail system other than at Sheringham. Trains remain good means of mass transport, aesthetically acceptable, relatively economic, relatively 'green'. The reinstatement of the line from Lynn to Hunstanton has long been mooted. It has the potential to take a good deal of pressure off the A149, and could do something to revive a festering resort. Similarly, restoring the line from Dereham to Fakenham would provide access from the south and east, and also help promote the town. These would be relatively small projects. A more ambitious scheme would be to re-open the West Norfolk Railway that ran from Heacham to Docking, Burnham Market and Wells; and the MGN from Lynn to the existing terminus of the private North Norfolk Railway at Holt. Third, the sea. Given the very existence of the sea and the coast's maritime heritage, it is surprising how poorly the coast is served by boat. The coast is difficult to navigate and most of its harbours are only accessible when the tide is in. Nevertheless, as a means of providing visitors with alternative ways of enjoying the coast, the maritime option has to be explored.

Is this a madcap proposal, or something desirable, legal, practicable, sensible and affordable?

It's certainly desirable. The coast really has reached the point at which the qualities that appeal to visitors – let alone residents – are being grossly compromised by the visitors. If it wasn't for these tourists, plenty of locals wouldn't have jobs, most would be poorer, and none of us would enjoy things like the butchers, bakers and candlestick-makers in an area without the density of population to support them in the twenty-first century. But enough is enough.

It may well be legal to close the access roads. A public road is a public road, but in 2000 the Countryside and Rights of Way Act made special provision to enable traffic regulation orders to be made for the purpose of conserving an area's natural beauty...to amend the law relating to nature conservation and the protection of wildlife; to make further provision with respect to areas of outstanding natural beauty; and for connected purposes.' An open sesame for all those QCs with fourth homes on the coast.

It would certainly be practicable to distinguish between visitors cars and those of residents. This is already done in London for the purposes of the congestion charge.

Establishing proper public transport on the coast would scarcely be cheap, but visitors bring a great deal of money into the area. According to the AONB partnership, a study four years ago suggested that annual visitors to six of the coast's nature reserves spent £5.3 million a day and £20.8 million on the whole trip. At the time, the Holkham reserve itself was attracting almost three-quarters of a million visitors a year. Clearly these comprise only a proportion of the visitors, and only a proportion of the £millions spent on the coast every year.

Ambitious though it might seem, integrated transport systems of this nature have operated for decades in more advanced European countries like Austria, Germany and Switzerland.

It won't happen today or even tomorrow, but it could happen.

As the country's economy continues to prosper and as the population in the south-east of England continues to grow, more and more people are going to want to live on, work on, and visit our coast. The consequences of this are visible here today and can be seen elsewhere in Europe, the developed and the developing world: the destruction of remote and beautiful places by the people who come to enjoy them. David Bellamy said years ago that the Lake District was being 'loved to death'; the Austrian explorer and mountaineer Heinrich Harrer was told equally sharply by a Himalayan peasant: 'A few tourists are a blessing, many are a pest.'

Change is inevitable but the sort of vandalism we are now seeing, whilst both typical and predictable, may not necessarily come to pass. There are communities that have seen what was happening to them and taken a hand in the change rather than just letting it happen. If you want to visit Zermatt in the Swiss Alps, you leave your car six miles down the valley at Tasch, and go up by railway. When you reach the village electric carts take you to your hotel. There are no cars. In Austria's Kitzbuhel the whole of the medieval old town is closed to traffic after 10.00 in the morning. We can't detach our coast, our precious stone, from the twenty-first century, but because of its relative isolation we can put a wall round it and restore a degree of control over the way in which it changes, and the rapidity of that change. Indeed, the coastal community is now facing the choice between allowing things to continue the way they are, or taking matters into its own hands. If nothing is done the destruction of the coast as a unique habitat, community and landscape is absolutely inevitable. If something is done, there is a chance that its essence may be preserved.

Personally, I think we have no choice.

John Penny

John Penny was born in London in 1943 after an air raid that sent his mother into premature labour. After a village school and a preparatory school, he escaped to Birmingham, Leeds University and the College of the Resurrection at Mirfield. He has served three Curacies, three Incumbencies, Chaplaincies at a Hospital, a Hospice, a Girls' School and a Convent, and for nearly four years was a Diocesan Press Officer. He retired from his North Norfolk parishes in September 2004. His wife Diana was one of the first women to be ordained Priest and was for many years an Open University Tutor.

The Church in North Norfolk

John Penny

'They are all a little eccentric around here; some would say quite mad,' said the Bishop. 'But,' he added, looking me straight in the eye, 'you'll fit in nicely!'

And with that two-edged compliment I became Priest in Charge of the parishes of Binham, Langham, Morston and Stiffkey and later Bale, Field Dalling, Gunthorpe, Saxlingham and Sharrington.

I have been in this post for seven years and it has been a happy and stimulating area in which to minister. But it is demanding; people are very discerning and often highly qualified. Luckily I have a wide and varied experience to support me, having been a Priest in town and city parishes, a girls' school, a hospice and a hospital. I also draw on my own experience of joys and tragedies, so time and time again I am aware that the present harks back to what has gone before.

It was as a child of three that I first wanted to be a priest. But the awareness of a vocation left me until I went to Leeds University to study English. The city was growing and fostered tightly knit communities, but there was poverty such as we do not know in this country today. I astonish people by saying that in 1963 I saw children playing in the snow with nothing on their feet.

As I said, when I first came to North Norfolk I had four parishes, later nine. Like many other clergy, I faced the challenge of ministering to several very different villages, each with its own history and life-style. The 'Multi-Parish Benefice', as it is called, is the order of the day in many rural areas. (The Raveningham Group where I served in the 1980s is now looked after by just one stipendiary cleric.) It provides a challenging ministry, not least when many of the churches want a Communion Service on the same Sunday.

Help comes from Readers, women and men who do many of the things a priest does, but cannot take Communion services. Their ministry is joined by that of the non-stipendiary (unpaid) priests. These clergy fall into two groups; the Ordained Local Ministers (OLMs) who stay in their own parishes and Non-Stipendiary Ministers (NSMs) who minister more widely. Our benefice is fortunate to enjoy the ministry of two NSMs, but no OLMs.

Ordained Local Ministry is centred, as its name suggests, on the parish or benefice of the Locally Ordained Minister. From the start, anyone seeking ordination as an OLM is part of a group of people who both form a Ministry Team and share part of a candidate's training. This link with their own parish or benefice continues if the person is ordained, and only rarely are they asked to minister outside this area.

Candidates for the Non-Stipendiary Ministry have little or no contact with their local parish or benefice. They train with others in a number of schemes operated by the Church of England. When ordained, NSMs begin their ministry in parishes or a benefice other than the one in which they live, though they may eventually find themselves taking services more locally.

Both schemes have tremendous potential, but one has a serious flaw. All candidates for ordination have to attend a Selection Conference before they can begin full training for the ministry. For NSMs, only the parish priest need know the date of the Conference. But for OLM candidates, the date *and* result of the Conference is known to the Ministry Team, and inevitably to the parish or benefice.

If an OLM candidate is not recommended for training, there can be a significant amount of distress and anger on all sides. The candidate believes that he or she has 'failed', and the Ministry Team think their support and recommendation has been ignored.

Sadly, those responsible for communicating the news of the 'failure' have not always appreciated the fragility of the situation. They are frequently high achievers who have never 'failed' anything like a Selection Conference themselves, and may grossly underestimate the pain felt by the candidate and the Ministry Team.

If a candidate is not recommended for training, a Ministry Team is free to present another candidate. This may be difficult; who will come forward and risk a very public humiliation? But if a second person *is* found, and they too are not recommended, the reaction of the parish or benefice may be comprehensively negative and the OLM scheme is dead in the water for a number of years.

There is, nevertheless, still hope that NSMs and OLMs may take the place of a significant number of paid clergy. But the number of candidates presenting themselves for training is less than anticipated, a result, some think, of low age limits and unrealistic academic expectations. In addition, both OLMs and NSMs have found that family life and full-time work leaves them limited time and energy for ministry.

Until more OLM and NSM candidates present themselves, rural dioceses will continue to rely on retired clergy to take Communion services. These retired priests are in fact indispensable. Some take services when a person is ill or on holiday. Others commit themselves to looking after a few parishes in return for free housing and expenses, an arrangement referred to as 'House for Duty'. It is a scheme similar to this that our benefice operates.

We have four retired clergy who minister in our parishes. Each is a homeowner, and all but one live outside the boundaries of the benefice. Each is assigned to a village and takes its service three Sundays out of four, as well as exercising a limited pastoral ministry. While I am recognised as the Incumbent of every parish, the retired priests are seen as 'belonging' in a special way to the community to which they minister.

These retired clergy are much loved, and their influence is out of all proportion to the time they give to parishes. While most clergy today are ordained after some considerable time in a secular job, our retired priests have many years of prayer and experience to bring to their ministry.

The use of retired clergy is not always welcomed in the Church of England. But as financial cuts bite, and fewer and fewer full-time paid clergy can be afforded, their ministry enables worship to continue in areas where financial difficulties are most acute. This is particularly true in the countryside.

There are, however, many people who see a widespread rural ministry as a waste of resources. They wish to promote a radical and aggressive policy of rationalisation, and suggest that a multi-parish benefice should close all but one of it buildings and worship in a single central church.

In practice, this works occasionally, though most of the time it fails because people's religious allegiance is bonded to the local church, the village 'holy place'. A proportion of the congregation may be willing to go elsewhere for a joint service, usually on a fifth Sunday. But this is rarely more than half the regular worshippers; the remainder stays firmly wedded to 'their church' and has a 'Sunday off'.

A policy of centralisation, therefore, may well be self-defeating. Smaller collections from smaller congregations would reduce the money a benefice could raise for parish clergy and diocesan administration (the Share). Worse still, the cost of maintaining closed churches may fall to the diocese, for which the combined effects of mounting repair bills and falling offerings would be ruinous.

Thankfully the church is beginning to see that a sense of 'place' is as important to our relationship with God as a sense of community. John Inge's book *A Christian Theology of Place* emphasises that a person's encounter with God is linked closely with the location of this encounter. Professor Timothy Gorringe in reviewing the work, powerfully endorses Bishop Inge's thesis, saying that the need for 'a new respect for place is vital in a world remorselessly globalised by the big corporations and the new imperialism'.

It therefore makes both financial and theological sense to retain village churches. But the provision of services is still a challenge for many areas. While lay people can take Morning and Evening Prayer, priests are needed for Holy Communion services, and they are in short supply. Many have seven, eight or nine parishes in their care, and not all are blessed with the abundance of retired parsons that we enjoy.

Nevertheless, there are other ways of providing Communion services, preaching, teaching and pastoral care than seeking more stipendiary or retired priests. The New Zealand Diocese of Christchurch has adopted an imaginative scheme called Local Shared Ministry (LSM) for parishes that cannot afford paid clerics. But LSM is not simply about replacing the traditional model of the clergy; it is a new way of thinking about the whole church.

LSM follows the teaching of St Paul, which says that every member of a congregation has some gift that can be used for the Glory of God. It also recognises that the work of taking Communion services, preaching, teaching and pastoral care should be shared. As St Paul says:

> There are varieties of gifts....and varieties of services. Are all apostles? Are all prophets? Are all teachers?

The scheme begins with a visit from a diocesan 'enabler'. She or he explores with the people the way God gives gifts and ministries for the mission and work of the Church. Each individual is encouraged to discover their own gifts. Only then does the congregation pray and 'call' members to a specific ministry.

Those who are nominated share the roles that previously have been given to one person. One or two people are ordained priest and preside at the Eucharist (take the Communion services) and the others are made Deacons. One looks after the pastoral care of a parish, another preaches and teaches and another takes on the parish administration.

Local Shared Ministry enables every member of the congregation to feel that they have something to contribute to the life and witness of the Church. It moves away from a traditional view of ministry, which centres on the clergy, and sometimes on their spouses as well! It enables men and women from the local communities to be ordained Priest in far greater numbers than under the OLM scheme.

Without this or another radical solution, it is possible that a significant number of people will push for Lay Presidency in the Church of England. This enables Communion Services to be taken by members of the local congregation who are not ordained priest. Lay Presidency is totally unacceptable to many, and has been a source of controversy in the Anglican Church in Australia.

For the time being however, maintaining ancient buildings will continue to be the major priority for the rural areas. At the moment, much fund-raising for this work relies on the efforts of a faithful few. Happily, local support is growing, and more and more groups of 'Friends' are raising money for church repairs. Sometimes none of these people would either call themselves 'believers' or worship regularly, but their efforts are heartfelt and generous.

The work of these 'Friends' reflects the way the church plays an important part in the life of a rural community. The school may have gone, the shop closed and pubs no longer serve the host of farm workers who populated many of the

Langham Church

villages. But people still want somewhere to be baptised, married and buried, and, as was found when Princess Diana died, a place where they can go in time of distress.

The church is at the centre of village life; it is the community's 'holy place' in a way that is rarely true of urban areas. Moreover, a rural congregation is often a much higher percentage of the population than that of the town. City parishes of ten to twelve thousand souls may attract congregations of a hundred or so. Benefices like ours, one sixth of the size, see a similar number worshipping each Sunday.

Clergy whose experience and ministerial 'models' come from urban situations, frequently ignore the high proportion of worshippers in the country, and focus on the small congregations and the relatively few people cared for by the incumbent of a rural benefice. To an extent this is justified. In the town, a parson may have over ten thousand people in his or her parish. In the country it is often much less than that.

But this assumes that only Church of England clergy operate in urban situations. In fact, when the work of people from other denominations (ecumenical ministry) is taken into account, a different picture emerges. Although my housing estate parish in Birmingham held twelve thousand people, I was not the only cleric in the area. There was the support and friendship of a Roman Catholic priest, a Methodist minister and the Leader of an Evangelical Church.

The Church of England has rarely recognised this very significant ecumenical ministry in urban areas. Indeed, the report *Faith in the Countryside* was severely critical of the way the Sheffield Report set targets for the number of clergy being deployed in the dioceses. The report is said to have had a 'hidden agenda', and to have ignored the needs of rural areas in favour of those in the towns and cities. The writers of 'Faith in the Countryside' state clearly that in the allocation of clergy to dioceses:

> The ecumenical approach was rejected because it did not assist those who wanted a more urban priesthood. Page 157 paragraph 8.48

Those who favour urban 'models' of ministry frequently ignore other factors at work in the country. In a multi-parish benefice, a priest is in charge of a large number of different communities, while in the town she or he has the care of one. Those who have studied the workings of small groups draw attention to the powerful influences at work in the dynamics of village life.

Knowing which 'language' to 'speak' to people of varying backgrounds and life-styles is very demanding. Moreover the variety of 'hidden agendas' in a number of very different villages, means that a cleric needs the sensitivity to discern the subtle interaction between what people say and do not say!

Keeping up with the many events and meetings in a rural benefice can also be exacting for a country priest. Each parish holds at least five P.C.C. meetings, its own harvest festival and supper, carol service, summer fete and/or a Christmas sale, plus other fund raising events. As well as this, rural parsons have constantly to work in villages with long histories and with people who need time to adjust to what is new. Change can take a lot longer in the country where the 'roots' of the community go very deep and resist disturbance.

This contrasts greatly with urban life where people take change in their stride, and congregations adapt to a new vicar or modern worship relatively quickly. Clergy who have no experience of the country can fail to take the difference into account, and may try to 'bulldozer' their people with disastrous results.

This may explain why so few clergy actively wish to minister in the country. Indeed those wanting an 'ecclesiastical career move' do well to seek positions in towns or cities where they can set an agenda relatively freely and so 'make their mark'.

Rural clergy on the other hand find themselves dealing with a way of life that has been in place for years. Moves to change this can be opposed with fierce and stubborn resistance. The country parson may well have to 'find which way people are walking and follow them!'

Salthouse

Small wonder that until recently much of the planning carried out in the Church of England seemed to focus on urban ministry. The excellent report 'Faith in the Countryside' attracted far less attention than its predecessor, 'Faith in the City', and some clergy have gone so far as to advocate a wholesale retreat from rural ministry.

But rural parishes have much to offer and the Church of England needs to value and cherish them. The parishioners are unsung heroes, deeply committed to the care of their churches, and the country's heritage. Wardens, secretaries, treasurers, members of the Parochial Church Councils and an army of helpers, regularly shoulder huge responsibilities.

I am very lucky in having a large number of retired people in our parishes. These highly trained professional people have for years used their professional skills to serve the church and community. But gradually, fewer volunteers are coming forward to take on their responsibilities. Indeed in some Parishes it is impossible to find anyone who will stand as warden, PCC treasurer or secretary, because the demands on their time and energy have increased enormously.

Our benefice, with a population of fewer than two thousand people, and one hundred and forty regular worshippers, has to maintain nine ancient churches and raise a Share of over fifty thousand pounds a year. Each parish has to comply with the requirements of the Charity Commissioners, child protection policies, disability legislation, risk assessments and so on. People who were hoping to enjoy a relatively quiet retirement are reluctant to take on these considerable burdens, and no wonder.

For those unacquainted with the recent changes, it is difficult to appreciate what a nightmare paper work can become. Two of the most intelligent, conscientious and diligent P.C.C. secretaries I know were driven almost to distraction by the correspondence made necessary by relatively few repairs to a church.

A radical simplification of procedures is necessary if P.C.C.s are faithfully to comply with diocesan regulations as the temptation to ignore them is, for some, irresistible. But unlike the Church in New Zealand, a web of regulations traps the Church of England. Andrew Bowden says that while the C. of E. is bound up with red tape, the New Zealand Church is held together with pink elastic!

There is of course a need for parishes to be run in a legal and business-like manner. The parishes with good financial resources often pay for an administrator, but not all can afford one. It then falls to the Parish Priest to spend more and more time on matters which have little relevance to the promises he or she made when ordained.

A way forward may be for several benefices to employ a group secretary on the lines of a Health Centre's practice manager. Such a person could handle many of the difficult and time-consuming administrative tasks. This is not a cheap option and the ever-increasing Share may see this and other solutions fall by the wayside, and back into the lap of the individual parishes.

But the daily round in a rural parish has more problems than the ecclesiastical obstacle courses. There is a huge need for affordable housing and sufficient employment. Many small dwellings are now second homes and these are unoccupied for much of the year. Few houses are being built for first time buyers, while more and more money goes into luxury developments.

North Norfolk needs more young adults if villages are to have balanced populations. (At sixty-one years old, I am in the lower age bracket in many of my villages!) It lacks housing for the professions; teachers, nurses and others who cannot afford the grossly inflated house prices.

Above all the villages need more people who can take part in community life and share the responsibilities now borne by elderly congregations. It is understandable that anyone coming to a holiday home, does so for a rest, and may not wish to get involved in village activities. Nevertheless those who do take part in local events, and are generous with time and money, help rural life to stay very much 'alive'.

A lot of these visitors, especially those involved in the IT industry, want to make their holiday house into a permanent residence and work from home. The introduction of Broadband and a change in Council regulations would make this possible and boost the local economy enormously. At the moment most rural communities rely on the tourist industry for income; 'a feast' in summer, but in winter 'a famine'.

Even if villages wait in hope for 'new blood', most still enjoy the efforts of an army of volunteers. These good people promote a sense of community and stability rarely found in other places. Where else do the able bodied provide such excellent community care, allowing the elderly and infirm, to receive help with transport and shopping?

But huge change is on its way. As the average age of village populations increases, the number of people able to give help, paid or voluntary, gets fewer. Support from children who live a considerable distance from their parents is limited, and many residents will shortly have to 'buy in' domestic repairs and personal care from people well outside the area. This could be very expensive. Steps need to be taken now which will enable an ageing population to receive proper care at affordable rates.

For the present, North Norfolk villages can be a joy for both residents and visitors, surrounded as they are by the remarkable beauty that coast and country have to offer. No wonder people from London see it as an escape from the jungle of city life!

The area has a long Christian history. The ancient Shrine at Walsingham and the incomparable Binham Priory, are but two of the places that share a unique spiritual heritage. Hundreds of people come to these and other churches, not simply as tourists but as pilgrims.

But more and more people are beginning to ask if a place of worship in each village is a luxury we can afford. 'Do you need so many churches in Norfolk?' People say: 'Is it worth the effort of meeting these endless costs? Surely it would be better to sell off the old buildings and give the money to the poor?'

I can only answer that these are the very words of Judas who criticised a

Binham Priory

woman for anointing the feet of Jesus with an expensive ointment. Compared with the amount spent on armaments, defence, alcohol, tobacco and entertainment, the cost of keeping a medieval building alive is small when its influence may be so very great. Even non-believers in villages consider the churches to be worthy of support because they are places of inspiration and beauty.

In a world constantly threatened by the Dark, there is a need for churches, holy places that are open to Christ, the Light of the World. These churches are far more than shelters for communal worship. Bishop Inge quotes T.S. Eliot in a passage from 'Murder in the Cathedral':

> For the blood of Thy martyrs and saints
> Shall enrich the earth, shall create holy places.
> For wherever a saint has dwelt, wherever a martyr has given his blood for Christ,
> There is holy ground, and the sanctity shall not depart from it,
> Though armies trample over it, though sightseers come with guide books looking over it.

The effect of prayer in these churches, like the intercession of the contemplative nuns in my home village of Langham, goes far beyond Norfolk. Moreover, the buildings are witnesses themselves.

And this witness will always be needed. Every religion begins by proclaiming the unconditional love of God. Yet these same religions can twist this message into a ghastly perversion of the truth, preaching false Gospels of rigid and inflexible rules, which condemn, punish and repel the poor and marginalised.

As in other places, the churches of North Norfolk succeed where organised religion fails. They are beacons, lights shining in the darkness, that call people to worship, encourage them to pray and tell the world that God is God, who loves us 'now and forever'.

GLOSSARY

Benefice: The Parish or Parishes in the care of a clergyperson: He/she may be known as the Vicar, Rector or Priest in Charge. Their first post (and possibly others) is a curacy.

Curate: Usually a clergyperson in training. Strictly speaking the title is 'Assistant Curate'. The post she or he holds is called a Curacy.

Deanery: A group of Parishes whose members meet regularly. The clergy hold 'Chapters' and the lay people meet at a 'Synod' which is also attended by the clergy. The Priest who co-ordinates the activities of the Deanery is the Area Dean (in the town) or Rural Dean (in the country).

Diocese: The area under the authority of a Bishop. This may correspond to a county, e.g. Durham and Gloucestershire. The name of the Diocese is that of the city in which the cathedral is found. e.g. Birmingham and Truro.

Ecumenism (Ecumenical): Co-operation between Christians of different denominations

Parish: The area served by a church. It may correspond to a village, town or district in a town.

Parochial Church Council (The P.C.C.): The body which governs the affairs of each Parish. This is elected each year after the Annual Meetings which choose Wardens and review the affairs of the Parish.

Chelsea-on-Sea

Lisa Reynolds

They call it Chelsea-on-Sea, a unique stretch of the East Anglian coastline for years dismissed as cold, dull and desolate. A place once considered too far from anywhere, but suddenly one that is the *de-rigueur* place to be seen at weekends and *the* place to have a holiday home.

North Norfolk has always been a favourite holiday destination for people from the East Midlands who, for decades, along with other hardy folk, have spent their summers here. But over the past four years the Saltmarsh Coast has taken off as the favourite weekend retreat, as its 'designer label' suggests, of the residents of SW3 – and other fashionable postcodes. Throughout the year thousands of the so-called Chelsea-set leave London for the North Norfolk coast, and with them comes 'London' money ... money that few would disagree is desperately needed to help boost the local economy. And the more time they spend here, the more they want to own a little piece of our wonderful coast. Surely this can only be advantageous to us all?

It has, without doubt, led to a surge in wonderful eateries, luxurious hotels,. delicatessens, art galleries and gift shops. The boom in designer tourism means that the area could and should be more affluent than it has ever been. But is this surge in outside interest in danger of ruining the area for the local people? Are we now so preoccupied with pleasing the 'outsiders' that we have forgotten the 'locals', the people born and raised in the area, those who need to live and work here long after the tourist season has ended?

In this chapter I shall explore the positives and the negatives of the new found popularity of North Norfolk and ask whether the 'real' residents of the area have any say in the way it is changing; should we be fighting change or embracing it; what are local councils doing to support the local economy and community; does the Government care; and what help can we expect from Europe?

I think few would argue that one of the most obvious impacts of the new-found status of North Norfolk has been on its housing market.

I should start by confessing that to most people in North Norfolk I am one of those dreaded outsiders. Born in south Norfolk, I left home at the age of 19 to head off to college, and I'm not proud to say that I planned never to return. I'd spent many a childhood holiday in Wells-next-the-Sea and had memories of biting

Lisa Reynolds

Lisa Reynolds was born in Norfolk. After Bungay High School she gained a certificate in newspaper journalism at Harlow College and worked on local newspapers at Kettering, Leamington Spa and Stratford-upon-Avon before joining the *Derby Evening Telegraph*. From there she moved to London and worked on the staff of *Today* magazine until Rupert Murdoch shut it down. She moved to the *Daily Express* as a news reporter and (briefly) religious affairs correspondent before becoming a general news reporter and health correspondent at *The Sun*. In 2001 she left Fleet Street and London to join the BBC at Norwich where she is Assistant Editor at 'Look East' and is responsible for producing the 6.30 p.m. news programme. She now lives in Wells.

winds, and rain-lashed campsites. I vowed never to 'endure' them again. And then I found myself in London, working on a national newspaper with savings burning a hole in my pocket. I lived in the heart of Clapham. Like most of London it never sleeps, there is no peace, no space, no fresh air.

I longed for a seaside retreat, somewhere to escape the big smog, and found myself returning to the town of my childhood holidays – Wells-next-the-Sea. So five years ago I bought a three-bedroom cottage in the town, an investment for the future, and like so many 'weekenders' I planned to renovate it and rent it out for a princely sum to others who wanted to spend time on the coast. That way I could live in London and enjoy the fruits of my labour with weekends by the sea in a cottage paid for by other holidaymakers. Then I changed jobs ... found myself working in Norwich and living in my 'investment' ... suddenly I started seeing things from the other side.

Three years on I now consider myself a local ... I'm sure the locals still view me as an outsider, despite the fact that I was born in the county and my family have always lived here. And as the coast becomes ever more popular I find myself enraged that people who genuinely call this coast home, those born in the area are being driven out ... by the rise in house prices. Homes which were on the market a few years ago for an affordable £60,000 are now worth three or four times that amount. The spiralling property prices mean that first-time buyers are unable to get a foot on the property ladder, and with a lack of affordable housing they are being forced out.

Tourism may be good for the area, but it is not one of the highest paid industries. It is on the whole a low wage economy, and many teenagers leaving school and setting up home for the first time cannot afford to get that foot on the property ladder. Estimated figures reveal that around 10 per cent of the housing stock in North Norfolk is now second homes, properties that are unused for large parts of the year. In some areas, like Blakeney and Cley it's thought that as much as 50% of the properties are owned by people who do not live in them year round.

There are two obvious adverse consequences of second homeowners on rural housing markets. First they restrict supply, and increase the cost of housing. Second, second home owners tend to make less use of local businesses. They arrive at their weekend retreats, cars laden with goods from their 'local' stores in London ... barely stopping to consider the impact on the local economy. But it means that village shops, once at the heart of the community, are closing because of a lack of custom. In some respects we are all to blame. Out of town supermarkets, the so-called one-stop shops are an attractive option. We fill our baskets once, pay once and load the car just once.

But often what we may have saved on the bulk buys we waste on petrol money, and so could have supported the shops on our doorsteps whose produce is often fresher and can be just as cheap. And so we lose the old fashioned High

Street, where once there was a butcher, a baker, and a greengrocer and their shops are converted into dwellings. A recent report by the Countryside Agency found that second home owners now not only vie for the quaint old cottages and period buildings but also for new build and ex-local authority housing.

It's a problem that has angered the residents and to some extent troubled the councils. But at last the North Norfolk District Council is doing something to redress the balance of power. The Local Government Act 2003 provided local authorities with the authority to increase council tax on second homes to 90 per cent. Until recently second home-owners were entitled to a huge discount of 50% on the amount of council tax they paid for the second property. But early in 2004 the North Norfolk District Council opted to bring taxes in to line with the new act and second property owners now pay 90% of the full cost. In theory this should be bringing in somewhere near an extra £1.7 million into the local budget; money that could then be ploughed into building more affordable housing for local people.

But as is always the case there was a pitfall, the County Council took a large slice (80%) of the cash proceeds, leaving a much smaller portion for the District Council. Some argue that second home-owners should actually pay more council tax, perhaps 110% or even 150% as a 'pay back' to the local economy.

North Norfolk MP Norman Lamb was one of those who campaigned rigorously to have the 'rules' changed. He is now pushing for the District Council to get a better deal next year, by citing examples from the West Country where local councils have successfully bid to retain the extra cash raised from increased council taxes on second homes.

Latest figures show that Norfolk, and in particular North Norfolk, is among the top five areas in the country for properties that are now second homes. Norman Lamb says the lack of affordable housing is now the 'number one issue' for North Norfolk, with no sign of a slump in the housing market. 'The perception is that North Norfolk is quite a wealthy and desirable place to live,' he said. 'But when you consider the number of second homes and the low wage economy, it's not that well off at all.'

One idea he has put forward, which has been explored in Devon and Cornwall, is for the local council to require that second-home owners apply for planning permission to change the use of their properties from permanent residences to holiday homes. That way the council could monitor, and limit the number of homes being taken out of the local housing stock and into the hands of holidaymakers. But it has been considered too difficult to police and is also seen as an infringement on personal liberty. The trouble is that because North Norfolk is the kind of place it is, with large parts of it protected because of its natural beauty, there are restrictions on building and development.

The Government is aware of the social needs of rural communities, but research has shown that rural housing schemes can take a long time to develop and often require sensitive negotiations between local communities, planning and housing departments and housing associations. The Countryside Agency and Housing Corporation, along with local support, is funding a national programme to establish Rural Housing Enabler posts across the country. The role of these individuals is to work closely with local authorities, housing associations, landowners and developers to help speed up the development process.

There are currently 36 Enablers in the country, one of them in Norfolk. Their role is to raise awareness of affordable housing needs, working with all the bodies involved in development to help influence the regional and local strategies.

In its recent report 'The State of the Countryside' the Countryside Agency highlighted the fact that as more and more people 'buy' into rural areas there are fewer and fewer affordable homes for local families and there is increasing homelessness in remoter areas.

Pam Warhurst, Chair of the Countryside Agency, says:

Life in England's countryside is good – for many people...More and more people are moving there to live, and why shouldn't they have that choice? There's nothing wrong with wanting a good quality of life, but this pressure on the countryside has an unintended impact....Those who exercise their right to move can reduce the choices of the less well-off in rural areas and affect the character of our countryside....That's why it's important to focus on what's been going on, to help national and regional policy makers better understand the impact of their decisions and initiatives on rural communities and our landscapes, and do something about it.

It's not all bad news. The report showed that there has been growth in rural businesses, that the incidence of crime and the fear of crime are much lower in rural areas and that rural people tend to live longer than their urban counterparts. But one obvious knock-on effect of the fact that young people are being forced out of rural areas by rising housing prices is that there has been a consequent change in the demographics of the area.

The latest census, published by the Office of National Statistics, shows that the elderly outnumber the young in the area by around ten to one. Statistics for Wells, for example, show that in a population of just over 4200, 48% are men and 52% women, but more tellingly only 3.6% are aged 16-19. The average age of the population is 47, and the over 60s make up 36.2% of the town's residents. The figures also revealed that 56.7% of people are employed ... 23.2% are retired.

Further along the coast, within the Burnham Ward, the figures are much the same. Here the over 60s represent a massive 39.4 per cent of the population, the average age is 49 and again less than 5 per cent of those living in the ward are aged 16-19. Says Norman Lamb:

> There is an inward migration of people coming here to retire and we have to ensure that the infrastructure is in place to support them. There are increasing health needs in the area and the demands on the NHS by people

Wells Cottage Hospital

over 60 are much greater. They are a huge strain on the health economy of North Norfolk. An increasing number of people are cared for in their own homes by a loved one and we have to ensure there is sufficient provision for them.

But it's not always that simple, with the biggest hospitals more than 30 miles away. For elderly people living alone there is the issue of transport, and North Norfolk is relatively poorly served by public transport. And, as ever, there is only a limited pot of money for health services in the region, and this means that local services, such as Wells Cottage Hospital, are constantly under threat.

At the beginning of last year the Cottage Hospital was forced to close for two months due to a shortage of staff. At the time the local health trust blamed recruitment problems on the lack of affordable housing in the area. Although the hospital is now open again its future remains uncertain. But the increase in the elderly population means there is increased demand for local services.

In 2004 a campaign was launched to get an osteoporosis clinic and scanner in King's Lynn. At the moment men and women who suffer from the 'brittle bone' disease face a journey of 50 miles to have a bone scan. The very nature of the disease means the majority of patients are elderly and such a long journey is to say the least, difficult for them. But, as ever, there is a limited amount of money, and it doesn't always go round.

There is some good news. Plans to rebuild Cromer Hospital would see some work switched to Cromer from the Norfolk and Norwich University Hospital and thus nearer to the people of North Norfolk. The services affected include elderly rehabilitation beds, day-case surgery and a minor injuries unit. But a series of delays means the new facilities are unlikely to be open before mid 2008 – at the earliest.

Norman Lamb says that as the North Norfolk MP he feels it's these types of issues that he has to take on:

North Norfolk is a fantastic place to live if you are young, mobile and healthy. I don't want to paint a bleak picture of North Norfolk but there are stresses and strains, and for people on low income, fixed income or in retirement there are real challenges there. I feel it's my job to fight, and find a way for those particular people. But there is only so much that one constituency MP can do.

Earlier I mentioned the question of whether the residents of North Norfolk should fight change or embrace it. As a nation we are very good at taking the NIMBY attitude to change: 'Not in My Back Yard'. We often welcome change as long as it doesn't affect us, the way we live, or the area we live in. But many of us forget we can influence change and find the idea of joining a parish or town council laughable.

Yet think of the power of service. Any decision that affects the area we live in can be influenced or changed by the people who live there if they care enough to stand up and be counted. A classic example of what can be accomplished occurred in the spring of 2004 in Blakeney where three mobile telephone networks, O2, Orange and Vodaphone, applied for planning permission to erect mobile phone masts in a wooded area close to the church.

Realising they would be an eyesore for miles around, the parish councils of Wiveton, Morston, Blakeney and Cley joined forces to 'protest' the applications. When the time came for a site visit by the District Council all four parishes were represented and their argument was so strong the District Council turned down the application. There was still a chance the companies could appeal the decision but the first round of the battle was won, even if the war was not over. The parishes could have ignored the application or failed to join forces to fight it.

This small example shows what 'people power' can do. Yet a recent survey revealed that parish council elections are in danger of becoming a thing of the past because so few people are willing to stand as candidates. It seems many have been put off by new rules brought in last year which mean parish councillors have to produce a declaration of interest. As the numbers dwindle so the number of parish councillors returned unopposed increases, but how long can this go on? Will we

eventually run out of people who are willing to devote their time to parish issues?

If there is no-one left to represent parish views there is a danger that people at the grassroots level will not be heard. There will be no-one for district councils to consult and decisions will be made without input from the 'locals'. For many, the idea of joining a parish or town council is a waste of time. But I think we need to get people more involved in the political process, especially the young.

In 2004 Steven Ward became the youngest-ever member of Fakenham Town Council, Yet before long he was pushed out, being deemed, at 19, too young to become involved in the political process. He had applied to join the council after a position became vacant due to a retirement. He was successfully co-opted and was looking forward to representing the views of the young people of the town. He says:

I wanted to have some effect on the community that I live in,' he said. 'I have an interest in issues and think young people should get involved because it's important to make your voice heard. I was invited to a meeting but someone heard about how old I was and complained. It seems you can vote at 18 but can't sit on the council until you are 21. I got the impression that I wasn't wanted by some of the elderly people because I'm young and they didn't want me trying to change things.

He hasn't been put off by the negative experience and says he will try again when he's 21. But what kind of message does this send to young people about getting involved with local issues? They walk away thinking 'Why should I care? Why should I vote, no-one listens to me.'

Many argue that the Government is too 'urban' and doesn't understand the ways of the countryside. A classic example is the ban on foxhunting. Will there come a time when parts of the country like North Norfolk have more say in the way they are run? Devolution is the buzz word at the moment. Will there ever be a day when we have our own small 'parliament'? Madness or food for thought? Only time will tell, but one thing that is important is that we don't squander our vote. It's our chance to have our say and yes we can influence the decision-makers.

The lack of interest in elections isn't just a local issue. There are poor turn-outs at general and European elections too. People ask, 'What's the point in voting; no-one listens to us anyway.' In the recent European elections there was no representative from Norfolk. Of the region's seven representatives not one of them lives in the county and many feel that, as a result, our part of the East of England is not fairly represented.

Robert Sturdy MEP, one of the seven, disagrees. He lives in Suffolk but argues that he speaks for and represents all the people of East Anglia, including the residents of North Norfolk. 'Once elected you work for the people of the Eastern Region,' he said.

Mr. Sturdy takes an interest in coastal erosion, the pollution of the North Sea and the dwindling fishing fleets off our coast. He believes that the only way to save the fishing industry off the Norfolk coast is to buy back the Spanish fishing quotas and stop the harvesting of sand eels, which are the staple diet of fish in the North Sea. He argues that without drastic action the fleets will disappear from the North Norfolk coast. He says people should care, and should vote because every piece of legislation passed in Europe has a huge impact on all of us and our lives in some way.

People complain of being made to feel like second-class citizens in their own home towns or villages. But why should they? Why squander the opportunity to make your voice heard? When we hear complaints about the lack of affordable housing, the influx of outsiders and the shortage of decent local health care, transport and employment, why not stop and think 'Is there something I can do to change it?' When you're asked your opinion on a local issue and given the chance to vote on it, take it. Let's not watch the erosion of the Saltmarsh Coast. Let's help preserve it for future generations. So that they too can experience the unique and enchanting land we call home.

Mine Hoste

Paul Whittome

When I purchased the Hoste Arms in 1989, I returned to an area with which I fell in love as a child when all our holidays were spent at a caravan site in Thornham. By the late 80s Burnham Market was slightly run down but it had a wonderful community and a thriving Traders Association. Whilst most shops in most villages had by then closed, Burnham Market had halted the exodus of retailing although Front Street, once a thriving retail street, had been reduced to one interior design shop.

By the end of the 80s a lot of local people and families had left the area because they could not find work after the decline of farming and fishing. In the 30s there were over 1000 people employed in agriculture within four miles of Burnham Market. Fifty years later there were probably less than fifty. Now there are no more than twenty.

Fishing had declined too. When I was a child we would drag a net off the 9th hole at Brancaster and catch enough fish to feed the whole caravan site of about seventy caravans. We would get dabs, flounder, shrimp, eels and sometimes plaice and sole. You could spear flatfish at low tide. And tope were plentiful. By the time I came back to live here you couldn't do that because the fish just weren't there. A once flourishing industry had been reduced to small amounts of shellfish and some sea trout and seabass and since then it's been reduced even further.

Upside

But tourism, which had been here since Victorian times, was about to experience a new upward surge.

From the 19th century right up to the Second World War there was a colony of huts on Scolt Head Island. Families would come down and spend the summer there and the local boatmen at Brancaster and the Lanes at Overy Staithe would take them across and keep them supplied with food and water. By the end of the war all the huts had gone. So families bought caravans and sites developed all along the coast. Some of them were exclusive. The caravans at Thornham for example were all owned by farmers and doctors, most of whom eventually bought houses in the area and in many cases sent their children to school here at places

Paul Whittome

Paul Whittome spent his childhood summers in a caravan at Thornham. After Glebe House School, Hunstanton, and Uppingham he developed a very successful potato trading business near Peterborough. In 1985 he decided he wanted to live in North Norfolk full time rather than only at weekends and became a full time resident of Burnham Market when he bought the Hoste Arms. Since then, the Hoste has earned an international reputation for innovative excellence and has played a not insignificant role in shaping the modern image of the village. He now lives with his South African wife Jeanne and his two stepdaughters in a home on the marsh and has another home in South Africa where he lives for part of the year.

like Glebe House School in Hunstanton where I went myself. Each village seemed to attract people from different areas. Thornham for example seemed to mainly have people from Peterborough and the Fens while Overy Staithe was all Cambridge.

Because tourism down here is steeped in history, those links have continued. Families, whether caravan owners or second home-owners, still have tendencies to gather in little compounds of their own. Most local villages are now dominated by London but Burnham Overy, which in my opinion has the most musical and artistic population, has retained its strong ties with Cambridge. Brancaster holiday-makers still tend to come from Leicester and Thornham still attracts people from Peterborough and the Fens.

As late as 1990 there were not many other places to stay. A few small hotels in places like Titchwell, Thornam, Wells and Blakeney but not much else apart from caravans and bed-and-breakfast places – that often meant a spare room in someone's house.

When I bought the Hoste I had no idea that it would become what it is today. Or that in less than fifteen years so many other places along the coast would develop as they have developed, offering outstanding accommodation and hospitality. But I did know that Burnham Market was unique and that it was the right place for high quality merchandise and services. The Fitzgeralds had already shown that in the 70s with their wonderful delicatessen (Bowers) which was known as the Fortnum and Mason of Norfolk and (after Fortnum and Mason) was probably the most famous delicatessen in England.

I have been absolutely flabbergasted by the rate at which things have changed. The growth of the Hoste has surpassed my best predictions. We have had fourteen years of fantastic expansion. And over the same period many good shops such as Gurney's Fish Shop, two book shops, Annas, Gun Hill and others have opened and are doing well. Burnham Market has become an extraordinary retail marketplace.

One reason for the success of the Hoste is that I was in the right place at the right time. In the early 90s several people decided at more or less the same time that Burnham Market had great potential and they acted on those decisions. To some extent I benefited from that. I rode the wave. As I was a bachelor, I decided to sell my three homes which I had acquired through my potato trading businesses and use all the cash to invest heavily in my newly acquired inn. It paid off.

A second reason was that Burnham Market was already a special place on account of its artistic life. As an amateur painter and musician, the thing I noticed most when I moved here was the artistic and musical culture of the area. Lady Margaret Douglas-Home had created the wonderful Burnham Concerts and many eminent musicians had graced Burnham Market. Both the estates of Holkham and Houghton richly support music, lending the setting of their magnificent homes for a great variety of events.

One day Rodney Slatford walked into the Hoste. I had been a double bass player at Uppingham and was particularly excited when England's Number 1 double bass player came to give a concert. As an 'A' Level art student, I had also done the posters of 'Rodney the Bass' with a caricature of Rodney as a double bass. Rodney's Yorke Trust is now celebrated in the area giving wonderful concerts in local churches and stately homes. The Burnham Overy Christmas Concert is a classic example of the musical and cultural talent in this immediate location.

A third reason for success is that whilst I had a general sense of what I wanted – my initial thought was to create a small, chic hotel – I remained flexible and adaptable. Instead of driving towards a preconceived vision I stayed open to new possibilities and changed my goals as the way opened. The result is something I could never have imagined when I bought the Hoste.

A fourth reason is that whilst I have been adaptable I have always insisted that the Hoste must reflect my personal tastes and preferences. I hate stuffiness and formality so it had to be informal (I never wear ties by the way). I can't stand sloppiness so it had to be immaculate. I have no time for incompetence and inefficiency, so it had to work perfectly. So the Hoste is a place I would want to come to if I weren't here already; a place where I feel comfortable; and a place where I find the things I want and the standards of service I expect.

In some ways creating the Hoste has meant recreating it by peeling back layers of modernisation to find things that had been changed for the sake of change. For instance I knew from the start I wanted the bar to be a bar, a place where everyone – and I mean everyone – could come for a drink and feel completely at home. That meant going back to something that had been here but had been changed in the name of progress. Bars are for drinking. So you won't find menus in my bar. And you can't buy food – you can do that in the restaurant. I now have what I believe to be the only bar in North Norfolk where there are no menus. And I did it that way because that's what I wanted myself.

The same thing applies to the hotel side and the rooms and suites, all designed by Jeanne, my wife. Upstairs is more formal than downstairs because that is the way people live now. At home they eat in the kitchen, perhaps a very large and luxurious kitchen but still a kitchen because it satisfies their need for informality. But their private spaces have become more and more lavish and in a sense more formal. And that's what they find here too, including the African themes in parts of the hotel that reflect our passion for South Africa – Jeanne is South African – where we now live for part of each year.

I listen all the time to learn how people are reacting to what we offer. I watch their reactions and I use the knowledge I get from that to make improvements – provided of course they are improvements that fit my own style and preferences.

Downside

The surge of tourism and second home ownership which has driven these changes would have been welcomed in most parts of the country where jobs have been lost due to the decline of industries like mining and the impact of agricultural mechanisation. Many such areas have lost their identities because all the young people have moved out of those areas looking for employment.

But here, as the property market boomed and the area prospered, becoming one of the most fashionable in England, there was a down side. People did not need to travel or leave the area to find work but were being forced to leave because house prices were so high it was impossible for the younger generation to buy them. We have to find a solution to this problem.

The Council tried to help by putting a covenant on a lot of Council properties saying they had to be sold to people who had lived and worked in the area for over three years. But this approach has been horribly abused by wealthy people who have bought Council properties and rented them out, getting round the covenants technically by stating that they have worked in the area for three years or more. In reality all they had was a local office address and they have used it to take advantage of the situation. They have created no benefit for the area whatsoever, and have profiteered by latching on to a scheme that was intended to help locals. I believe we should have a register of the people who have been involved in this outrageous abuse because they are depriving potential local first-time buyers of a chance to get on the property ladder.

Some locals feel there should be no second homes. I have worked very hard for what I have. I was brought up in a very unattractive part of England amongst the brick pits of Peterborough and was able to fulfil my dream of having a second home on the North Norfolk Coast before I reached the age of 30. But I had to live among the brick pits in the week and I saw no reason why I and others like me should not be able to share this place with those fortunate enough to have been born here.

It is very important, in a democracy, that hard working people can achieve their goals. A great friend of mine, who was brought up in the North West in a family of seven in a tiny flat, succeeded as a great lawyer. Yet he has experienced resentment at having a second home on the Norfolk Coast. The next stage will be a group of people trying to dictate the size of the house one can own and soon we will be on a slippery road to communism. So I think we need an equation whereby those who aspire to live in this area of outstanding natural beauty can do so whilst those who have been born here and wish to continue to work in the area are also able to do so.

I believe there is a solution to the housing problem and that we must resolve it because it is getting worse all the time and because the survival of this community depends on it.

In my view we need a two-tier housing market along the lines of schemes that have been adopted in Jersey and Guernsey. A good percentage of good housing should be available for local people who have been brought up here and have lived and worked here for, say, at least six years out of the last nine, thus allowing for the fact that many people move away and come back. These properties should never be sublet and the covenant should continue indefinitely. In that way we would be able to create more affordable housing.

The solution would not be difficult to finance. Agricultural land is worth between £2000 and £3500 an acre. Building land is worth between £200,000 and £500,000 an acre, so on grey area planning belts landowners would get planning permission for new housing – for which there is so much demand – on the condition that half the land was available free for starter homes under the covenant I described. Two bedroom houses could be built for under £80,000 (the interest would be similar to an open market rent), and the other half could be sold on the open market. Both the land-owner and the first time buyer would benefit enormously.

Governments and Councils seem so slow in implementing things that seem so obvious. Take the rates paid by second-home owners. For many years they paid only half the council tax. Yet only a small percentage of them objected to paying the same as everyone else. Recently the rebate was cut to 10%. The debate over rates and the resentment quite rightly felt by locals had been going on for a decade. Yet it took the Council a long time to take action.

I also think that for the good of the community and the local economy we have to be open to new ideas in other areas and be more willing to consider radical proposals. Take the churches. From the tower of Burnham Westgate Church in the middle of Burnham Market you can see six churches. Like churches elsewhere, they have few worshippers these days. The growth of tourism and the influx of second-home owners does not seem to have boosted their congregations or helped them in other ways. So it occurred to me that something could be done with near empty churches that would preserve them and adapt them to new uses.

I rang the Vicar and asked him whether we could talk about one of the local churches. So he came to join me for coffee. Immediately he sat down the vicar, on learning of my interest in the church, asked me if I would read the lesson on Sunday. He was rather upset when I said my interest in the church was that I wanted to buy one and create a hotel out of one of these magnificent buildings.

He immediately lost interest. But I have studied several incredible conversions around the country – in Hereford, and Nottingham amongst other places – where such conversions have been made. I still think it would be a good idea to change their uses provided it was done in the right way. The converted churches I am talking about have retained their religious aura and have remained tranquil and peaceful places in their new uses. I know this is a radical and for some people unacceptable idea. Maybe the arrival of Alpha courses on the Norfolk Coast will revive the fortunes of local churches. But if I look at the challenges of maintaining these wonderful buildings, it seems to me the idea of adapting some of them to new uses – for instance replacing village halls with the pews on castors to move in and out – is well worth considering, not least because if something of the kind is not done they will eventually be ruined.

I passionately believe in the need for adaptation. People have to adapt. Institutions like the Church have to adapt. Retailers have to adapt. We have to make it possible for local people to stay here. Not because I need them to work at the Hoste but because without them, this place would not be what it is.

Sometimes people ask why, if I have so many ideas, I don't go in to local politics. I tell them I've been there and done that. At one time, when I lived near Peterborough, I was the youngest councillor in England. John Major helped in my campaign. But I can now do more by doing what I'm doing. The Hoste employs 70 staff and if you think of the impact of their wages on the local economy it's obvious that I'm making a real difference. I can also influence things by speaking out on the need for adaptability, the need to solve the housing problem and the need for fresh ideas.

And I can do this partly because I've set things up in such a way that I have no constraints. I own this business. I have no shareholders, no board, no committees. And I can give vent to my impatience for progress as I please. The thing is though, I am radical and conservative at the same time. I think things must change because if they don't we shall die. But I don't want change for its own sake. I want change that preserves the essential qualities that make this place, this village, this coast, so special. Above all I want to preserve its slowness. I want people to be able to come here to find Norfolk. I don't want them to come here to find London. If they want London they should stay there. And I am absolutely convinced we can have conservative change. Keep the economy moving, create new jobs and provide affordable housing while preserving the unique character of North Norfolk.

I'm also asked sometimes about what would be the best and worst things that could happen to Burnham Market. The best thing would be to solve the housing problem in a way that would benefit everybody and would include seeing the silly prices people are now paying for local property come down. The worst would be the arrival of a supermarket because that would wreck our wonderful shops.

For myself I never forget that, as a child, sailing in Brancaster Harbour, I always dreamt of one day living and working here. Many other people have those dreams too. But I have had the luck and privilege to have the dream come true.

A More Acceptable Part of the Fens

Roger Law

Growing up in Littleport in the heart of the Fens in the early 40s and 50s gave a young man certain advantages – an immunity to the chill factor and a strong determination never to get that close to the work ethic again. I have never been cold since I left the Fens and as far as my working life is concerned if my father was alive I'm sure 1 would still be referred to as the 'rake'. He considered me as about as useful to a Fenland village as an out-of-work actor.

I was a wartime baby but I cannot say I knew much of the privation. Living close to the land we never went short of fresh eggs and vegetables which my father grew on an acre of land shared by chickens, ducks, rabbits and a pig. At Sunday lunch it was my father's proud boast that the only purchased ingredient was the flour to make the Yorkshire pudding. For a time he was away with the army but by all accounts he spent more time fighting his own officers than he did fighting Hitler and a high proportion of his Military Service was spent in the glass-house. The army, he explained to me, was a bad idea. Soldiers were not encouraged to think for themselves and became essentially lazy. My only graphic memories of the period were a scary effigy of Hitler being burnt in the centre of the village and being strapped to the balustrades of Burnham Overy Staithe windmill, looking out to sea through the sails, whilst my father painted the brickwork with pitch on one our frequent visits to North Norfolk.

Even as a child in the Fens I had the sense of living on the edge. There was always a feeling that the water might one day reclaim the land and that Littleport, a landlocked little town-cum-village of some 5000 inhabitants on the Norfolk/Cambridgeshire border, might easily revert to its island status. As kids we would go out to certain fields and poke the apparently solid surface of the earth with poles. Three or four feet down it would be like jelly. And if the place did not sink without trace there seemed a good chance of it being blown away by the icy winds that came howling across the open spaces straight from Siberia. These days, like most places within a couple of hours from London, the Fens has its share of second homes. I often wonder if the weekenders realise the ground beneath them is being pumped out 24 hours a day – although they must notice the banked rivers

Roger Law

Roger Law used to be famous – he was responsible for the sweat shop success of 'Spitting Image'. Having seen Thatcher out he had the decency to deport himself to Australia. Born and brought up in the East Anglian fens in the middle of the last century, the old has-been now migrates between Wells and Australia, painting and drawing.

are often higher than the land.

The character of the people was less wintry than the terrain but it was to some extent shaped by it. From Roman times onward, Fen country has been a natural refuge for outlaws, as the bogs deterred hot pursuit by the forces of law and order. Hereward the Wake held out against the Norman invaders in the marshes around Ely before he was betrayed by a greedy abbot. In Regency times the Fens were a popular hideout for runaway black slaves which probably accounts for some of today's more exotic physiognomies. The inaccessibility of the area was also prized by its more law-abiding inhabitants who could live entirely by trapping, shooting and fishing the teeming water-lands. When the Dutch started to drain the Fens there was endless trouble with the local labour hired to do the work. They would dig trenches for money by day and fill them in by night for free – they were the original Fen Tigers. Eventually Irish navvies were brought in to do the job.

The workings of central governments were regarded with distrust, sometimes with good reason. It was an uprising in Littleport that sparked the bread riots around the country in the wake of the Napoleonic wars. These were stamped out with great ferocity. As the captain in charge of quelling the Littleport riots remarked at the time:

"Last year the battle of Waterloo, this year the battle of Hullabaloo."

In 1816 five Littleport men were hanged for their part in the rioting and 75 others were deported to Australia. I was well acquainted with their descendents whose family names still appeared on the school register. A sense of being at odds with the world beyond the Fens, even though many people made a living selling produce to it, was very much part of growing up. One consequence of this peculiar solidarity was that there was not a lot of class feeling, nor was there much display of professional arrogance. The fens being such a grim, flat and damp place to set up shop, the ranks of Fenland doctors, solicitors and teachers seemed to contain an unusually high number of rejects from elsewhere.

Remnants of past ways of life were still in evidence when I was a child. Old people still drank poppy tea, an essential escape from ague and the irritation of mosquitos and as they became a burden on their immediate family there was much whispering about giving them the black teapot. I had bad dreams about this mythic black teapot and eventually exorcised it by making one – covered in poisonous scorpions, spiders and snakes – which can be found in the Norwich Castle Museum.

My own family tradition was essentially muscular. My grandfather Robert, who died when my own father was eight years old, was a revered figure. He had originally been a blacksmith and broke in horses as a side-line before making a great success as a general dealer. He invested all his money in cattle and a large chunk of Welney Wash. He prospered to the extent of opening a couple of butcher's shops in the village and even sold his meat pies in London. His business was then completely wiped out by a foot and mouth epidemic. Soon after, he died a typical Fenland death. A horse and carriage had crashed through the ice on the Wash and my grandfather helped to rescue the trapped driver. He went home and died of pneumonia. His eleven surviving children (he had 13 children in all) were farmed out among various families in Littleport which gave me a tremendous range of aunts and uncles as a child.

I felt my father was a driven man and his drive was to restore the fortunes so cruelly washed away from his father's grasp. At one point in his construction business, which profited highly from the post-war council house boom, he had three of his brothers and his youngest son working alongside him. But there were no family favours. The workers were expected to work at the double but George's nearest and dearest were expected to die for the cause. Any request for time-off for good behaviour was met with cocked eyebrow and a gruff chant of 'if the dog hadn't stopped to crap it would have caught the hare'. It could safely be said, Law Brothers of Littleport, or Claw Brothers as they were known in the village, did not architecturally enhance the Fens.

My father's approach to his work made local hero, Oliver Cromwell seem frivolous by comparison. A similar attitude was expected from his off-spring. Any innocent or pleasurable pastime taken up by any member of the family would be escalated into venture capitalism in a trice. My pet rabbit, a large Flemish Giant called Zambuck, and his doe became a rabbit farm peaking at 300 rabbits – all needing to be fed and watered twice a day.

My uncle Tom's tiny grocery shop became a supermarket years before Tesco's. And my brother Martin, whose aversion to real work was slightly less than mine, had a talent for intricate restoration carpentry only to end up on an industrial estate on the outskirts of March punching out office furniture for the government. Any venture started had to be seen through to the bitter end and very bitter some of the endings were too.

As a boy I would escape from all this industry by disappearing with my dog Scrap across the fen. The sky would start at the top of my boots and soar to the heavens. The rich black of the fen droves, undiminished by distance, would stretch forever in front of us. We'd dig out rabbits and rats from the dykes and ditches, chase moorhens and pheasants to the sound of larks hovering above. Sometimes a mate would bring a lurcher and we would course for hares, rarely catching one. We would cover miles until it was too dark to see and return home exhausted but imbued with a sense of freedom that is important to me to this day.

A more cosmopolitan side of my upbringing came from my mother's family. Her parents ran the dairy in Littleport but were acquainted with the wider world. They had run a shop in London's East End and my grandmother, Jenny, had worked for a number of years in Birmingham as a forewoman in the rag trade. She was word perfect with all the music hall songs and was a lot of fun, if sharp with it. My grandfather, a local man, seemed to know everyone in the Fens. He delivered milk seven days a week. Sometimes at the weekend I would help him out on the isolated Fen rounds, down tracks with names like Burnt Fen and Coffee Drove, to black pitched shacks and fletton brick bungalows flagged by a couple of desolate poplars as wind breaks. To survive the work it was necessary to judge, within a gnat's whisker, the length of the ubiquitous Alsatian's chain.

On Saturday afternoons my grandmother, bottle of gin to hand, would do the books and wages on the kitchen table, the scrubbed surface covered by piles of coins and wads of notes. When the work was done and more than a few drinks had been taken I was allowed to work my way through several bottles of 'Ely Ales' from the crate in the pantry. Pleasantly inebriated I would listen to grandma's tales of the city. The session would end with music hall songs, the bawdier the better, with titles like 'Keep your Hand on your Ha'penny' and 'A Little Bit of What you Fancy does you Good'.

Then there were the school holidays when we would visit what I like to think was a more acceptable part of the Fens, the North Norfolk coast. Day trips to Holme, Old Hunstanton and Wells-next-the-Sea. Later, as my father made money, we would take a week's holiday in Sheringham or Cromer – 'I can see the sea', Punch and Judy shows, sandcastle competitions and sunlit prayer meetings on the beach with the Evangelists, my brother and I singing 'Jesus Wants me for a Sunbeam' at the top of our voices. Now I'm over sixty I rather hope Jesus has gone off the whole idea.

My father was a strong swimmer and consequently was always rescuing people from the treacherous North Sea. He was also a good high diver specialising in the Swallow dive (you throw both arms back like wings and arch your back in imitation of the bird). He was teaching me to do this from a breakwater at high tide when, intent on being a swallow, I hit my head on the breakwater's hidden prop. I was drifting out to sea unconscious, more swallowing than diving. My father pulled me back to shore whereupon I immediately had to Swallow dive again in case I lost my nerve.

When the tide was out my father would walk us for miles across the sand bars, digging for cockles, catching shrimps and watching as he hauled crabs as big as plates out from under rocks until his hands ran with blood from their powerful claws. At dusk we would return home to Littleport in a convoy of cousins, uncles and aunts, to my grandparent's dairy to boil up the crabs and shrimps until they were as red and ready to peel as the skins on our backs. The raucous feast would be washed down with 'Ely Ales'. At last, too exhausted to complain, we would be sent to bed.

One year we took a week's holiday in Sheringham staying in a flint-knapped town house trimmed with hollyhocks. It was here that I met one of my first artistic inspirations, Tom W. Armes. His wife ran the boarding house while the old boy painted all day in his studio – comfortable interiors and beachscapes – the best of which he would submit to the Royal Academy Summer Exhibitions. He also had a lucrative bread-and-butter seam – quick portraits of the boarding house guests. He painted a couple of telling portraits of my brother and me commissioned by my mother. Posing for Tom W. Armes as a properly brought up little boy and breathing in the exciting smell of turps I thought the old RA had it made. His relaxed way of life, was so much more appealing than my father's plans for me – running 'Claw Brothers' and trying to compete with my father's only hero, the contractor Sir Robert McAlpine, whose dying words he would quote whenever the going got tough: 'Keep the big mixer rolling boys.'

I was so impressed with the artist's life I tried for a scholarship to Cambridge School of Art and got it. The only fly in the ointment was the academic catching up they insisted I do – boring chores like learning to write. But I loved art school. I thought I had died and gone to heaven. I hastily abandoned the family home and the Fens to concentrate on learning enough from my tutors to insure I would never have to work again.

My only remaining contact with the Fenland work ethic was limited to the strawberry season. Father would buy a field of strawberry plants in the spring for a good price. When the strawberries began to ripen I was summoned to pick them and sell them, punnet by punnet, around the council estates of Cambridge. This was by way of supplementing my student income and his wallet. His master plan had one fatal flaw. This high-summer work was very thirst making and my end of the profits tended to be soaked up by Cambridge publicans. In my final year at art school the closest I got to Norfolk were the tiny vignettes I drew for the *East Anglian Magazine*.

Since I left college in the late 50s, I have managed to make a living as an artist/ buccaneer liberating gold coins in cities world-wide. In four decades I am happy to say I have rarely had to earn a crust doing what my father so rightly called 'real'

work in the 'real' world – I simply refuse to live in it.

My childhood in the Fens and North Norfolk fashioned my rebellious attitude which served me well as a satirist and also instilled in me an affinity for wetlands and endless skies. When the time came to scuttle the ship and hang up the skull and crossbones I decided to return to that most acceptable part of Norfolk. And now, like artist Tom W. Armes before me, I have a studio by the sea and submit my work for the Royal Academy Summer Exhibitions. I'm not so far from the windmill at Overy Staithe where I looked out to sea from the crows-nest while my father painted the mill black. I am so close to the sea that in a generation my studio could well be under water.

The grandchildren visit in the summer and for a few hectic weeks I live in the past, present and future. When thousands of pink-footed geese lift off the salt marshes and spread like quivering streamers across the early morning sky it's a signal for me to migrate to warmer climes. A Norfolk winter is just a little too much like life in the Fens.

Photo by Michael Festing

Sally Festing

Sally Festing's family arrived in Burnham Overy Staithe in 1947 to find families they had known in Cambridge – several of which, like Sally's, are still there – had discovered the North Norfolk coast before them. She embraced the landscape by pounding barefoot through marshland towards the open sea. Yellow sand, green marsh – all decolorate, and leached blue skies – interrupted by little boats, pine trees and the ears of Holkham church. Sally later stayed in other village houses including a bright green railway carriage and the wooden single-storey School House. Her Overy days are governed by tide and weather and her family's priorities remain those of mucking about on sand and in water. Her first book *Fishermen* (published in 1977 and republished with photographs in 1999), was about inshore fishing between Brancaster and Great Yarmouth. She says writing about a place she inhabits gives her insights such as the fact that fishermen seem naturally to know the landscape belongs not to them but to its birds.

Voices from Wells Quay

Sally Festing

Wells's attractions are manifestly inclusive. Early June until September, a chain of crabbers straddles the quay, east and west. From miles away, on day trips or in touring family groups they arrive to stand or sit, legs dangling over the water. Squatting on reed mats, surrounded by buckets, nets, bait, fish-and-chip trays, dizzy dogs and half-drunk mugs of tea, they are engrossed by the mysterious borderland between air and water. Up and down, the quay is strung with orange lines dangling hunks of whelk and Tesco's bacon tied in washing powder bags.

'Normally you get one every three minutes. You're just lucky where you pick.'
The unpredictable nature of the hunt is as implicit as respect for the crab's clumsy, warlike demonstration.

'He's lost three of his legs.'

'When they have the gilly competition here, you're disqualified if you use a hook.'

'Some of the shops take the hook off, but not all of them,' said Wells resident, Myrtle French, who frets about the swans.

The background is a spread of pale yellow sand, pale green marsh, boats, sails and skeletal pines. From the Lifeboat House on the tip of the western promontory to the old whelk sheds at the far end of the East Quay, the landscape unites the waterfront. Myrtle with her swan crusade and a reluctant crabber from the edge of the quay, carried off screaming by his mum, are part of Wells's activity on the land, both participators and scene. The water too provides constant busyness, and busyness is part of Wells's attraction. To harbourmaster, Bob Smith, it is vital:

A harbour needs things happening, it needs boats moving. People bustling around on the water. The shipping virtually finished in about 1990, 91-92. *Albatros* was the last we had, but she was a very small ship. The harbour looked dead on its feet. There's nothing worse than when you see a harbour run down. So we thought we're going to have to change. If we didn't, the place would have silted up and with the greatest respect it would have ended up like Blakeney, Brancaster, Overy. There's a few boats pottering about but it's not happening. It's the only accessible harbour [Wells] between the

Humber and Great Yarmouth, twenty-four hours a day during the tide. The place is special and we want it to be buzzing.

Of eight people I spoke to about the future of Wells, Bob's vision is the most single-minded. His family go back 300 years in the town. It was his grandfather's stories that inspired his deep love for the place. A place, he feels vehemently, whose future should be determined, not by developers nor outsiders ('the wellyboot brigade') but by Wells people. Any reservations he has about tourism are outweighed by a robust confidence in managed affairs. Why else would he trot along to council meetings on a Monday night when he would far rather stay in? I met him at the present HQ of the Harbour Commission, a very small room in the 'old' lifeboat house in which one wall establishes, in red and green paper stick-ons, all the boat moorings in the harbour.

We now have over 400 moorings in the harbour and yachts waiting to come here. We're lit all the way from the Fairway buoy to Teesside. Never in history has it been lit to this degree. And we've now got boats coming from all over Europe. The year 2004 was the highest we ever had. Sixty yachts more than the year before. But we can accommodate a few more. We have the fishing boats here and we've now got a leisure industry. The two can work in together. We're not changing for change's sake, we're changing it because we need to go forward. We can't stop people coming and we better accommodate them the way we want to. Nowadays when people come to a harbour and they expect a nice warm shower. Expect to be able to go to the loo. They expect that instead of having to tie up against the quay wall, which was fine twenty years ago, when you went up a ladder, they can moor at a pontoon. Now you can't have people scrambling up a ladder in case somebody falls off and breaks their leg. You could be sued. So we put pontoons in. There again, we haven't gone over to the fancy pontoons of the south coast. We've made our own out of timber, in keeping with this old rustic harbour.

We've now got seven staff with the Harbour Commission. The place is busier and busier and it generates more for the town. I don't care what anyone says; when people come to Wells, they make for the water. We are conscious we don't want to spoil it. We won't spoil it. So we're doing it in a sensitive way. Doing it slowly. People are frightened of change. I think we've been in this cocoon, or Wells has. Or the North Norfolk coast has. This is a place like no other. We know that. So let's share it, but then let's keep what we've got. Keep what the attraction is.

Long ago, Roman Catholic pilgrims, on their way to Walsingham from the Midlands and the Lake District, dropped in at Wells to spend money. Visitors have continued to arrive although the scale and suddenness of the town's popularity has taken even its dwellers by surprise. The Harbour Project is a three-phase overlapping programme conceived before the new century that attempts to cater for such change. It embraces a Maritime Heritage Centre, the restoration and adaptation of the carrstone Old Lifeboat House, new facilities for harbour users and improved recreation facilities. Bob sees the project as a forward leap that would simultaneously cater for increased numbers of visitors, catch up with conservation, provide more accommodation for the Harbour Commission, and house the Museum he set up in 1990 with Lorraine Marshall, his 'chief exec', and Graham Walker, with a pair of oars from the Wells lifeboat. The Harbour Project is a topic on which most of the town's inhabitants have an opinion. But change is a sensitive issue and Bob admits, 'There's a lot of people who don't want it.'

Here is Wells. Mid-September is as good a time as any to walk the steepish incline of Staithe Street which opens directly on to the quay. At the top, the highway is not what you would call broad and the last third narrows even more, emphasising alternate bands of gull-specked marsh and blue-blue water. In sun and at high tide, the sharp hulls of sailing boats tack left and right, carving the water's ruffles. People pass, though inevitably, you focus ahead. Most of the coloured flags that criss-crossed the street during August's carnival have been taken down. An old crabber chunts by with a tiller so long it appears to reach half way into the boat. A 20-foot yacht with a cabin and a long mast moves away as the view stretches.

One or two people sit, backs towards Staithe Street, on a wall that edges the quay. On either side of them, strips of blue and scorched green appear between cabins of commercial fishing boats, their rails billowing a festival of pink, blue and orange buoys.

On the coast road, you can look left (west) or right along two very different perspectives. West finds, at the base of the sea wall, the pretty 19th-century Old Lifeboat House (a Grade 2 listed building). At right angles to it, the quay gives way to a jaunty kingdom of amusement arcades run by families of settled travellers. This is Wells's flip side, a Wells of inexpensive toys and knick-knacks, souvenir shops, chippies, Bingo, restaurants, coffee and burger bars.

Eastwards, a gantry on stilt legs protrudes from an old brick granary monopolising the skyline. Beyond it, the road closes in between the hipped roof of a Chandlery and what was once a potent symbol of Wells's inshore fishing community, the Shipwrights' Arms. Fishing hasn't stopped. About a dozen boats go out from the harbour, mostly crabbing, but, like men of other callings, fishermen began to watch TV in the evenings and their particular haunt stopped trading.

I haven't mentioned a congestion of metal. To some extent familiarity fuddles aesthetics; congestion feels 'homely', and some shrug shoulders, grunting that cars have always parked on the quay. Others would dearly love to erase the clutter of vehicles, spreading so close to the edge that recreational crabbers tie their fishing lines to bumpers. Behind them rises the ice-cream coloured paint, occasional pebble wall and old red brick of the town's buildings.

Wells's social diversity is significant, compared, for example, with the neighbouring Burnhams. At the top of Staithe Street there is a polite square of Georgian houses round the Buttlands, some of whose inhabitants seldom see the sea. The resident spectrum runs from the odd native inshore fishermen to long-standing family trades-people, couples who have moved in from surrounding villages for town amenities and academics in second homes. Regular visitors might be natty yachtsmen or Manchester United nylon-clad Midlanders. Like every community, the town has divisions. Small groups of dwellings once clustered round separate yards with their own bakers, fish shops and vegetable stores. On a larger scale, Staithe Street divided fishermen to the east and mariners to the west, without a great deal of intermingling.

'Everybody says hello, especially in the winter,' says Myrtle, whose grandmother, a midwife at East End, found time to mother thirteen children. Some of her ability seems to have passed down. Myrtle married into French's Fish & Chip Shop, started by her father-in-law in 1925. She keeps voluminous scrap-books of cuttings on affairs in which she has participated as town and district councillor and a governor of three schools. Her prowess as a Sharpie helmsman for thirty years is commemorated by tiles on her kitchen walls, an activity in which she engaged as a founding member and first woman commodore of the Sailing Club.

We used to have meetings in the Shipwrights when that was a pub. Then the little place you go through with a sort of archway. Then we got this bit of land' (between the Shipwrights and the whelk sheds).

A hundred pounds raised by members was matched by a council grant. Land bought, materials accumulated and the Club House was built by its members. With a current membership of more than 150, the club might be cited as a model of social interaction. Indeed, it would be possible to compliment the whole town, some 2500 people, for its wealth of clubs and societies, for so much *bonhomie* and intermingling. At the same time, there are pockets of intolerance. Lack of tolerance reinforces self-interest and self-interest limits vision because important things can only be seen from a larger perspective. The disadvantage of restricted vision is that it allows people to act against their own best interests. What happened to Wells's whelk shed area is a good example.

I first knew this mysterious corner of Wells as an oasis of wooden buildings, rough grass, allotments and an occasional chicken where windswept fishermen arrived in darkly silhouetted boats to boil their catches in steamy sheds. It is getting on for thirty years since I squatted outside what was then the most distant whelk shed while Jack Cox, skipper of one of the boats, spelt out his engagement with place and the exactitude demanded by his work. Despite which, he reckoned, the sea was his feast, one moreover that keeps man in realistic subordination to the natural world. Jack combined fishing with painting, and painting reinforced his sympathy with the constant flux and turns of seasons, weather and wildlife.

Paradoxically, and Wells is full of paradoxes, Jack's whelk shed – an old brick factory – was demolished. Its site lies inside one of two large imprisoning wire-link boat storage yards. Jack's nephew, David Cox, had a long career in fishing and service to the Wells lifeboat. Fittingly, he reflects the regret those involved feel, as much as anyone, that bureaucratic bungling led to irreversible vandalism. 'It [the family whelk shed] would have been a marvellous thing now. It could have been a maritime museum. It would have been ideal. So it was a sad day when we took notice of the planners to pull it down.'

It is not unusual for Wells people to identify an almost spiritual belongingness to their home. If the best of the whelk sheds has gone, those which survive are a testimony to the inshore fishing.

I think there's a great attachment to the whelk sheds by the people of Wells because they knew them when they were producing whelks. They could go down and see the black smoke rising from the chimneys. It's one of the places which is irregular – the soul of Wells. I've used one for my own trade without changing anything.

This speaker, another artist, took up residence four years ago in a town he has known from childhood. Since then, John Richter has purchased an old whelk house to use as a studio.

It's perched between the busy little town and the open marshes. On one side you can see the town and hear it. On the other, the open expanse of marshland and creeks. It's a very beautiful setting. The light is excellent. You not only get the direct light but the light reflects off the water onto the ceilings down there. So you get a dappling on the ceilings which gives a very consistent strong white light.

It was extremely difficult to find space in the town in which he could work. One aspect of providing for the future is to conserve visually meaningful buildings and John feels responsibilities to the shed that has become his workplace.

To maintain old buildings is very labour-intensive. The roofs fall off, the wood rots, they subside. The creek undercuts the quay. The northeast wind can be ferocious with a spring tide. Repairs require far more work than bulldozing and putting up something new.

Vividly alert to the social forces that shaped the setting, John has spoken with many local people about the fishing, brick-making and the railway which traversed almost the entire quay until 1963.

The line ran down as far as the Shipwrights' Arms, but it only had an engine up to the Sailing Club. Past that the carriages were horse-drawn and they mostly took coal because there were a whole lot of coal yards on the south side of East End.

'There's a lot more people come to North Norfolk than there used to be,' said David Cox who finds himself surrounded by newcomers in the East End cottage which snuggled among fishing families when he bought it from an uncle in 1949. 'This 'Harbour Plan'. Up to a point it's a big improvement because they've got to have toilets and things for the visiting boats.'

If Wells's natural resources predispose the town to tourism, clarity, foresight and adaptability are prerequisites to benefiting from change. Certainly they characterise the approach led by the Pinewoods Campsite. About a mile from the Quay, along a straight windswept drive behind the sea wall, the site feeds into Wells harbour by car, foot and miniature railway. At full capacity it holds 4000 people, which is getting on for double Wells's population and is obviously significant to trade. Holkham Estates own all the reclaimed land between Holkham and Wells and since 1996, when they plucked back the campsite from the local authority, the Estate has also been responsible for jumping so effectively on the tourist bandwagon.

The day I went in, out of season, a gaggle of Brent geese had taken up station in the centre of landscaped grounds catering for what the Pinewoods call tents, tourists and statics (permanent caravans), and Yorkshire recruit, David Shelley, was about to receive from David Bellamy, on the camp's behalf, a fourth consecutive Gold Medal award for conservation. 'They use solar panels, which don't pollute the night sky,' he said, 'and they don't run a bar so that visitors head for the town and support local businesses.'

Not that the railway or amusement arcades are a priority for all its clients. Daryl and Jane Saunders have been coming to the Wells area from their tiny East Leicestershire village since discovering North Norfolk ten or twelve years ago. Ninety-five percent of the caravans, like the 200 beach huts, are privately owned, and theirs is on a 16-year lease. The town's amenities are appreciated:

We like that street that goes right up the middle (Staithe Street). The hardware shop is brilliant. Bookshops and shops for cheap underwear and socks and stuff. Good butchers there as well. Nice little coffee shop on the left-hand side as you walk up. The pub right at the top's very good. Lot of people on the caravan site recommend it. French's do superb fish-and-chips. We always pick up our crabs and lobsters from the van on the quay.

Still more important to them are the natural surroundings.

Our walks go from Titchwell Marsh to Holkham and the other side you've got about the same distance to Cley where their bird reserves are. So Wells is about midway. We visit all the bird reserves but we also like the walks in between them. It's a nice caravan park. We're actually backing onto pine woods. Wells beach is superb. Such a big beach it's never crowded. You can walk from our caravan right to Holkham Bay and up to the top to Holkham Estate and the walk through the woods from the Lifeboat Station is superb. The best times to go are early spring and autumn when you've got migratory birds. The winter's good for all the thousands of geese. When they're coming in to roost at night and you're standing underneath them, the sight's unbelievable. You're talking of 50–100,000 geese. All coming in, landing in the fields round Holkham Bay and the Wells area. Make a hell of a row.

Not only Wells's resources but the lack of alternative employment reinforces the wisdom of developing the tourist trade. There are no manufacturing or service industries and it seems difficult to get a foot in on the small industrial estate. If David Cox hadn't wanted, since he was young, to fish, he'd have had difficulty, he says, to find a job in his home. The prospects for his grandchildren, living in Warham, aren't rosy either. Since the future of farming and fishing became uncertain, dearth of opportunity for the young has been a recurring refrain.

There will always be some fishing. Alan Frary, Lifeboat Coxwain and one-time fisherman whose father went longshoring with Jack Cox, spoke for the odd dozen Wells boats crabbing on the Race Bank in 2003. It's for 'the glorious uncertainty', not the returns, the inshore fishermen goes to sea, and crabbing is so governed by regulations as to make it, in his estimation, 'mind-numbing'. As to trawling for shrimps – for local fishermen the cost would be pro-hibitive.

'You need damn great big boats to make it pay'. Important as fishing remains to tradition and to the visual impact of the har-bour, the trade never made men rich and the quarry has proved fickle. Set against the prolif-eration of crabs and lob-sters in recent years, mus-sels and whelks tailed off somewhat abruptly before the 21st century.

The explanation for slump and flux has always perplexed. From time immemorial, people have con-jected reasons for occurrences they don't understand, not least the fisherman with his wealth of superstition, for the disappearance of fish. David addresses a significant cause:

> The fishing like I was brought up to was more communal. 1945 onwards there was the Pegg family, the Cox family, the Cooper family and the Grimes family. They was all getting a fair living. But the grounds could only stand so much because with any fishing you can clean the grounds up with over-fishing.

Older generations used techniques that conserved stocks, he clarified, methods neglected by 'cowboys'. There are, of course, many reasons for the depletion of fish, environmental factors, both natural and man-made being also involved.

So fishing is unpredictable and jobs in Wells are scarce. This makes half an equation with potential for at least partial balance, because a lot of people fancy the place. Willy-nilly, they are arriving and tourism spells opportunity. Can the town both protect what it values and adapt? Given the damage caused by mass tourism, David's caution is understandable.

> I think before long the Harbour Commissioners are going to have to think how many boats they can have in this place because they can overcrowd it. When you get to the height of summer and look up and down the harbour on the creeks, the place is full. It's revenue what counts, mind you. It seems to me that is what counts in lots of things.

The social change that causes most objection in Wells is common to all beauty spots; a problem to which, for lack of easy answers, adaptation is particularly prudent. Ownership of holiday accommodation and second homes has depleted some surrounding villages out of season, increased the average age of populations, and already cut numbers in Wells schools. Demand is rising, house prices are rising. Since 1991, national statistics show, while the number of dwellings in Wells has increased by over 400, a significant proportion have become holiday homes. Myrtle deplores the threat, especially as she would like to think that the people who were born in Wells could afford houses to live locally. The situation is complicated, one of the twists being that some second homes are bought and run as investments by local people. Another consideration, at least arguable, is whether those native to a locality should have special privileges. Will people born *in situ* necessarily contribute more than those who choose to join a community? The issue involves divisions between incomers and natives.

The importance of the distinction is basic to some of those with whom I spoke, since they prefaced every description of a fellow inhabitant with additional information, that he or she was or wasn't a 'local'. These references were so habitual, they had become second nature. Yet discrimination impoverishes the ability to discover what people have in common. Housing decisions based on the type of settler most likely to benefit the community could bring long-term rewards. Has the town considered, for instance, providing affordable studios? Making the industrial estate more accessible?

Ray Hewitt dubs himself a 'Holiday Home Proprietor'. Starting out as a carpenter, he now does 'a bit of everything'. Four sons and a daughter were raised in an old end-of -row cottage, in the starkly white but aesthetically pleasing Brigg Square at the west end of the coast road or 'Freeman Street', bought when he arrived from Briston in 1969. A little cash plus a little imagination at the right time have done him well. As Ray says, he was 'in on the ground floor' with one of Wells's first holiday developments. Why, then, is he suspicious of larger adaptation to change?

'I don't see how the Maritime Heritage Centre is going to protect salt marsh. The salt marsh isn't in danger of disappearing, quite the reverse, it's building up. There's a lot of scaremongering going on.' The whole project, he implies, is some kind of ruse. 'We're now at the mercy of people from cities with vast amounts of money ... They want to create this as a yuppie harbour ...'

Ray wasn't the only man who cited overspending or 'wastefulness' as part of his objection. 'I can't think how they can make it pay,' Myrtle worried. 'What about money to run the place once it is built? We've got a community hall which is run by locals, the old Malthouse down the street. All we have on there is a caretaker and someone else to help. It pays for itself.'

John Richter's considerations are partly financial and partly about governance. 'It is the economics of these bodies [the County and District Councils] I do not support. Burnham Market and Holt have developed into flourishing towns with very little intervention from governmental policies whereas places such as Fakenham have had continuous revitalisation plans thrust on them with vast sums of money spent over 20 years and have very little to show for it...'

'The old way's still the best,' David Cox opined, comparing the immediacy of marketing fifty years ago (of whelks) with current centralisation through a shellfish factory in Cromer (crabs and lobsters). There are many subjects he might have been addressing: the notion is partly a matter of one's flexibility. As regards marketing, Alan Frary sees two sides to the case. 'This factory's got the lads by the short and curlies. It pays them by the kilo. On the other hand, if it wasn't for the factory some of these boats wouldn't be going to sea now. There's good and bad in it.'

For Alan, it's the same with the lifeboats. He appeared from the top of a shiny pinewood staircase beside a shiny blue lifeboat in the sand-coloured, corrugated iron lifeboat shed with red trim, at the far tip of the west bank. He has been in the Lifeboat Service for twenty-seven years, coxswain for seven, and has splendid rope-pulling arms to show for it. In the past all his men knew the sea. Today, of a possible crew of twenty-five, only four have maritime backgrounds and they include Alan's brother and his son. The twenty-one who 'don't pick up a piece of rope from one week to the next' take a training course at Poole and end up with a National Certificate. 'So there's plusses and minuses,' he said. The modern ingredient that does most to spoil his job satisfaction is one that affects a great number of service professions; the requirement for accountability. 'I do a fifteen-minute job on the boat and spend an hour writing up what I did. All the papers have got to be catalogued.'

The boom of Wells's maroons takes me back thirty years to the tales of fishermen-lifeboatmen and the generations in Sheringham churchyard, lost at sea. Ninety percent of today's callouts are to 'Leisure', but still there is the excited scramble, the pulling on of shirts and gumboots. Until recently a 'Name & Shame List' was pinned up in the town. 'Everyone wants to know what the story is. It's like Chinese whispers, all the links,' said John. And as did the old ways, the new ones have limitations.

Progress needs broad sweeps, though broad sweeps have dangers. Bureaucracy can too easily stifle imagination and bureaucratic bodies are by nature insensitive to minority needs. Fear is roused especially in those who feel their interests have been neglected in the past. Ray sees as an anomaly that people who say they want to protect the coast should simultaneously bring in more visitors. In a way, of course, it is. More specifically, he approves neither of the site, size nor visual impact of the prospective Maritime Heritage Centre. 'It's over the top. It will cost too much money and become a white elephant.' Again, there is a sort of frugality. Having learned the 'hard way', the 'old way', Ray prefers situations he can understand and control. Still more specifically, he claims the Centre would encroach on the adjacent childrens' playground that he considers a vital part of what Wells owes its young. This is a perfect objection because it embodies a moral element. Ray can not allow that negotiation involves developing terms. Reasons for partisanship may be deeper and more emotional than he realises. The territory, a powerful undercurrent, is 'them' and 'us'.

What Wells is looking for are compromises rather than solutions, despite which you feel the impact of an open creative mind, feel how it differs from the frightened and prescriptive one. I will never forget two principles made in a talk given by one of the great landscapists of the century, a woman who worked most of her life for the Forestry Commission, designed Uppingham Reservoir and some of Britain's major highways (Dame Sylvia Crowe). We are obsessed by 'tidiness', and change doesn't have to be bad. Both these tenets were addressed directly or indirectly by the people I met in Wells.

John Richter's affection for the whelk sheds stems partly from their functionalism. He isn't a stick-in-the-mud, but he is worried that development in the name of progress should embrace a single issue rather than a variety of needs:

Most of my work, preceding even moving to Wells, was maritime scenes. Boats, harbours, sea and sky. So this was a continuity. Even the paintings which are abstracted are of that same experience of being in that whelk shed with the tide, knowing the creeks, and hearing the sea in the distance. I find I didn't want to paint one little camera view but to include all the elements, particularly the flowing and ebbing of the tides which is not one second but a rhythm which seems to affect my life and that of everybody else down there. People come to sail boats. Fishermen go out. The tide recedes and boats lie on their side, people come out on the sand. This pattern is repeated twice a day and it is my inspiration.

Bob Smith spoke with challenging enthusiasm of current difficulties, and of an earlier creative mind.

The car thing is a massive issue. Hopefully we'll get over the problem using land further down the town. But that has been an absolute nightmare and that's gone on for about eight years I should think now. Many times you think, is it all worth it? But it's got to be, because if we all say 'I can't be bothered with that', you'd never get nothing done. When Lord Coke or Lord Leicester in them days – what was it, 1845? – reclaimed all the land, to me that's the biggest inspiration. He planted all those Corsican pines. He knew he was never going to see them. But the vision of the man to plant something that gives so much enjoyment to people. And he knew he was never going to see it. Now to me that was stuff on its own. He built the embankments, reclaimed the land. OK he did it commercially because he wanted the land, but the trees is something else. What a legacy to be left. Now what we're trying to do is leave a legacy. Our legacy's got to be a small building across the road. Simple as that. May sound a bit strange but it's about protecting our heritage for future generations.'

A Farmer's Tale

Teddy Maufe

Norfolk has been my home since my birth fifty years ago and I have lived in the same house ever since – a common occurrence in England until the middle of the last century. Now I realise I am something of a dinosaur; being a farmer makes the dinosaur comparison even more poignant.

My childhood was spent on this farm on the Holkham Estate where my father was a tenant. The farm enjoyed relative prosperity after the war when food producers were held in high esteem and the population still remembered real food shortages. I grew up in an immensely sheltered environment – spending most of my time when not at school on the farm amusing myself; friends always had to be imported by car.

I had three older sisters who were a force to be reckoned with and I quickly learnt to keep a low profile. Growing up on a Norfolk farm in the 1950s and 60s was a very different experience from that enjoyed by my children now. For a start the farm had enough staff to field a cricket team and did. Now we are down to just two arable workers and a lorry driver.

My childhood life of boarding school and long holidays on the farm – in the summer a lot of time was spent on the coast, picnics at Gun Hill and swimming in the North Sea – was suddenly and cruelly blown apart when my mother died when I was only fifteen.

Teddy Maufe

Teddy Maufe was born at Branthill, a 1000-acre arable farm on the Holkham Estate in 1951. After school at Greshams he spent a gap year as a 'jackaroo' in Australia where he acquired a passion for lightweight sailing dinghies. Returning to England he built a Lightweight 12 Square Metre Sharpie, *Southern Aurora*, and still sails it at Brancaster Staithe. It is, he says, 'rewardingly fast when the right way up' and with three crew 'a very stable boat'. After Agricultural College he took over the running of Branthill Farm where he lives with his wife Sally and their three children.

From then on my father no longer had his heart in the farm and was just ticking off the days until I could take over and he could sail away over the horizon, literally! So my education was cut short but I was lucky enough to squeeze in a gap year 'jackarooing' in Australia before a one year course at Agricultural College

Being a 'Pommey Jackaroo' on a mixed station 550 miles west of Sydney was a steep learning curve, not least the horse riding element of the job. But while out there I realised that working in open spaces suited me and several months working for an accountancy firm in Jersey reinforced that.

I returned to the farm, fell in love with a California girl whose hippy lifestyle was an utterly entrancing new world to me. But I soon realised the hippy pace of life was fine if someone else was subsidising it but that on its own it didn't stand up; nor did it suit my restless temperament.

We had a son, Zac, just as our marriage was breaking up. He has kept close ties with his Norfolk home. At that point I bought a majority share in the farm company and my father who had remarried a much younger woman with whom he had children the same age as Zac, moved away from the farm. This move suited both parties. On so many East Anglian farms the son carries on in the father's shadow for too long, slowly sapping the enthusiasm for change of the next generation.

After my divorce, amongst frequent trips to London to collect Zac for weekends in Norfolk I was so lucky to meet and later marry Sally. She was running a cooking partnership with another girl (who also went on to marry a Norfolk farmer) which proves I suppose that Norfolk farmers love their food…Sally and I have two boys, Bruin and Max, and a daughter, Amber.

Until 1997 the Branthill farm clock ticked round as usual.

The year starts in September with drilling winter barley for beer and oats for cereal bars. In October the sugar beet harvest begins with some wheat for the local mill planted behind the first lifted sugar beet fields. In November, drilling finishes until after Christmas but the sugar beet campaign goes on until the New Year. In January the last of the sugar beet is lifted and, if the soil is dry enough, spring barley (for lager) drilling is started. Spring barley drilling continues in February. March and April bring fertiliser dressings and sugar beet plantings plus fungicides against diseases and herbicides for weed control. In May, more fertiliser. June is a time for the corn to swell and sugar beet to grow. In July, the grain harvest begins and finishes in August with long hours and, hopefully, rewards for the farming year.

This farm rotation has been the mainstay for many Norfolk farms for the last half century. But in the 1990s this viable pattern began to wobble. First came a series of crippling droughts in the mid-1990s. Then the EEC fiddled with the subsidy system with their usual ineptitude and UK farmers suffered a bonanza. I say 'suffered' because we have never quite been able to live down those three years. The media had a field day with stories of East Anglian barley barons running out of ideas where to spend their ill-gotten gains that were gained at the taxpayer's expense.

Now we are in the grip of the worst UK agricultural recession since the 1930s. You may well ask what this has got to do with this beautiful part of Norfolk; I would reply 'everything'!

The North Norfolk countryside has been moulded by man over the centuries from the scrub and heathland that was slowly established after the last Ice Age. The Enclosure Acts of the 18th century helped pull together the final picture we have today, driven by the great landowners of the time like Thomas William Coke, Lord Leicester.

His ancestor's famous remark that the Holkham Estate was a place 'where two rabbits fight over one blade of grass' gives you an impression of how impoverished this part of Norfolk was. There was no beautiful Holkham Park and the undulating countryside was not protected by the miles of hedges you see today. Yes, there was a period when farmers grubbed out some hedges to make field sizes more adaptable to modern agricultural machinery but now many more hedges are being planted than lost; the same is true of trees.

But if this environment is to be protected and continue to flourish, farmers, the custodians of the countryside must have viable core businesses. My slogan 'Bankrupt farmers make poor environmentalists' becomes a more vital message month by month as UK farming slowly bleeds to death on the alter of global trading and a strong UK currency.

The very fabric of the Norfolk countryside is under threat and its destruction would be a catastrophe to most of the people who live in or visit North Norfolk and value it so much. The problem is that it will not unravel in front of peoples' eyes until it is too late for lasting damage not to have been done. Already there is enormous and growing financial pressure on farmers and landowners to seek planning permission to develop their land for anything but agriculture.

That may mean housing developments, caravan sites and golf courses, which is

so sad. We have kept this part of Norfolk relatively unspoilt partly because the relative prosperity of farming meant the land had agricultural value and there was no pressing need for farmers and landlords to develop it.

Do we really want to go down that development route?

We are so lucky North Norfolk has remained relatively unspoilt while so much of England has been tamed. And having survived thus far what a bitter pill it would be to lose it in this century. Another repercussion is that if the core business of farming is haemorrhaging there is no money to spend on such things as planting hedges and trees and restoring ponds and even if a grant is available there is no longer the time or staff to undertake it.

The mood of the nation is that farming should be more environmentally friendly. As a LEAF farmer (Linking Environment and Farming) I have no argument with that. We are always looking at ways to cut back on sprays and fertilisers as well as safeguarding the farm's natural features. With judicious application, timing and inherently healthier new varieties we are constantly cutting back on active product, yet we are still seen in the public eye as stalking the land, scattering prodigious amounts of chemicals across our fields.

What a public relations mountain we have to climb. But climb it we must if farming is to survive in anything like its present form and if we are to protect the North Norfolk countryside. The alternatives are either a few farming companies managing huge tracts of land with no input from the very people who now live and breathe the land, or a landscape of sad scrubland with thorns and brambles the dominant features. Neither scenario is very attractive.

But we have a government that is totally out of touch with the countryside and which believes that we as countryfolk are just obsessed with hunting and shooting. A huge disaster is in the making. But, sadly, I have to admit some of the blame rests with us farmers. We, by the very nature of our jobs, tend to be an insular group of people and this is proving our downfall because our public relations skills tend to fall very short of those of Issues Groups like the Soil Association and Greenpeace.

Organic farming has its place as a niche market but to try and drag us all back a century in agricultural progress would debase any potential organic premium there is and eventually require yet more virgin land to go under the plough. Surely the opposite intention of most of the green lobby groups. We do not call for the withdrawal of antibiotics and anaesthetics. So why should we call for the tested advances of modern farming that have led to the end of food shortages in most parts of the world and rapidly rising life expectancy?

Yet again farmers and the NFU have failed miserably to fight for conventional farming that is not organic. A lot of farmers are showing a similar mentality to that of rabbits when under threat, that is to go down their burrows and hope the present farming crisis will blow over. Sadly, this plays into the hands of the present government's spin doctors who propose 'diversification' schemes as the way out of the present crisis. They are patently not the solution.

If a lot of farmers embarked on these schemes there would be an over supply of bed and breakfasts, horse livery and holiday lets. If their core business is losing money head over heels, none of those alternatives is going to save the day (as our own, bed and breakfast, though busy, proves). As for the government's much vaunted environmental payments they are just scratching the surface. If the cake mix (core farming) is a disaster, covering it with the icing of government diversification grants and environmental payments will not provide the answer.

What is also frustrating to me as a farmer is that a lot of us cried wolf in the better times and gained a reputation for always moaning about something from the comfort of a new Range Rover. We now have to overcome that stigma and move on.

Is Norfolk worth saving? I realise as a Norfolk farmer I have a slight vested interest here. However if you value the Norfolk countryside as it is and also value an assured indigenous food supply, then it certainly has to be. Consider too that the existing rural infrastructure that is already stretched so thinly would disappear. Tourists to North Norfolk would be visiting a cultural museum in which no actual living members would be left. Is that what we want?

As farmers, have we lost the plot? Are we producing commodities nobody wants? The answer is no! Our high grade malting barley, acknowledged as some of the finest produced anywhere in Europe, is still sought after every year by maltsters. But we now receive half the price we did before 1997. Obviously this is unsustainable. Yet the price of beer continues to rise in line with the global brewers' profits.

As far as sugar is concerned, the UK produces 50% of its needs but since the recent currency swing and the rise of sterling the price for this crop is down 30%. We will never be able to compete with the extensive sweeping grain fields of the mid-west USA. Our fuel costs and price of land/rents per unit preclude that on this crowded little island where every lowland acre is coveted. But surely a secure, safe domestic food supply is worth hanging on to? Do we want to be at the beck and call of other countries for our food? Or is globalisation sacrosanct?

Other European countries take a much more sympathetic long-term approach to their agriculture and realise that letting it go would do desperate and lasting damage to their rural economies and the tradition of their national heritages.

As Norfolk farmers we do not deserve to be feather bedded. But I believe we run the risk of becoming a dying breed unless the government moves to help counteract the effects of the present currency imbalance. We need to get our message across to the rest of the population or these golden fields of ripening barley enclosed by our hedges and speckled with copses will be but a distant memory to the next generation.

On this farm I must try to arrest the relentless slide into losses by redirecting more of the farm's focus to niche market crops. In 2003 grain prices were better but this gain proved very short-lived.

In a recent initiative I approached the micro-breweries of East Anglia and together we are starting out on a new venture. In the past, Branthill Farm has supplied Maris Otter specialist malting barley for the real ale breweries. But we are now taking that concept several steps further. To start with, with one other farmer, we are setting up a supply group to grow specifically for real ale producing customers, offering barley that can be traced right back to an individual field. The 'package' will also include a totally assured crop grown with the utmost care and diligence using only the minimum of modern agricultural inputs on increasingly environmentally friendly farms.

To provide a shop window for the East Anglian brewers we have opened a real

Branthill

ale outlet off-license shop in a redundant building on the farm and will thus bring in to the public eye the forgotten connection between the fields of prime malting barley and a valued pint of real ale in their local pub.

My long term goal is for this region to be totally associated with the production of top quality malting barley for top quality real ale, as was the case in years gone by. Visitors to the region will want to seek out the real ale just as visitors to the wine growing regions of France and California seek out their finest wines.

For far too long the connection between East Anglian produce and the food and drink people buy has been lost. We will allow that to continue at our peril. Everyone stands to lose: farmers will be slowly eradicated on the anvil of world prices and the public will be denied a safe and assured quality domestic food supply. I sincerely hope we make that reconnection sooner rather than later.

As I watch the geese fly back in perfect formation from the beet fields to the marshes against a cold Norfolk January sunset I pray that this beautiful part of Norfolk in which I am privileged to live and work will survive.

The Incomers

Tessa Courage

Norfolk, one of the last bastions of rural life within spitting distance of London? Spoilt beyond recognition by the dreaded 'incomers'? Unspoilt in spite of waves of holiday makers that clog up the coast road during the summer? Sophisticated suburb of Islington? A time warp set forever in the 50s?

It's Friday night somewhere in Islington, the 4x4 is almost loaded, the chassis sitting low on its axles. The boot is groaning with goodies from Waitrose and the cat is sitting bad-temperedly in her basket, wedged between the green wellies and the foul smelling dog. Rowena and Justin are crammed in the back, almost submerged with the goodies surrounding them as 'fend-off' material for the inevitable 'are we nearly there yet' whine. Strange that although this ritual takes place virtually every weekend; they are never able to stop the war of attrition on their mother's nerves. Fiona thinks she has everything organised, after all she has been doing it for the last ten years, but still there is a nagging thought that the Worthys who are coming for the weekend may find the whole thing a little foreign. Giles, having ambled back from the city just in time to change into his country clothes, expects Fiona to be grateful as he manfully slides behind the wheel for the conveyor belt run up the M11 to Norfolk. The weekend progresses and for all the difference it makes to the Arch-Jones in the way of interacting with the locals, they might just as well have stayed behind in Canonbury and had a film of Holkham beach played against the wall in the sitting room. The Worthys indeed do their best to 'fit in', but somewhat to their amazement, when helping with the weekend chores they find that the local grocer fails to stock fresh coriander....

Drive through most villages near to the coast at night, and many of the houses will be 'dark'. It appears at first to be some form of selective power cutting exercise, but on looking more closely this is because a great deal of them have become second homes or holiday houses to the 'incomers'. These glamorous people sashay up from London for the weekend in their 'done to death' four-wheelers, packed to the gunnels with shopping bought from town, linen collected from the local laundry, and arrive just in time to make the place look 'lived in' before their imported guests for the weekend arrive. The weekend is spent in glorious oblivion to what is going on around them. Well perhaps not quite, as it

---

* *Note* All the names of those mentioned have been changed – for obvious reasons

Tessa Courage

Tessa Courage (sister to Teddy who is a fellow contributor to this book), was born in Norwich and grew up at Branthill Farm outside Wells. After school in North Norfolk she lived and worked in London and Europe. Later, with husband James, she lived for two years in South Africa and another two in Hong Kong and has travelled to most parts of the world (I first met her in Bogota, Colombia – ed). Although she lives in London her home has always been in North Norfolk. In the 1970s Tessa and James acquired a cottage at Branthill, a long stone's throw from her childhood home where her own children have grown Norfolk roots. She is slightly worried that, because she does not live here all the time, she might come across as an incomer, but says nothing can change the fact this is where she comes from.

is important that the weather behaves and that they can get a table at the local restaurant. On departing on Sunday night, do they give a backward glance, (apart from the one that checks whether the security light is working), at what they are leaving behind?

It was not ever thus, back in the early 70s when Julia and her husband moved to North Creake they were a rare thing. Firstly they had moved there on a full time basis, and neither of them had any connection to Norfolk and as Julia wryly puts it, 'I knew it would take a while to be accepted, but hadn't realised quite how long until the plumber told me that he was still regarded as an outsider after 35 years, having come all the way from Hunstanton!' At that time Norfolk was truly another world, it was like returning to the best part of the fifties. Now Julia feels that perhaps for those that journey up from London, it might seem like 'being propelled forward to some bucolic Knightsbridge of the future.' A case in point is Burnham (Up) Market, it used to boast two butchers, a baker, a greengrocer, an ironmongers, and a drapers, and the Hoste was a 'deliciously run down alehouse.' Not anymore, Julia like many others avoids Burnham Market from May to October. Going any near the popular villages in the summer leads me to believe that there is a slot for a reality programme called, 'I'm a local, get me out of here', or perhaps it should be called, 'I'm a local, get them out of here?'

Life in the satellite villages has changed radically. The litany of abandoned villages has been heard before and perhaps the time has come to pray to that old fallback – the god of compromise. Would there be a way in which there was a limit to how many houses per village could be given over to second home owners? It's ironic to think that the council estates, which are generally tucked away out of sight from the main heart of the village, (so as not to spoil the view?) are bursting at the seams, with never-ending waiting lists. Local children who grow up and wish to live in the same village are invariably priced out and have to be prepared to move well inland.

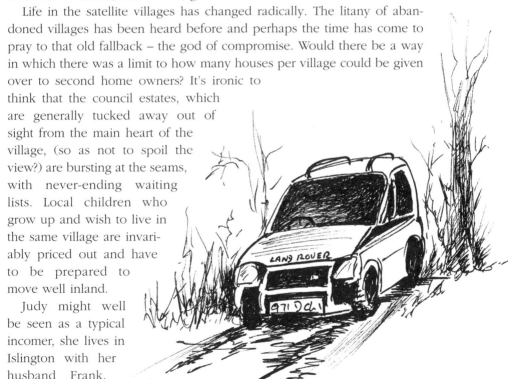

Judy might well be seen as a typical incomer, she lives in Islington with her husband Frank.

They have three children and spend quite a few weekends and holidays in Cley. (On talking to various people, I began to notice an interesting anomaly, inasmuch as if a couple decided to buy a place in Norfolk it was invariably because the wife had spent time there as a child or had family there; so where do all the men come from? Or more to the point where do all the men with Norfolk connections go to?) Jane had spent many happy weekends and holidays in Baconsthorpe as a child, her parents being ahead of the masses by having at the time, the only weekend cottage in the village.

Judy was pregnant in the hot summer of 1995 and had originally decided to rent a cottage in Cornwall for a month, until she realised that she could rent a place in Norfolk for one year for the same amount as one month in Cornwall. Being a sensible girl, she opted for Norfolk and that was the beginning of her connection with Cley. Judy feels that there are roughly four categories that make up the face of Cley. These are locals, retirees, weekenders and lastly those that 'buy to let'. Judy and her family have entered into community life with enthusiasm, from being determined not to load up the car in London, therefore supporting the local shops, to running a stall at the village fete. Interestingly, there are two summer fetes held each year, both emanating from the village hall, but held by two different groups, the church fete being run by the village hall and the car boot sale and barbecue by the Cley Club. Unlike many incomers, Judy has clearly given thought as to how the locals feel, and to how she thinks the current status quo was arrived at. 'The knock on effect that the mechanisation of farming is huge and has caused the biggest impact on the local way of life.' She goes on to remember that as a child in Baconsthorpe, 'Nearly all the cottages in the village were lived in by people who worked on the land.'

Cley has not suffered to quite the same extent as a lot of the other villages; it boasts amongst other things a smokehouse, deli, and a pottery shop. It also is a haven for 'twitchers' and many of the cottages that are let to holidaymakers in the summer, do not suffer the sadness of being left empty in the winter, as 'twitchers' are made of (and clad in) pretty strong stuff. On being asked what Norfolk means to her, the reply came quick as a flash, 'The beautiful beaches, the lovely countryside and the good fresh local food.' She also seems to have a love affair with Sheringham, and waxed lyrical about a place that I can only associate with going to the emergency dentist from school....

Further along the road from Judy live another London couple. The Butlers live in one of the oldest houses in Cley and are lovingly restoring it. They regard it as home, despite living in London during the week and having never spent more than two and a half weeks at any one time in residence. This feeling is genuine and it is reflected both in the feel of the house and the way in which they use it. Virtually every Friday night the picnic (to be eaten in Brandon) is made and the car is loaded to make an automatic pilot trip to the coast. Their connection with

Norfolk slightly bucks the theory of it being the female who initiates the introduction as they both have links. Michael is the nephew of a local train enthusiast and Suki's mother is from Norfolk, and she herself spent summer holidays along the coast at Lowestoft.

Despite having been in Norfolk for eighteen years, with fourteen of them being spent in Cley, they are still regarded as 'newcomers'. A recent incident has acted as a 'rain check'. Suki and Michael live beside a public right of way, but this has been somewhat restricted by the advent of a sea wall blocking the path. Michael has been parking his boat up against the sea wall in the knowledge that it is no longer practicable to use it as a right of way. Nothing daunted, the locals have taken action by parking a tractor to block his ability to move his boat. On politely remonstrating they met with, yes you've guessed it 'a brick wall'. Observations about the outrage have appeared in the parish notes, along with misnaming the house (a quiet nod to litigation?). The Butlers have been described as newcomers, and this has reinforced what they already felt. They are warm and hospitable and yet most efforts to integrate with the locals have been met, according to Suki, with no success.

Although they clearly love the area and have made a few good friends, breaking into local society has been difficult, to say the least. Invitations are met with polite refusals. Perhaps there is some sort of misunderstanding? It also seems that the longer they are there, the more difficult it becomes to get to know the locals. Like many others they feel that Norfolk will 'expand and is on the road to be ruined'. It seems such a conundrum. On another level there seems to be a locked interface. The small shops are closing down, this is seen as a direct result of the incomers bringing their food from London but looking closer, it is also because the locals have given up using them as well, preferring the easier to use and cheaper large supermarkets.

On being asked for their reasons for choosing Norfolk, apart from the childhood links, it seems that Michael was keen to find a place where he could follow one of his two loves, (apart from Suki) which are climbing and sailing, possibly the sailing won in this case? He wanted 'a none too stressful journey from London', and it was essential to find a place without a garden. On being pressed on this point, it was in order to stop Suki from 'whinging on about the problems with the mange-tout'.

Julian, who is in his mid-fifties, has lived in Norfolk for over twenty years and has witnessed the changes made by the advent of incomers. He feels this part of Norfolk is going the way of Hampshire and Gloucestershire, inasmuch as the 'big house' in the village tends nowadays to be lived in by strangers, who come only for weekends and holidays. He says, 'A sense of continuity is being lost, a continuity that up until now we've always had.' He feels that nothing can be done as, 'They have no sense of responsibility as to what their obligations might be.' He is saddened although resigned to the inevitability of market forces. Julian has also observed that the incomers as a race hate to stray too far from what they know. He calls the weekenders in Burnham Market 'marketeers', and has noticed that their lack of research when renovating their newly acquired property has had a negative affect on local craftsmen. If you drive around you will quite often see that, 'The signs relating to who is doing what on a house being done up, are from as far afield as Rutland.' He feels that no real village life exists anymore, and that it never will again. He points out the paradox that if a local does manage to buy a cheap house, when the time comes to sell it they will obviously sell it for a profit. Therefore the locals will not be able to afford it and it will yet again go to a second-homer.

Christine grew up in Wells, and apart from one six month stint in Hampshire has never lived away from North Norfolk. She is in her mid thirties, living in Salthouse and is a single mother of two sons. In Salthouse nearly a third of all the houses are second homes. While this gives the locals work as cleaners and caretakers, it also deprives them of the home from where to begin the journey to these jobs. The irony appears to be lost in translation as far as the council is concerned. Not only are they not building for the locals, but they have augmented a curious scheme to deal with earlier council houses. Old council houses which were originally built as 'temporary' accommodation after the 1953 floods have been renovated but strangely not for the locals. Christine points out that the Housing Association and Council have 'put the wrong-uns in from North Walsham', these being the homeless clearly not from Salthouse, and it would seem people who sadly bring their own problems with them. There are twenty houses involved in this project, with only two of the original families still living there.

One of the many things that I love about Norfolk people is their deadpan humour, which Christine has in spades. Without a change of expression she relates that most of the incomers own houses built on the flood plains, a part of the village which the locals would not touch with a barge pole (perhaps leaving it as a navigational kindness to the incomers when the waters rise?) Bearing this in

mind, guess how the incomers feel about the quandary of the flood defences? Currently Salthouse is defended from the sea by a shingle bank. This is constantly eroded by the wind and tide, and always needs to be rebuilt, which is a veritable Forth Bridge project, involving ongoing expensive maintenance. There has been a ten-year debate as to whether to build a clay wall which, although not as aesthetically pleasing as the shingle bank, would be a far more practical solution to the problem. The village is divided on this, which is not too surprising. No, the surprise is that some of the dwellers in the flood plains whose very homes are the ones that would benefit the most from the added security of the clay wall are some of the fiercest opponents. Conclusions to be drawn on a postcard?

Although Christine is not 'against' the incomers, recognising amongst other points, that their money helps to support the pub, the crab shop and the village store. However she feels that some of them don't have an awareness of how their wealth affects the less affluent, perhaps unintentionally, having an 'in your face' mentality. It has occurred to her that perhaps what is deemed to be good for the goose might also assist the gander? Namely that in order to buy a council house one has to have lived in Norfolk for five years before one is eligible. She feels that it would be a good idea for second homers to have to rent a house for the same number of years before being allowed to buy a property.

Living on one of the local farms for nearly forty years has given Julie and Edmund a clear vantage point from which to bear witness to the story. They have watched the way in which farming has gone from a way of life that remained largely the same for a hundred years or more through to rapid and unforgiving change. No longer for them is there a real feeling of community both on the farm and radiating out from it through the local villages. Mechanisation has had a profound effect, when the first tractor ploughed its first field, little did it realise the ghosts to come that would trail behind vying with the seagulls it its wake. When Edmund first started working on the farm there were 15 others working alongside. Now there are just three of them, and they are all nearing retirement age, with no eager youngsters chaffing at the bit, or even the ignition key, at the gates to take their place.

As the labourers have disappeared some of their cottages have been taken over by second-homers. One day the postman told Julie that there was a burst water-pipe in one such cottage on the farm. Julie and Edmund immediately set about trying to help, by locating the previous tenant and getting a message through to the present owners the problem was solved, and did they get thanked? Sadly not. However as a balance to this tale, Julie told me of a time years ago, when she worked up at the farmhouse. She was sent by the farmer's wife to go and give some very bad news to Kathy, one of the people living on the farm. Why she sent the sixteen year old Julie rather than go herself will become clear. The bad news was that Kathy's mother had died. Kathy having an unpredictable reaction to any news at any given time was to be approached with caution. Julie called from outside the house and Kathy's face appeared at an upstairs window. She explained that there was some bad news and would Kathy be kind enough to come downstairs and let her in. 'What is the news?' Julie tried every approach to cajole Kathy into coming downstairs. Finally she blurted out, 'Your mother has died.' Silence as Kathy stared at Julie, suddenly disappearing only to return moments later, to lean out of the window and pour a bucket of water over Julie's head. Possibly why the farmer's wife had elected to delegate the bearing of the bad news? As to the farmers wife? It must have been a deeply 'out of character moment', as she was my mother!

Although Christine and Edmund have never met, it is interesting to note that there is a similar thread that weaves through their views of the incomers. Which is a resentment which burns with a low flame in Christine's case and as a towering inferno in Edmund's. He feels that the people who buy holiday cottages should live solely on his and Julie's wages for a year. Currently, after taxes their joint take home pay is £17,000. Edmund has a pet name for the incomers; when pressed he just smiled, later on when he left the room, Julie leant forward confidentially and said, 'He calls them the Haemorrhoids.' It doesn't take a rocket scientist to make the correlation!

The supposed infiltration of the local council is another thorn in the flesh. Edmund feels that the second-homers visit Norfolk and like it for its beauty, wildness and air of being unspoilt and decide to buy a property.

They think it's great, but perhaps not exactly to their supposedly good taste. So they try to alter it, by getting a place on the local council. From then on they try to change everything, because although they like the idea of coming to Norfolk for its differences, they rapidly find the reality is not to their liking. So instead of blending in with the locals, they want the locals to blend in with them.

As a local, he is no longer surprised (and the irony is long since lost) to find himself going off road as the ubiquitous 4x4 bears down at speed towards him in the centre of the country lane. 'The only mud that it encounters is when it splashes the locals as it majestically passes by.' It would seem that this feigned or real indifference has seeped into the whole relationship between the two factions and is in danger of turning into the 'them and us' cliché. Julie grew up in Burnham Market and says that as more and more of her family have been forced to move away, the only people she knows there now are her mother and a couple of aunts. This would have been inconceivable in her parents' generation.

The displacement has gone further into their everyday lives. Each spring just before the season starts, the prices go up in most of the shops and as if to add insult to injury, they are often overlooked when queuing up to pay in favour of a holidaymaker. As Julie says, 'We feel like strangers in our own town.' Although there is the much-touted argument that the second homers bring money to the

North Norfolk coast, it fails to filter down to the lower-paid wage earners. Julie and Edmund now go to Norwich to shop and only go to the local town when it is 'released' to them for the winter months. On reflection, they feel certain that as much as 75% of the locals feel the same way, but hesitate to say anything, partly because they are not sure to whom to say it and partly from wishing to keep the peace. Edmund, musing on how he thinks he is viewed by 'them', quoted the refrain, 'Norfolk born and bred, strong in the arm, thick in the head.'

The scales have fallen from my eyes, and the other scales have been found to be out of balance. It would appear in general, that the incomers wish to 'gentrify' the Saltmarsh Coast. Instead of blending in with the locals, they want them to do the blending, and are only tolerated in order to play 'walk on parts' in their lives, possibly to add 'a bit of colour' and as a reminder as to where they are. The local councils do not appear to be helping keep the very people in Norfolk that make it what it is. Every local I spoke to talked about the lack of new council estates. Maybe it's a naïve and unworkable view, but perhaps each time a newcomer buys a house maybe a tax specifically payable towards local housing could be levied?

How to reconcile the two factions? There seems to be a fear of the local unknown and the unknown local. Will the further reduction of labourers on the farms, which inevitably leads to greater mechanisation and huge fields, create mini dust bowl prairies? Will the motorway finally encroach and, as we hurtle on the road to nowhere, will we glance out of the window and see the gigantic combines and wonder whether we are after all in Idaho? Are the incomers great big fat spiders that have hijacked the web, and who sit waiting for a few more flies to succumb so that they can make the web just that little bit more chi-chi? Do we all

want too much and give too little? Is it that places like Burnham Market are merely a theatre, where the players are afraid to stray too far in case they fall off the stage?

It was so much easier when everyone knew their place in the scheme of things. When the 'haves' did not live in such close proximity to the 'have nots.' When the local 'big house' was lived in by the same family for many generations, who knew what was expected of them – inasmuch as they took an active part in the welfare of the locals. Now we have so many aspirational magazines and television programmes, we are made to feel a failure if we don't have what the next door neighbours have and seem to feel that happiness can be bought along with the consumer goods that bay for attention.

Norfolk means so much to me. I left when I was seventeen and apart from sporadic visits back didn't return until I was in my early thirties, when I became one of those ambivalently regarded 'incomers', inasmuch as we bought a cottage on my brother's farm where I had grown up so many years before. Many happy summers were then spent as the children grew up. Time was shared with friends, both local and imported, and it was wonderful for me to see the impact that Norfolk had on people who had never been before. For some it has entered the blood. A South African friend came for the first time one Christmas. We went down to Holkham beach after a big snowfall, and she was so struck by the way in which one couldn't tell where the sand, sea and sky had merged, they seemed to form one huge grey landscape, which was both forbidding and enticing.

As to my relationship with Norfolk, it's part of 'the air that I breathe' even when I am not in the county. However, on arrival, there is always a 'buzz' when I see the line of trees that marks the turning into the lane. The ritual walk to the sea at Holkham beach is my form of therapy. Whatever the season or the weather or my mood, I walk there to celebrate, commiserate, alone, with family, with friends, it is my solace and consolation in times of sadness, and my joy in times of

happiness. I have taken my young children there with their buckets and spades and as 'oh my god we don't have to the walk to the sea again, do we?' teenagers, and now watch them go down voluntarily with their friends and sometimes even with me!

One night not long ago I was going to have supper with a friend in Holkham Park. It had been snowing during the day and I drove up the avenue under a brilliant moon and a star-studded sky. The snow lay 'deep and crisp and even', the trees were dusted with snow and the deer were sheltering underneath – they looked ethereal and there was a dream-like feeling as I slowly drove by the obelisk, with no sound except for the crunching of my tyres. I stayed the night, and on drawing the curtains in the morning, was met with the stunning sight of hares dancing on their hind legs on the white frosty lawn.

It is the landscape that has such an effect. The huge open skies, the still unspoilt tracts of countryside, the sea with its seemingly limitless horizon. Where else can you go in England and feel such a sense of space and closeness to nature? It makes a mockery of us 'matchstick men' who are such insignificant and temporary beings, who nonetheless have the power during our limited span to ruin this stunning backdrop to our lives. Instead of trying to manipulate the scenery into something resembling a theme park, and begrudgingly allowing the locals to play minor roles, we should be making attempts to step back, appreciate the astounding beauty of the coast and to do all that we can in order to protect it and to help those for whom it is their natural heritage, so that they are able to live there alongside the incomers.

I have such a strong feeling of being at one with nature on my walks along the shore that I have written into my will a clause that asks for my friends and family to walk to the sea, after my death and to return to one particular dune and drink a toast and know that this place meant everything to me.

Richard Worsley

Richard Worsley is co-Director of the Tomorrow Project, a charity which helps organisations and individuals think about the long-term future of peoples' lives (www.tomorrrowproject.net). He co-founded the project in 1997, following a series of jobs in large companies and organisations. He works with some 20 government departments and agencies and voluntary organisations to explore emerging social trends. Richard and his wife count themselves extraordinarily lucky to have been able to build a new house overlooking the marsh at Burnham Norton. Although the house is only eight years old, visiting barn owls, oyster catchers and the occasional marsh harrier suggest it has settled well in to the landscape. Richard is churchwarden at Holkham and is a Trustee of various local and national charities and chairman of two. He is obsessed by his vegetable garden.

Reflections and Conclusions

Richard Worsley

No one who has read these accounts of the Saltmarsh Coast can remain in any doubt that this is very special place. Each writer has described this in a different way, telling of its open skies, its marshes, its landscapes and seascapes, and its people. These people know about the Coast because their lives and their views have been formed by it. But they also know that it is vulnerable and under threat.

In this chapter I have tried to draw out from their writing and from conversations with them the essence of what is happening here, to look forward at the forces that will shape its future, to think about what could happen as a result, and finally to ask what we can do to help this extraordinary place into a future in which it continues to be loved, respected and understood – and not destroyed.

Not just one, but many places

What jumps out from these chapters is that this is not just one place but many – not just a summer place, but a very different one in winter; a place of villages (and a town) as well as countryside and coast; a place where some live all the time and to which many come to visit; a children's place. That is all true of many areas in Britain – but there is something peculiar and hard to pinpoint that makes this part of North Norfolk different and so much loved.

It is certainly due in part to that combination of differences, but it goes well beyond that. It is the feeling of excitement when you come back here that Tessa Courage describes, the knowledge that out there is the sea with its mystery, dangers and beauty so sharply observed by Frank and Margaret Dye. It is the smell of the sea air, the extraordinary change in the colours of the marsh throughout the year, the amazing light that draws painters here, the harmony, unless we shatter it, of its buildings of pantile and chalk, brick and flint.

If you take your time to find it, this is also a place of exceptional expertise. The chapters by James McCallum on the area's wildlife and by Christine Abel on its history are just two examples. There is extraordinary musical, painting and poetical talent on display throughout the year within a radius of just a few miles.

It is also an unusual community. Even though we are remarkably near London compared with other places of such natural beauty and isolation, this coast also has its own qualities of wilderness, excitement and mystery – alongside an indigenous community of hardy, tough, skilled, knowledgeable and self-sufficient people. Janet Beckett describes how 'end of the world' places such as this 'often allow individualism to develop and are tolerant of eccentricities'.

Three things have stood out in the conversations that have led to this book, and in my own experience of North Norfolk.

The first is the open sky that provides the permanent background – the extraordinary feeling, when you are only a couple of hundred feet above the sea level on the high ground inland that you are on top of the world. While you can go to Scotland, Wales or further afield to sense the excitement of great mountains and their shadows and waterfalls, here the landscape lays itself out before you – nothing to obstruct it for miles and miles. You can see three church towers in a single vista.

Second, this is one of those few places where, if you want, you can be alone and quiet. If I stand on my doorstep in Burnham Norton before going to bed on a windless night, the only sound is of the rolling waves in the distance and the cries of the marsh birds. The sky is an amazing bowl of stars, unpolluted so far by any artificial light. Or I can sit on a dune on the seaward side of Scolt Head (with an eye to the tide) and look along the beaches for miles in both directions without seeing a single soul.

The third and final quality comes from the sea itself which so strongly influences and defines this place. We probably wouldn't have written this book about an inland place.

Everyone who knows this coast will have different affections and memories. But when you put all those feelings together, they produce a powerful instinct to protect a place that so many people cherish. Concerns and fears, and sometimes anger about its possible future, are as strong as the affections and memories.

Can it last?

Sustainability is an ugly word that can confuse people and reduce understanding. But it is also a useful shorthand for many of the issues that confront us here.

What can we do to underpin the future of this place with new sources of income and economic opportunity for tomorrow? Will those opportunities be widely shared between all those with a stake here, or will they be enjoyed only by a few at the expense of others? Is this a place that can offer jobs and homes to young people now and when we are all gone? Will we be able to maintain communities that can work together for the common good? And will we be able to provide good answers to those questions without damaging the natural environment that is at the heart of what we value here?

There are all sorts of forces for change at work here which worry people: some of them are human, social issues such as the shortage of affordable housing; the impact of those who have second homes here; the steady growth of traffic on country roads never designed for such numbers; the radical change in opportunities for employment. Others are natural threats, for example of climate change (itself partly impelled by man) and flooding, bringing back tragic memories of the floods of 1953.

Will those who farm here, whose role in preserving the landscape we can too easily take for granted, be able to adapt their farming sufficiently to economic pressures to continue that role? Teddy Maufe's initiative in creating a retail outlet for the beer brewed from his barley tells its own pioneering story.

'Incomers' is a word loaded with emotions. It is fascinating how people talking about the future of rural Norfolk seem to feel that they must first present their non-incomer credentials. I do it myself, making the most of my mere 15 years as a resident here and my wife's Norfolk forebears. What we easily forget is that one of the strengths of this place is the number of people who come here from time to time, who may be writers or painters, naturalists or musicians, and who bring with them huge knowledge and expertise. They are in their way very much part of the place, some of them doing a great deal to help people understand and respect it. And yet so often they are seen as being on the wrong side of the incomer/indigenous fence.

We easily forget too that if there were no incomers there would be no one here – we were all incomers once.

There is no doubt that the Saltmarsh Coast is the victim of its own special qualities. Susanna Wade Martin's concern that 'Norfolk's beautiful coastline, historic towns and villages and wide empty landscapes' should not be 'spoilt by the very people who come to see them' are even more real today than when she said that 20 years ago. Understandably, people in large numbers want to share that beauty. They buy their houses and inflate house prices; they fill the roads and car parks, and they also contribute to the local economy. The fear is that those numbers will one day exceed what the area can absorb – and some would argue that they already have.[1]

An area such as this will always depend on a delicate balance between nature

---

[1] 352,000 more people have moved into England's rural areas than have left them over the last four years (State of the Countryside, 2004, Countryside Agency)

and man's encroachments on it. It is nothing new. Christine Abel tells the story of man-made changes over the centuries – including the reclamation of land from the sea (why reclaimed, she asks, when it was simply claimed?), the creation of ports from natural harbours and the embankments which led to their eventual decline, for example at Wiveton and Cley. As James McCallum observes, 'in a county largely sculpted and manicured by man, nature most definitely won't look after itself'.

The last century saw the encroachment of 'modern' farming practice on hedgerows and headlands, now thankfully in reverse. Today, as Jim Ring warns us, the invader is the car as a result of booming visitor interest in the area. He reminds us that for a while at least we have been spared by the inadequacies of our transport system from invasions which have destroyed other places – but warns us that it cannot last.

But man's activities are not always damaging – and need not be so in the future. Our writers remind us of the great human contributions to this part of the world – the magnificent churches, windmills, and barns, and the shaping of the landscape itself. Are we up to the job of saving them and even creating their equivalents in the 21st century?

Meanwhile other forces are at work. Gloria Hurn's account reminds us that with courage and determination, it is possible to create new businesses here. Who would expect to find Europe's largest stock of hats in North Norfolk?! And there are more and more self-employed people (like Jim Ring and myself) making a living here through being able to work online from home. (My commuting journey is 15 yards.)

The second home arouses intense emotions – with its threat to weekday life in many villages and its effect on house prices and availability. But the second home owners are also providing employment for builders, plumbers, electricians, increasing the turnover of local businesses, and improving the housing stock – but

for whom?

There is a brighter side. Christine Abel doesn't rule out the revival of Wells as a port. Jim Ring reminds us what intelligent transport planning could do for North Norfolk. (Our writers were evenly split over his suggestion that, if we could have an efficient public transport system, we might follow the examples of similarly besieged places in Europe by banning all cars except those based here.) And though we moan at the bureaucrats, they are busy doing their best to protect our landscape, to keep our beaches clean and to protect both flora and fauna. Next time you hear stories of planners' intransigence and unreasonableness, just remember what unrestrained development can do to a landscape – like parts of Ireland where bungalows chosen from catalogues dot the landscape like measle spots.

It is significant that one consequence of our visitor numbers and habits is to create a less seasonal economy. For all its critics and mockery, Burnham Market, which 20 years ago was in economic hibernation in the winter months, is now busy all year round. That may not suit those who want it to themselves, but it is of great importance to those who depend on it for a living.

What might happen?

Reading these chapters leaves no doubt that, unless great care is taken to safeguard all that is special about this place, it could be overwhelmed. The worst fears are that the Saltmarsh Coast would lose control of its identity and be transformed into a playground for visitors, offering no real future for young people, becoming increasingly exclusive and expensive and divorced from its history, its services stretched beyond their capacity and its inhabitants and visitors polarised by bitterness and resentment.

These fears, though very real, are countered by the positive view that comes through these chapters and was reflected in our discussions. The alternative is based on a collective determination to keep this place not unchanged, because change it must, but still true to itself; to be constantly vigilant about the things that make it special – the landscape, the foreshore, the wildlife, the buildings; to welcome visitors, but also to help them in all our interests to preserve the essence of the area.

What can we do about it?

Perhaps the biggest threats to an area such as this are the ones that polarise those who live here and those who come here: anger, arrogance and self-indulgence. No amount of frustration about the impact of incomers is going to keep them away. We have to come to terms with them and what they bring.

But we can reasonably expect something in return: good manners. It's an old fashioned term but I use it to convey the essential courtesy that I suggest is our best hope for a viable future: a willingness to talk, listen and understand; taking time to do so rather than tearing through in a hurry; saying thank you when we let the other car go first on a narrow lane. (An American visitor recently asked whether this strange raising of hands between cars was some sort of secret society communication.)

Good manners cost nothing, but they do reflect something much more profound and necessary for this place to survive all the pressures which face it: a recognition that any community is interdependent. If its members do not communicate and work with each other, it could easily be destroyed by self-interest, greed and withdrawal into separate camps.

At a gathering of the writers for this book we heard a revealing series of questions and comments that speak for themselves: 'How do we get to talk to 'them'?' 'Most people who come here want to feel that they belong – and are willing to play their part.' 'Our Parish Council doesn't want incomers as members.'

Some of our writers talked of 'disincentives' to check the invasion – perhaps a Saltmarsh congestion charge or punitive levels of council tax. But the effect might simply be to change the wealth profile rather than the number of visitors. And we cannot simply ignore the value of the business that visitors bring to our hotels, shops, caravan parks and places open to the public – and the jobs that those businesses support.

The issue of affordable housing is difficult, but not insuperable. The negative side of it is deeply disheartening, especially to young people who see no hope for getting onto the property ladder and no alternative but to leave the area. It's about shortage of land for building, about the limited supply of affordable homes being sucked into profiteering development (see Paul Whittome's heartfelt plea for those who threaten this all too rare asset by buying up and exploiting affordable homes to be named and shamed), and about 'not-in-my-backyard' attitudes by more fortunate people in communities.

The opposite side of that coin, however, is that if those problems are made into opportunities, it is not impossible to provide at least some housing at reasonable prices. What is needed is a fourfold combination of landowners being ready to identify and make available small pockets of land, perhaps of limited agricultural value at agricultural rather than development prices; the use of the housing association regime to create affordable homes that cannot be sold on into the private housing market at inflated prices and will always be kept as affordable housing (the Blakeney Neihbourhood Housing Association and current plans for a housing association development in Bellamy's Lane, Burnham Market are shining examples of what can be done); recognition by existing communities of the short-sightedness and self-indulgence of turning their backs on the need for cheaper housing and expecting 'them' to be housed somewhere else; and a benign and far-sighted planning regime.

Another issue which concerned our writers was opportunity for young people, not just in housing but in jobs and in starting up new enterprises. Can we clone Gloria Hurn?! There are plenty of difficulties facing anyone starting a new business, but the early requirements are premises, help in preparing a basic business plan and help in crossing the bureaucratic hurdles. Then there is a crucial task of helping small businesses which have managed to establish themselves to get through the next, very difficult stage of survival and growth.

Role models are important here: a few more good examples of young people striking out (as John and Fiona Griffin have done in Holt with their fishmongering business). There is no shortage of people well qualified to offer help and advice on the lines of the Prince's Youth Business Trust (a valuable potential role for retired and regularly visiting professional people wanting to make their contribution).

In some ways the issues at stake here are about power. Are we being overwhelmed by urban power, with rural issues well down the political agenda? Or is it financial power – the feeling that as long as you have money, you can enjoy life here, but that there is a gloomy future for those without it. There are certainly grounds for both sorts of fear. But there are also individual and collective examples of people standing up in the face of such power. Think of the Wyre Forest where an independent MP was elected on a platform of saving a local hospital. Think of the Norfolk parish which took its governance and finance out of the hands of the diocese. And think too of the examples of people like Gloria Hurn who have battled their way through to success. Perhaps the future lies in a combination of the characteristics which typify the Norfolk character – determination verging on stubbornness and warm-hearted courtesy.

The history of the area has shown its capacity to weather change on a big scale. None of us advocated a 'drawbridge' response to today's pressures – rather a firm determination to manage change on reasonable terms (like putting a mast for mobile telephones inside the church tower at Blakeney – a classic case of adapting to today's technology without spoiling the landscape, a nice little earner for the church and a happy conclusion to Lisa Reynolds' account of local resistance to the initial location plan).

A lesson from the sea

This is not a place to be experienced at speed – whether in cars, powerful speedboats or impatient shoppers. The slower the better if you want to enjoy landscape, sea, skies and wildlife and each other. This is a place in which to take time to listen, learn and watch. That is why this book has been a slow, reflective process, I hope the better for it.

People who live near the sea know about its beauty and its unpredictability. They know that it can be perilous and even bring tragedy, especially if we fail to respect and understand it. But respect and understanding also have their returns – in livelihood, beauty and peace.

That is the plea of this book – to all who come here, whether to live or to visit. Take your time, listen, watch and understand and the Saltmarsh Coast will give you plentiful returns. But if you come here to challenge the place, seeking to change it or impose your will on it, or to take more from it than you give to it, it will be as unforgiving as the sea which defines it.

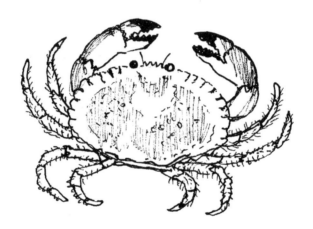

Campbell MacCallum

Campbell MacCallum, Photographer, was born in Arbroath and was forcibly anglicised at 12 when his family moved to London. Three years later he decided he wanted to be a cameraman. His started in a West End studio, turned freelance at 22 and his professional life as an advertising photographer has been based in London. He says he would still be in his last studio, in Carnaby Street but for the greed of landlords. Most of his assignments are now on location. In 1961 a close friend was shipwrecked off Wells, was rescued by the lifeboat, and rented a cottage near Wells Church. Campbell borrowed it, fell in love with the place and found a cottage of his own in Stiffkey for £25 a year. In 1971 he and his wife Dorothy bought the derelict Rectory Barn in Wells, converted it and moved there full time in 1973 when Campbell became a reverse weekend commuter, returning to Carnaby Street each Sunday evening. He says life is less hectic now but he still gets a buzz when the film comes back from the laboratory and plans to go to the Great Studio in the Sky clutching a camera.

Index of place names

N

W   E

S

KNOCK

MORSTON

WELLS-NEXT-THE-SEA